MEXICO

MEXICO
Chaos on Our Doorstep

Sol Sanders

Madison Books
Lanham • New York • London

Madison Books

4720 Boston Way
Lanham, MD 20706

3 Henrietta Street
London WC2E 8LU England

British Cataloging in Publication Information Available

Trade paperback edition published in 1989

Library of Congress Cataloging-in-Publication Data

Sanders, Sol W.
Mexico, chaos on our doorstep.

Originally published, 1986. With a new preface.
Bibliography: p.
Includes index.
1. Mexico—Politics and government—20th century.   2. Mexico—Relations—
United States.   3. United States—Relations—Mexico.   4. Mexico—Economic
conditions—1970–   .   5. Mexico—Social conditions—1970–   .   I. Title.
F1234.S187   1989   972.08'3   89–8260

ISBN 0–8191–7296–0 (pbk: alk. paper)

All Madison Books are produced on acid-free paper.
The paper used in this publication meets the minimum requirements of American
National Standard for Information Sciences—Permanence of Paper for Printed Library
Materials, ANSI Z39.48–1984.   ∞

"The idea the Mexican people have of the United States is contradictory, passionate, and impervious to criticism; actually, it is a mythical image rather than an idea. The same can be said of the vision of our intellectuals and writers. Something similar happens with North Americans, be they writers or politicians, business people or only travelers.

I am not forgetting the existence of a small number of remarkable studies by various North American specialists, especially in the fields of archaeology and ancient and modern Mexican history. Unfortunately, praiseworthy though these studies are, they are no substitute for what we need most: understanding. This is all the more difficult because understanding, which is an art and a science, is also a passion. Without any passionate attraction (sympathy or sometimes antipathy) for the other, the encounter from which the spark of understanding springs does not take place."

—Octavio Paz

Introduction: "Mexico and the United States," *Mexico Today*
The Institute for the Study of Human Issues, Philadelphia, Pa., 1982.

" . . . [T]he secret imaginative background of the philosophizing characteristic of America is, on the one hand, the tragic sense of life rooted in Latin American existentialism and, on the other, the epic sense of life rooted in Anglo-American pragmatism. However, distinct these two philosophies of the good life may be, I should venture to say that a synthesis or meeting of North and South America is possible on the ground that they complement each other and share a common faith, namely, a humanistic attitude towards life, together with an heroic conception of man. Such is, at any rate, my vision of the two Americas, a Brave New World big enough and free enough to leave room for two kinds of human heroes, epic and tragic."

—Patrick Romanell

Making of the Mexican Mind (University of Nebraska Press, Lincoln, 1952).

Contents

Acknowledgements

The opinions, presentation of facts, and judgements—are those of the author alone and may be at odds with views of some of his many friends, Mexican and American, who helped in the preparation of this book through interviews, criticisms, and suggestions. The author wishes to thank particularly Elizabeth Pease who helped with the research, Roger Kaplan, Midge Decter, Cristobal P. Aldrete, Augustín Navarro Vazquez, Luis Olmos, John E. Smith, Jr., Lewis Tambs, Peter Maffitt, Luis Aguilar, Leonard Schiller and a host of other friends and acquaintances for their encouragement. The author also wishes to express his gratitude for the support of the National Strategy Information Center, 150 East 58th St., New York, New York 10155.

Preface to Paperback Edition:
Another Look

Like any other exotic organism that has led a rich and long life, the authoritarian regime of Mexico is going into that last full flowering, that Indian summer, when just before death, the effervescence seems to fulfill the organism's finest promise.

A young (39 years old as he was chosen) president, the heart of the Mexican system, has taken power. Carlos Salinas de Gortari is the apotheosis of the intellectual-technocrat that has been at the heart of the regime for a generation. And although he came into power under the cloud of as corrupt an election (July 1988) as Mexico has had, he was nevertheless able on Dec. 1, 1988 to assume office[1] after a three-way contest that may have given him, according to most neutral observers, less than a plurality of the votes cast and almost certainly not the majority that the government claimed.[2]

Salinas moved swiftly on Jan. 10, 1989 to consolidate his power by striking against Joaquin Hernandez Galicia ("La Quina"), for 37 years the boss of the powerful and incredibly corrupt oilworkers union. With his imprisonment and denunciation of La Quina, the new president accomplished several purposes simultaneously: He evened old scores. La Quina and he had battled continuously when the younger man served as secretary of budgeting and programming in the de la Madrid government which preceded Salinas' own presidency. Salinas' efforts against La Quina's *cacicazgo* was part of an effort to find a winning economic strategy in the endemic economic crisis which had griped the country since 1981. Increasing efficiency at Pemex, the country's state-owned oil monopoly producing 5% of Mexico's GNP, is an essential part of any such strategy.

Furthermore, La Quina had spent large sums of money and used the union's 350,000-man national voting machine to support Cuahtemoc Cardenas, the candidate of the leftwing-populist coalition in the elections against Salinas and the ruling *Partido Revoluccionario Institucional (PRI)*.[3] The oilworkers, as the richest and most powerful union in the government-affiliated sindicalist structure of the corporative state, had been one of the main underpinnings of the *PRI* from its earliest days. In retrospect, such a move against La Quina seemed almost a necessity were Salinas to try to clean up the growing corruption[4], try to increase the efficiency of the government's oil monopoly, Pemex, and above all, to reestablish the traditional, overwhelming paramountcy of the once all-powerful Mexican presidency.

Salinas' move was generally viewed first with surprise, then with satisfaction and hope by the great mass of Mexicans. Only the remnants of the American Lyndon Larouche's *Partido Laboral Mexicana* had the audacity to defend La Quina. And only the Communists—led by that maverick old warhorse of the Party, Valentine Campa—and a few on the populist left questioned the way the move was made, whether use of the armed forces for a criminal arrest was justified.[5]

Yet the fact that the action against La Quina had to be carried out in stealth, by military forces (although the government claimed police accompanied them), and with the accusation that La Quina was plotting a *coup d'etat* (which few Mexicans believed), could be interpreted as at odds with Salinas' professed aim of moving toward more respect for the law, a more libertarian, liberal, and decentralized Mexico. Equally contradictory is the *realpolitische* of the move: Salinas strikes at one of the key organizations which has kept the small elite of the *PRI* in power for more than 60 years.

Salinas apparently intends to move on many fronts to restore the prestige and the power of the presidency and at the same time to move toward solving almost a decade of economic crisis. As expected, he followed up the move against La Quina, ostensibly the left in the Mexican political spectrum, with investigations and indictments of some private sector businessmen, generally considered the right in the Mexican context.

Salinas has promised, too, as did his predecessor Miguel de la Madrid, to move toward more democracy, toward pluralism.[6] That promise will be tested quickly in a series of city and state elections in the spring and summer of 1989—just as it was in the early days of the de la Madrid Administration when, initially, it resulted in a string of losses for the *PRI* until de la Madrid, the regime and the Party went back on its equally forceful promise of "transparency", returning to old, crude and sophisticated practices and procedures for stealing elections.

But if de la Madrid's six years can now be looked back on as a period of drift, or more magnanimously, as a period of calm if uninspired recovery from the wild gyrations of his predecessor, Jose Lopez de Portillo, Salinas no longer has that lead time. He will not have the same ability to keep options open. The years of no growth, the piling up of foreign debt on foreign debt, the growing internal debt[7], growing unemployment, the steady erosion of living standards as well as a fall in *per capita* income brought on by the continuing 2.5%-plus annual population growth, rising criminal violence, and a growing desperation about the future of the economy and the country—all threaten whatever any temporary political settlement Salinas may effect. It was also ominous, too, that one of the first actions of the new administration was a 2% capital levy—a "tax" which hit hard at the confidence of the largest corporations in the private sector without changing the fundamental fiscal situation of the country. There were reports, from the government and some private U.S. sources, that there had been an inflow of capital in late 1988 and early 1989—perhaps a function of the hopes for the new administration, perhaps a result of the psychological effects of the $3.5 billion "bridging" standby loan offered by the U.S. Treasury in November 1988.[8]

The offer of the loan, which had surprised even the New York banking community when it was suddenly leaked to the press, seemed to be an indicator of what policy toward Mexico would be in the new U.S. Bush Administration. The then Secretary of Treasury James J. Baker had been known as a partisan of the view that Mexico was passing through a difficult period, that the U.S. must coax the Mexican administration toward new policies with encouragement and monetary aid. Presumably that would be, at least in the early part of the new Bush Administration, U.S. policy. The choice of John H. Negroponte, a career diplomat with widereaching social connections, appeared to be an effort by Baker to put an activist but professional diplomat with expert talents into the Mexico City embassy. Negroponte, who had been the U.S. ambassador in Honduras during the U.S. buildup of the Contra opposition to the Nicaraguan Sandinista regime enthusiastically supported by Mexico's leftist foreign ministry, had old (Vietnam) ties to former secretary of state Henry J. Kissinger and his stable of collaborators in the U.S. foreign service establishment, including the new Deputy Secretary of State, Lawrence Eagleberger, a Kissinger protege in the State Department career service and former president of Kissinger Associates, a New York consulting firm. Baker's Mexico policy would likely be a continuation of the Reagan Administration policy of occasionally bringing pressure to bear on the Mexicans on specific issues, but accepting the proposition that there was no alternative to the *PRI* regime. That, again, would depend on the Mexican president himself and his very personal policy choices and their success.

While Salinas has undoubtedly improved his public image with the move against La Quina, the prevailing belief among Mexicans in the street is that *el sistema*, the way Mexico has been ruled since the 1920s, is no longer working. That growing perception may eventually prove to be the real test of the regime. Salinas, whatever his *bonafides* and his true aims, faces a cynical, tired, and frustrated Mexico which is willing more and more to speak out against what is generally considered to be misrule. Perhaps only a kind of Jungian race memory of the terrible bloodletting of what has been called the Mexican Revolution between 1910 and 1922—when more than a million civilians and military died and 10% of the population of 15 million escaped to the U.S.—has kept violence at a minimum until now.

Given the traditional all-important role of the Mexican president and Salinas' attempt to restore its validity in this crisis, his own personality, abilities, and ambitions are overwhelmingly important. Most observers of the Mexican scene, inside and outside Mexico, admit to considerable puzzlement about the man himself. He is urbane and well educated (with two degrees from Harvard University). Although no charismatic figure on the political platform, he has the respect of the Mexican elite as a member of that small band of intellectuals and politicians who dominate the country. He is generally conceded to be a brilliant analyst, particularly when economic issues are concerned, a quick-study, and a dominant personality in smaller gatherings of policymakers.

But he has a reputation for being highly emotional, erratic, and vengeful. And his youth hardly gives him a track record for decision-making through a series of crises.

It is precisely for this reason that Mexican politics today—including the future of the *PRI*—have never been so confused. The crucial and unanswerable question is: Who is Carlos Salinas de Gortari, what does he think, and where is he trying to go?

Is he the reformer who promised an *apetura democratica*—or a traditionalist who came out of elections last July proclaiming victory before the vote was in? Is he the innovator, the compromiser, the moderator among the various currents of the PRI and the Mexican elite? Or is he simply a new autocrat who, as he told an Italian periodical recently, takes his *pensamiento* from Michaevelli, Gramsci—and Reyes Heroles?

Is he, as he has promised some Americans in private conversations and some of his young economic advisers claim—like Gorbachev, Deng

Hsiaopeng, the French Socialists, and the Japanese Ministry of Finance—one of that new host of world economic policymakers who are converts to liberalization, market mechanisms, and decentralization, *i.e.*, capitalism? Or is he simply another Mexican *technocrat* armed with North American business school degrees who wants to "fine-tune" the Mexican economy out of its present morass, but preserve its state capitalism?

Is he, finally, the brainchild of his senator father, a *PRIista dinasorio?* Or is he the child of his mother's well-publicized ultra-leftist views and the intellectual nephew of his uncle, one of the two Marxist-Leninist professors arrested during the student revolution at *UNAM* in 1968?

One overwhelming question *was* whether Salinas was to be the weakest modern Mexican president, brought into office in a widely contested election in July 1989. On January 10, only a few days after his inauguration, President Salinas settled that question—at least temporarily.

When he moved to wipe out the power of La Quina, Salinas had proved to a surprised and largely admiring public that his manhood is intact—to put the question in more polite terms than most Mexicans commentators would do privately. The action was imaginative, bold, decisive, and generally applauded across the Mexican political spectrum. When the oilworkers and their supporters on the left folded quickly, at least for the moment, he had an enormous victory so badly needed to shore up his presidency after its initially poor beginning.

With this action Salinas seems to have signaled that he intends to use the full power of the presidency (unlike his predecessor, de la Madrid), that he intends to try to restore it to its pre-Lopez Portillo prestige and effectiveness. And that, of course, has important implications for whether *el sistema* is intact and still functioning.

But at this juncture, Salinas' action against La Quina has posed as many questions as it has answered. Had the action been taken as part of an enormous general and ongoing cleanup of such fiefdoms? Will he now go after the smaller but equally corrupt and powerful empires that exist in other unions in the *paraestatal* enterprises like the *CFE, Telefonicas Mexicanos, UNAM* and the whole educational establishment, particularly the union of primary school teachers, etc.? Or was the President's action simply revenge, a lesson to be taught and learned by members of the Revolutionary Family who stepped out of line in the last elections? And conceding that probably only draconian measures could accomplish his purpose, are we to witness a continuing abuse of constitutional and legal powers that have too often in the past marked the rule of strong presidents of Mexico and the *PRI?*

Was the La Quina affair a stroke of genius, setting the pattern for the coming sexennium? Only time will tell. Time is probably running against the President. If he intends to restore the power of the presidency—what ideologues in the *PRI* once proudly called *presidencialismo*—he must act quickly on many fronts. No strategy of throwing a battalion at a time into the battle will succeed. It has got to be a *blitzkrieg* against the powerful centrifugal interests in the dilapidated corporative state, the enemies of presidential power, if Salinas is to be successful. For there is a creeping rot coming from below—the slow but steady erosion of Mexican standards of living, the growing unemployment, the growing communal violence, and growing demoralization and cynicism and lack of confidence in the future of the country and the society.

Yet, any attempt to break the power of the corrupt union leaders is a bitter pill for the *PRI*, and perhaps for Salinas. Not only have the unions been in theory one of the tripod of labor, *campesinos* and professionals on which corporative power has rested, but the party, as its roots have rotted, has increasingly counted on the *paraestatal* unions to work out the mechanics for winning elections. That was as much a part of *el sistema* as the *paraestatal* deficit operations, used to pay off political debts to the middle and upper classes. If, and there is going to be increasingly strong pressures at home and abroad for that, Mexican elections are to become more transparent—as Salinas himself has promised—the power of these mass organizations will be needed to stem the erosion from both the right and the left, an erosion so apparent in the last elections. And the growing economic crunch means that the slush funds once available to grease the machine will no longer be available.

The *PRI*'s power to win, or to manipulate, this new demand for transparency, will be tested in a series of state and local contests where the opposition shows signs of great strength. Furthermore, the highly publicized success (and I believe exaggeration) of a price control pact with the unions and the private sector in stemming inflation in 1988—a policy that Salinas had masterminded for the previous de la Madrid Administration and one which he has continued, at least temporarily—is in no small part due to the loyalty of the *PRI*-government unions. Cracking the heads of the present leadership could lead to new, more representative union leadership which would be under increased pressures to reflect the growing discontent of workers who have seen their purchasing power drop by more than half in the past five years. And at almost any moment the highly personalized rule of octogenarian Fidel Velasquez, the super-*cacique* of the *CTM*, the government federation of trade unions, could come to an end adding new problems and instability.

Nor is a campaign against the government unions the only cleanup that awaits Salinas. There is growing evidence for American authorities that the growth of the drug traffic from Mexico to the U.S. has brought with it the kind of penetration of the higher echelons of politics, the police, and the military, that has taken place in Bolivia, Colombia, and other Latin American countries. While the Mexicans are justified in their complaint that so long as a lucrative market exists in the U.S., the temptation of easy and huge amounts of profit will corrupt their services, it becomes increasingly hard for Salinas to defend the position of the Mexican government that it is an American problem, that Mexico has extended maximum aid in rooting out the problem, and that there is lack of cooperation from U.S. authorities in providing Mexico with information on Mexican nationals accused of being implicated. The movement of cocaine, not grown and produced in Mexico, from South America to the U.S. indicates that the organization and collaboration in Mexico has reached levels of sophistication not required to move native-grown marijuana and Mexico-produced brown heroin to the U.S. With the drug epidemic reaching new and deadly proportions in the U.S., this source of friction between the two countries appears certain to grow and become a major issue for Salinas' administration.

How will Salinas handle these and the myriad other problems he faces? The betting now is that Salinas, the self-proclaimed child of Michaevelli, intends to use all the *PRI* elements—or if you will, all the remnants of the corporate state—to try to remake a crumbling political and economy structure, in part by playing one major current against another. Thus his government contains some of the strongest personalities of contemporary Mexican politics, most of them 25 to 30 years his senior, on what is called in Mexico the right. On the left, his government is heavily staffed at lower levels by Echeverristas, populists and Marxists who look to the former president for inspiration. Salinas has preserved the economic posts for his own technocrats, some of them more experienced in doctoral theses from North American business schools than in practical government operations. And there is also a sprinkling of *neo-Alemanistas* and former followers of Lopez Portillo.

Riding all these horses and playing them one against the other appears to be the game plan. The President is a well-known, if reportedly impatient, horseman. But this is a set of very fast horses to ride.

New York City
Feb. 10, 1989

Notes

1. It is perhaps significant that in Spanish the ceremony by which a new president of Mexico is inaugurated is called "to take possession" of the office. For the first time in many years, the ceremony before the Mexican Congress took on the rough and ready aspects of dissidence and opposition that characterize most democratic assemblies from time to time. Opposition members, both from the leftwing coalition that had supported Cuahtemoc Cardenas and the moderate-conservative *Partido Accion Nacional (Pan)* staged protests in the assembly.

2. The abstention of voters, a growing indicator of the lack of support at the grassroots of a regime that once could turn out millions at its beck and call for any sort of demonstration, grew proportionately in this three-cornered race. This abstention, despite more enthusiasm than any electoral contest in Mexico for generations, could only be understood as a growing consensus among voters and citizens that the whole performance was farcical.

3. A question for the coming months is whether Cardenas, and his mentor behind the scenes, Pofirio Munoz Ledo, once a *PRI* presidential aspirant, a former chairman of the *PRI* and Mexican ambassador to the United Nations, can "institutionalized" their coalition which ran well against Salinas. Cardenas, despite his post-election autumn 1988 successful tour of U.S. foreign policy. establishment fora, is not considered a shrewd politician but able to exploit his father's, Lazaro Cardenas', name. Munoz Ledo is said to want to affiliate a new party with the Socialist International of Willy Brandt and President Carlos Andres Perez of Venezuela. But the *Cardenista* coalition was built around the Mexican Socialist Party, *née* the Communist Party of Mexico, and a group of splinters—many of them created by the *PRI* to cultivate its "revolutionary" image—ranging from Trotskyist to orthodox Stalinist. The binkering after the election did not bode well for such a development, but the continuing deterioration of Mexico's living standards and the government's continuing "austerity" program certainly seemed to offer a fertile ground for an agitational political grouping on the left.

4. See *La Silla Embrujada: Historia de la Corrupcion en Mexico*, Carlos Elizondo, Edamex, 1987.

5. That the army was used may have far more important political as well as constitutional implications: The move against La Quina was planned and executed through Salinas' new secretary for *Gobernacion* (interior), Fernando Guttierez Barrios, a 67-year-old political veteran, a graduate of military schools and considered by himself and the military as one of theirs despite his long government service in civilian police and intelligence operations, and more recently, as governor of the state of Vera Cruz. For the first time since the 1940s, Mexico has at least a candidate for *caudillo* if the crisis should continue to deteriorate.

6. "My administration will respect citizens' demands with respect to pluralism and effective participation. The most urgent guarantee is in the political aim

of transparency of the electoral process. I will calm this civic concern. We guarantee to everyone that his political weight, transmitted in the free decision of voters, will be counted and accepted on all sides. These are needed by us for confidence, openness, and acceptance by others." "Mensaje de Toma de Posesion", Carlos Salinas de Gortari, Dec. 1, 1988.

7. Salinas, his economic advisers, and much of the private sector business community have convinced themselves in early 1989 that a "solution" to the foreign debt problem is a touchstone for solving the crisis of the country's economy. That omits the enormous problem of the internal debt. Louis Pazos, the prominent Mexican market-oriented economist, estimates that of the 60% of the current 1989 budget devoted to debt repayment, 46% goes to pay the costs of funding the internal debt and only 13% goes to service the foreign debt. In other words, he says, 22.7% of the total resources of the government's debt budget go to pay the foreign debt and 77.3% go to pay for the internal debt. In early 1989 the Mexican government was paying a real interest rate of almost 4% per month for its borrowings which were rising at a phenomenal rate. All of this would explain why Mexico's foreign reserves at a record high after another successful restructuring of the foreign debt in 1987, had fallen by as much as $10 billion from May to December 1989. "At this time, the Mexican government's principal problem is to cover interest accumulated by an enormous internal debt, *not* (author's emphasis) by those of its foreign one. It follows that if the necessary measures to control the internal debt are implemented, any type of renegotiation and payment facilities of the foreign debt will prove to be of little consequence. Fresh foreign credit would merely help sustain the current exchange rate and postpone the real problems; it would not solve them." "Mexico's Economic Options in Perspective", Luis Pazos, Conference on "The U.S. & Mexico—Setting a New Agenda", The Heritage Foundation, January 25–27, 1989, Washington, D.C.

8. It was assumed at the time of the brief announcement that the loan was a psychological-political ploy to prevent a massive devaluation at the end of the de la Madrid Administration, or even worse, as an opening of the new Salinas Administration. Rumors were current in December and January that the loan had not been drawn upon. And by early February, 1989, the Mexican government said he had "refused" to take up the loan. There were reports that conditions set by the U.S. requiring to International Monetary Fund regulations had not been met, that the loan had not, in fact, been signed. But since it was originally announced as "standby" and "bridging", all this seemed to be more doubletalk about the real nature of reserves, Mexican and U.S. policy.

Preface to Cloth Edition:
From Vietnam to Mexico

In May 1975, just after the fall of Saigon, I looked around the U.S. political scene from Washington, D.C., after returning from a long residence in Asia, much of it in Southeast Asia, to find a curious phenomenon which united almost all Americans, wherever they found themselves on the political spectrum in regard to the U.S. tragedy in Vietnam: there existed a common, subliminal belief that with the end of the Vietnam War and the horrendous controversy it had set up inside the U.S., Americans could somehow get away from the problems of the so-called underdeveloped world.

For, the reasoning went, those problems were, after all, geographically remote. Guerrilla warfare, nihilistic terrorism, counterterror, abject poverty, epidemic disease, and—most of all— the excruciatingly difficult moral choices of the "Third World" posed for the casual interloper were far from America's shores. (Even that French term *le tiers monde*, has a romantic bent that somehow softens the curse of poverty and ignorance and suffering in backward societies for those who hold cocktail parties in New York and Paris in support of, often dubious, Third World causes.)

That spring of 1975 there was a widely held, almost unconscious hope that all those horrors might be held at arm's length. There was some substance for that: my own view was that even the Vietnam imbroglio had always been a distant horror. For despite the death of 54,000 young Americans and the enormous treasure we expended on the war, on my frequent visits home from Southeast Asia I found that the "Vietnam debate" was rarely about Indochina but more often about basic attitudes and moral concepts in the U.S. with little relevance to what was happening out there. Those problems were "over there," the unspoken consensus went, somewhere in Southeast Asia, black Africa, the Middle East or South America, far from the secure and prosperous U.S. The Vietnam disaster, it was thought, would be a catharsis, however painful, that would put all those problems behind us and leave us free to move on to other pursuits, or even to other problems nearer home.

As I became increasingly aware of this assumption on the part of my countrymen, I was fearful. I knew the wish-logic was false. And I began to test it by poking around in an old interest of mine—Mexico. I had had a Latin American "incarnation," as the foreign policy establishment puts it, in the late 1940s, when just out of university with college Spanish and a yearning to go abroad, I had worked on the United Press Latin American desk in New York. Later, in the 1950s, a rather unusual job as account executive and writer for a New York public relations firm specializing in U.S. industrial accounts in Latin America took me on extended travels and research to Mexico.

I knew from that experience that Mexico had many of the classic characteristics of "underdevelopment." And with my long Asian exposure to the difficulties facing preindustrial societies trying to move into the twentieth century, I was dubious that all the good news out of Mexico was true. A little probing among the experts in Washington proved that I had not been wrong. For even in 1975, despite its rapid growth and stability—"Mexico is the most stable country in Latin America" went the cliché, and for once it was probably correct—the country just south of the border was facing an uncertain future.

Mexico had already become the classic example of population explosion. Never in history had there been such a large group of people increasing at such a fast pace, growing at almost the biological maximum, with the concomitant explosion of its cities as poverty-stricken *campesinos* poured into their slums. (For example, not only has Mexico's population growth rate been substantially greater than that of her huge Latin neighbor Brazil, but in the 1970s and 1980s the growth in her labor force was almost twice Brazil's with every prospect that it would continue to grow into the next century, while Brazil's has been declining due to a sharply declining fertility rate.)

There was the muddle of Mexican agriculture, once a classic *latifundio*, which had been transformed by the violence of 1904–1922 but had never come to terms with the land tenure question. Part and parcel of that was the inability to satisfy the demand for food despite the introduction of new seed varieties of "the green revolution." Paradoxically, this revolutionary plant genetic breakthrough, which with the use of fertilizers and irrigation held out the prospect of plenty everywhere, was developed first in Mexico.

Not only was the snowballing urbanization creating new and perplexing problems but there were signs that the rapid industrialization, flawed by its highly protected narrow markets and high costs, was not being matched by a developing sophistication in Mexico's political institutions.

I was anxious to investigate what was happening and how it might possibly affect the U.S. For the Vietnam entanglement had demonstrated how America, for so long largely impervious to much that happened outside its borders, could become a victim of other people's follies, "of far-off nations about which we know little," not simply the machinations of European bloc politics which had pulled us into two world wars. I proposed to several publishers to research and write a book about all this speculation, for it was clear that Mexico's troubles were our troubles. Some time in the future, Mexico would pose a new and vexatious problem for U.S. policymakers. But there were no takers; my agent and I gave up the ghost when one large publishing house replied that the subject was interesting, that I seemed qualified to write about it, but, after all, it would be a three-year project, and by that time the problems I had enumerated in the outline would have been solved!

Needless to say, ten years later, not only have Mexico's problems not been "solved," but the country is in a full-blown crisis of confidence. It has taken a stark human tragedy, two major earthquakes in the older parts of Mexico City, to capture some attention. This incredible drama has evoked large-scale interest, at least temporarily, for it is the kind of spectacle that attracts the trendy media maven.

And while there is a far wider appreciation of Mexico's difficulties and their portent for the U.S. in Washington and New York —and certainly in the Southwest—the general American public, living cheek-by-jowl with all of Mexico's problems, is almost totally oblivious to all but the most obvious manifestations of trouble south of the border. The purpose of this book, then, is to present a panorama of Mexico's problems as they relate to the U.S. It offers no solutions but contents itself with an effort to draw the line between what appears to be the onset of a new tragedy in Mexico and our own lives and considerations.

New York City
May 1986

Introduction:
The Threat from Mexico

Nineteen eighty-five–1986 has been the winter of Mexico's discontent.

Along the Paseo de la Reforma, once the most beautiful boulevard in the world, the trees are slowly dying. Clouds of unfiltered pollution from the millions of motorcars in the world's largest city have burned the trees and shrubs. During the winter a series of inversions in the oxygen-light atmosphere on the high plateau on which the city is situated threatened human beings as well as the foliage.

At both ends of the Paseo, in Chapultepec Park where the president resides in the executive mansion of Los Pinos, and at the other end in the Zocalo square where the bureaucrats govern at the Palacio Nacional, a regime that calls itself "the institutionalized revolution" is also dying. To clouds of incompetence, corruption, and venality that have hung over the regime has now been added the critical ingredient for any form of governance, indecision—that fatal hallmark of a bankrupt government.

In the January 1986 cold, the worst in a decade, tens of thousands of homeless, victims of two earthquakes that shook the old heart of the city in September 1985, shivered in temporary tent housing on the northern fringes of the vast megalopolis. Despite all the hoopla at home and abroad to help them, they were virtually forgotten along with their more traditional homeless companions on the streets in the growing economic crisis that threatens the incomes if not the livelihoods of all Mexicans. An increasingly restive press—perhaps freer than it had been for 50 years—brought up scandal after scandal, ranging from the tricked municipal elections in the states, in which the government insisted on "winning" all contests, to the theft of $6 million from the luxurious cell of a drug kingpin, under custody only

1

because he was implicated in the murder of an American antinarcotics agent in Mexico.

At the center of the unfolding drama was Miguel De la Madrid Hurtado, almost a pathetic figure, a man who had succeeded to the all-powerful Mexican presidency but lacking charisma, had sought to substitute pseudo-technical expertise for political acumen. How long could a system which had at its heart the strongest executive in the Western world survive these centrifugal forces tearing it apart? And how long would it be before Mexico's problems, so intimately bound up with the United States, became a primary concern of Washington policymakers?

For more than a half century the United States has been able to treat Mexico, to use Sen. Patrick Moynihan's famous phrase from another context, with "benign neglect." But a sea change has taken place in U.S.-Mexican relations. The old relationship—a virtual ignorance of Mexico on the U.S. side of the border, and a controlled resentment of North Americans by Mexicans—has metamorphosed into a new and more volatile ambiguity. The traditional lack of understanding, in a new world where the interrelationship has become so much more intense, could easily develop into a confrontation—even should both governments do their best to try to diffuse it.

U.S. policy has been ostrich-like in the face of four disastrous trends that have overtaken the Mexican polity:

1. The demographic and historical currents that point toward instability.

2. The unsettling geopolitical situation in the Caribbean and Central America which redounds onto Mexico.

3. The chronic but escalating economic crisis.

4. The merging of the growing influence of Marxist-Leninism with the traditional autocracy on Mexican institutions, including the all-powerful presidency.

All these point to the likelihood of a coming destabilization in Mexico, inimical to the United States.

The option that history gave America's leadership during World War II and the decades that followed to relegate Mexico and its problems to a policy back burner has given birth to dangers that can hardly be exaggerated. Our southern land boundary of 2,000 miles has gone virtually undefended, which of course permits us to use our military resources elsewhere. Perhaps even more importantly, Washington's foreign policy planners have been free to devote their brain power almost exclusively to the problems of American interests in Europe, the Far East, and the Middle East.

During those years, Mexico continued to be a major customer for our goods and services—during the oil boom years 1981–1982 Mexico was our second most important trading partner—and a supplier of valuable raw materials, oil and metals, as well as cheap manufactured goods which helped fight our inflation.

True, during the past half century the Mexicans have nursed old wounds and old grudges stemming from their disastrous encounters with American arms in the nineteenth century and with U.S. efforts to police Mexico's internal law and order well into this century. Yet for all the inflammatory rhetoric against the *gringos* built into modern Mexican nationalism, Mexico and the U.S. have grown closer together in the post-World War II decades. That is partly the result of physical changes. Communications and travel between the two countries are enormous—the Houston-Monterrey air corridor was, before the economic crash of 1981, almost as much a routine flight for American and Mexican businessmen as the Boston-New York-Washington shuttles. But it also has cultural aspects. English is now the acknowledged second language—even of the intellectuals—as the traditional influence of France and French doctrines has been eclipsed. Both countries have worked for mutual advantage in many areas with a minimum of friction since the onset of World War II. This collaboration has even included, until fairly recently, counterintelligence operations that began in the fight against fascist totalitarianism in Europe and East Asia and developed into cooperation against what had been considered the new common Soviet enemy.

But as the relationship has changed, the U.S. perception of events in Mexico has dimmed. In part, this is because analysis of what is happening in Mexico and its significance for the U.S. is largely limited to Latin American academic studies. And these academic circles are heavily weighted, if not dominated, by Marxist interpretations. Because commerce between Mexico and the U.S. is so diverse, and because so much of it moves at regional levels in the Southwest, there is no major spokesman or theme around which the business constituency can coalesce, a phenomenon which has so much to do with other foreign policy decisions in Washington. In government itself, Latin America, including Mexico, has been traditionally neglected—the State Department's Siberia where relationships are parochial and inbred.

The Reagan administration, though caught up in the Central American crisis, has had neither the foresight, the time, nor the energy to place the Mexican question front and center. An internal squabble in the Central Intelligence Agency over how to analyze events south of the border—the question of Mexico's future and its portent for the U.S.—has polarized the agency, the "technocratic" analysts on the one hand and Director William C. Casey and former station chiefs in Mexico on the other. John Horton, a national intelligence officer working on Mexico, says that he resigned due to pressure from the director to change his estimate of what was happening in Mexico.[1] Horton's complaints are, however, only the tip of an iceberg of complex and fundamental concerns that divide those few Americans who have worried themselves with Mexico at all.

In fact, the official compromise line (despite pressure from Casey and the White House for a reevaluation) that came out of a 1984 task force investigation was that for the short term Mexico will remain stable and present no new problems for Washington, but that the long-term outlook is extremely dangerous. The failure of logic here is self-evident: long-term problems can easily become short-term through totally unpredictable events. One has only to ask what would have been the result if the assassination attempt against President Miguel De la Madrid Hurtado on May 1, 1984, by a group of radical students, possibly supported by the Cubans, had been successful? They threw firebombs at the Labor Day reviewing stands and came within a few feet of striking the president. Mexico has no experience and very few legal and protocol provisions for handling such an emergency succession. The whole course of Mexican history would have been changed by such a "short-term" occurrence.

It may well be that the earthquake of September 1985 will prove to be the proverbial last straw that will sink the present Mexican regime, just as it was the 1972 ground tremor that in no small part destroyed the Somoza dynasty in Nicaragua. Corruption, incompetence, arrogance, and cynicism—hallmarks of the Mexican ruling elite—have been demonstrated during the earthquake's aftermath.

Indeed, Mexican history and its lessons for the future are badly in need of revisionist approaches. The period 1910–1922, labeled the Mexican Revolution, represents an era of nihilistic chaos rather than a period of reformist revolution as conventionally presented. When a six-year drought brought famine to many areas of the country, and henequen and minerals prices collapsed after the panic on the New York markets in 1907, a senile old dictator lost his grip after a thirty-five year rule and, in 1910, the *Porfirista* (named after Porfírio Díaz) regime dissolved. Into the vacuum strode local warlords, who fought a long and cruel guerrilla war for control with few if any larger political concerns.

When it was over, Mexico was put back together by nonideological regional leaders in a fashion not so different from what had pertained until 1910—a highly centralized regime with an all-powerful executive. Such an outlook on the events of the early part of this century is important in analyzing what is happening now. For it is quite likely that the outcome of the present crisis will be the acceleration of the process of ossification of the government apparatus of the Party of Institutionalized Revolution (PRI).

With perhaps 65 percent of Mexicans now living in cities of over 100,000 people, the old methods which suited the rural and isolated Mexican countryside and villages have become increasingly ineffective. There is growing evidence of the regime's inability, in the face of modern communications and the sophistication and expectations of a highly urbanized population, to use the old methods of cooption and brutal suppression with enough efficiency to stem the rising tide of frustration and dissidence.

The world of the *caciques* (local leaders who evolved out of Indian and Spanish colonial societies) has been heavily eroded by the new mass communications and the movement into the cities. Since the De la Madrid administration set out a pattern in 1983 in Mazatlán, on the West Coast of Mexico, and in Puebla, one of Mexico's largest cities, to steal all the municipal elections, the fraudulent processes have become more and more clumsy and well publicized. Furthermore, the reaction has been stronger than in the past.

Mexico is no longer as isolated as she once was; her calls for pluralism in other countries—a ploy so often directed at the U.S. by Communist fellow-traveling Mexican intellectuals—is beginning to boomerang. The concentration of all power in Mexico City, which was effective with a smaller and more isolated population, makes it increasingly difficult to implement decisions in cities of over a million, some a thousand miles from the capital. The system is, moreover, crippled by corruption. That corruption, as old as the Conquest and the ruthless sacking of the Aztec capital by the Spaniards, exceeded all bounds in the last administration. President José López Portillo personally may have stolen as much as $3.5 billion, more than the total reserves of many smaller countries. All this might have been tolerable had the bubble of oil riches—which Mexicans were led to believe would solve all their problems—not burst. The falling real price of energy meant not only that all Mexicans had to face lowered living standards, but the whole "solution" of their international debt crisis, trumpeted around the world as the model for other creditors, collapsed.

Mexico City was an exotic never-never land when Leon Trotsky sought refuge there, because he was unwelcome elsewhere in the 1940s and wanted to be close to the U.S. But today the outside world, that is, the geopolitical struggles outside the Western Hemisphere, have reached into Mexico. Just as Stalin's killers extended their reach into Mexico and murdered Trotsky, the outside world has come increasingly to impinge on the U.S.-Mexican bilateral relationship. The coming to power in Cuba of a Communist regime and Soviet client in this Hemisphere in the 1960s placed new strains on the cynical Mexican political strategy of talking leftist revolution to the outside world while maintaining an oligarchic authoritarianism at home.

There has been from the outset of Fidel Castro's dictatorship a question of whether the Cuban revolutionaries, with their Soviet sponsors, would not exploit the rhetoric of the Mexican Revolution and the problems in the nonindustrial society in an attempt to set up a pro-Soviet regime in Mexico. Thus far, Havana has generally gone out of its way to assure the Mexican government that so long as it offers its territory for operations against other Latin American governments by allowing pro-Moscow exiles to gather and plot there, and so long as it takes anti-Washington stands in Latin American multinational councils, Mexico City will have earned an "insurance policy" from Moscow and Havana. But as revolutionary opportunities present themselves in a deteriorating Mexican political environment, that guarantee may have run its course.

Nor can any Mexican regime, whatever its professions of revolutionary camaraderie, look with equanimity on the creation in 1979 of another Marxist-Leninist state in Central America, Nicaragua, so closely allied to Cuba and the Soviet Union. That part of the Americas has always been intimately connected with Mexican history, both before and after the Spanish Conquest. Today, Mexico has a running sore along her southern border where Guatemalan Communist guerrillas squat along the 1,500-mile isolated and jungled frontier and operate against non-Communist Guatemala, the largest of the central American states. Not only are they based on Mexico's territory, but it is often with the aid and comfort of Mexican nationals, not the least important being local Catholic clergy of the liberation technology persuasion. This situation has the approval, of course, of Mexican leftists —even of some factions of the ruling party. And the federal government in Mexico City has tolerated the situation, impotent to do much else.

Denying the thesis that in the contemporary world situation all regional conflicts tend to become a part of the superpower confrontation, the standard Mexican rationalization is that the revolutionary movements in Central America are only latter-day manifestations of the same currents that drove Mexico's own earlier revolution, and that they will, in time, become "domesticated." But the truth is that

Mexico neither has the will nor the power to police that border. And it is certainly arguable that any Mexican government (even one backed by U.S. power) could fend off a campaign of guerrilla subverison waged against it from a Communist Guatemala. It is the classic guerrilla situation where the Communists exploit various elements: old resentments against a central government, an extremely difficult terrain, a frontier that artificially bisects kindred peoples, and smuggling and clandestine migratory crossings dating back over the centuries.

Mexico, too, has had internal changes—political, social, and economic—which have impacted on the bilateral U.S.-Mexican relationship, first and foremost the incredible demographic explosion. The Mexico of the Revolution of 1910–1922 of 15 million people has mushroomed to 80 million in 1985 with the expectation that it will exceed 100 million people before the end of the century, and perhaps 130 million in the ensuing decade.

It is doubtful that any regime could have handled this expansion with equanimity; that is, it would have been difficult under the best of conditions for Mexico to maintain both stability and material progress for its people. There is growing evidence that the present Mexican regime has not been able to accomplish the latter and the former is increasingly in question. Statistics in Mexico, as has been said about all Latin America, are poetry. But there is every indication that even before the onset of the current international debt crisis, the per capita income in Mexico was dropping rapidly. And the need to rein in the roaring inflation through austerity—or permitting the alternative of run-away inflation—promises that all Mexicans will see their living standards fall rapidly in the immediate future. Nor is there much hope that even the long-term pattern can be reversed, for it would require, as a minimum, an early and complete about-face in the government's economic and political strategies.

Those now include a growing commitment to an inefficient government ownership of much of the industrial sector, protection for highly inefficient import-substitution industries and a morass of ideologically naive policies and corrupt practices in agriculture that more than anything else resemble the food disasters of Central Europe and the Soviet Union. In 1982, the nationalization of the commercial banks—the chief conduit for private investment in the country—annihilated confidence. Although the Mexican government has officially devalued the peso, or periodically let it float free over the years since the economic crisis struck, capital flight continues— as much as half of the $100 billion international debt may be savings owned by Mexican nationals used as collateral abroad for continued short-term borrowing.

More significant, however, than even the shambles of the Mexican economy is the ballooning political crisis that the nation faces. Contrasted with the enormous economic and social changes is the regime's failure to evolve a political process fit for a major, modern state with a large and diverse population living in a country devilishly designed by nature with a proliferation of climates and peoples. The regime's failure is fuel for the growing indignation of a small but burgeoning lower middle class that has a new set of values derived from its exposure to the world outside Mexico. A decentralization and a distribution of power is absolutely essential, and, although Mexican politicians pay lip service to the idea, the traditional centralization of the regime continues apace.

Mexico is run today as it has been run for more than a century, with the interregnum of the chaos of 1910–1922, by an autocrat, the Mexican president. The Mexican presidency is a unique institution that comes out of its Spanish and Indian past, and, although the Mexican constitution is wholly imitative of the U.S., it functions in an entirely different way. After two failed six-year presidencies which left the office tattered and under a cloud, the present incumbent, President De la Madrid, still has more relative power than any chief executive anywhere in the world, perhaps excepting North Korea's Kim Il Sung.

The choice of who is to be president of Mexico had degenerated into the selection of a successor by the incumbent, with little input from either the ruling party, the bureaucracy, or the military, much less the ordinary Mexican. Once nominated, he is assured office by the monopoly of the one-party system—whatever the window-dressing of a plural electorate. Once elected, he is not accountable to the Mexican parliament, which rubber-stamps his budgets and his political pronouncements. The governors of the thirty-one states are merely puppets of the president, since he chooses them as candidates and assures their election. He is not accountable to the courts, for he has only to proclaim amendments to the basic law and send them to the Congress—as in the case of the *ex post facto* legalization in 1983 of the nationalization of the banks in 1982. His command over the armed forces is absolute for he checkmates their commanders through a Byzantine command structure crowned by the presidential guard, the only units in the country with really modern arms.

The incumbent, De la Madrid, is the quintessential Mexican technocrat without political experience. And, alas, he is partially a product of Charles River Scientism, that post-World War II American dictum that the world is logical, that a highly motivated and intelligent policymaker can, with "systems," plan his way out of even sociological and political crises.

But is this not all a domestic Mexican situation that precludes the U.S., especially given the history of Mexican-U.S. antagonistic relations, from a close examination much less an attempt to influence events there?

The thesis of this book is that, given the intimacy of our relationship, there is no way that Americans will be able to avoid the impact of a Mexican breakdown. To think otherwise is to lull ourselves into a false sense of security, one that has been carefully nurtured in our psyche since we withdrew our troops from the horrendous engagement in Southeast Asia in 1973.

For a few weeks in March 1985, the front pages of the major U.S. newspapers were aflame with the brutal kidnapping and killing of a U.S. antinarcotics agent in Mexico. The revelations which came out of that one episode showed the extent of the corruption and venality of the Mexican drug scene, in which both state and federal police are implicated. And it was clear that high Mexican officials had to be aware of the connection with a morass of drug-related crimes. Then came the tragic earthquakes which struck Mexico City in September 1985. Americans were appalled as the miracle of satellite transmissions brought live TV coverage of at least 20,000 Mexicans buried in the ruins of ultramodern buildings in the old section of a modern city. And then there was the spectacle of Mexican officialdom rejecting U.S. offers of massive help; this was somewhat mystifying to the average American who is unaware of the long tradition of Mexican antagonism toward the *gringo* so exploited by the political elite. Later still came the revelations of inefficiency and corruption, the hallmark of the regime, and the attempts by both Mexican officials and interested U.S. parties to use the natural catastrophe as the alibi for decades of wrong-headed policies and cynical manipulation of the Mexican people.

Cognizance of Mexico's difficulties remains miniscule relative to the enormity of the implications a possible Mexican destabilization implies for the U.S. The financial crisis of 1981–1982 indicated what could lie in store for Mexico—and for the U.S. Greedy and foolish U.S., European, and Japanese bankers had lent Mexico upwards of $100 billion based on unrealistic estimates of oil development.

Neither the horror story of Iran nor the decades of mismanagement of oil in Venezuela were included in their calculations. When the world markets adjusted to the higher oil prices of the Organization of Petroleum Exporting Countries (OPEC) with worldwide inflation, an international recession, and, finally, fuel economies in the major consuming countries, which reduced the long-term possibilities of higher real oil prices, Mexico floundered. And the bankers in New

York—as well as in Mexico—were in deep, deep trouble. So were suppliers in the U.S. who had turned Mexico with its oil boom earnings into a second market for American exports. Suddenly there were newspaper accounts of depressed U.S. border towns and cities in the Southwest; these had lived high-on-the-hog during the years when, as Mexico City wags put it, the only cheap thing in Mexico was dollars, years that saw Mexican secretaries vacationing in Paris and middle-class Mexicans buying condominiums in San Diego and Vail.

Soon the bankers, in order to cover their tracks, were assuring everyone that Mexico had only "a cash flow problem." But that was not the case. The financial crisis over international debt repayment was only the most apparent aspect of the politico-economic crisis —the culmination of a long period, going back to the 1950s, which had dynamited the highly touted "Mexico Model." It will take future psychohistorians to explain the complete demoralization that overtook Mexican President José López Portillo, the outgoing all-powerful chief executive, who dramatized the crisis with a massive devaluation of the peso and the nationalization of Mexico's private banks.

As for De la Madrid, it became fashionable among those interested in Mexico to assure one another that the new president was an honest, sane, technocratic, middle-of-the-roader, who would restore the balance to the government and within the Partido Revolucionario Institucional (PRI). Few remembered hearing the same logic and glib predictions when López Portillo was ushered into office after the disastrous presidency of his predecessor, Luis Echeverría.

What was actually being played out was the old Mexican morality play, wherein the outgoing autocrat takes the blame for the mistakes of his sexenium of total power, and the new ostensible political virgin is inaugurated with high hopes for his success in ushering in a new era of enlightenment.

What simply was not being faced—in Mexico or in Washington or in New York—was that something fundamental had changed in Mexico during the two failed presidencies of López Portillo and Echeverría, that the famed Mexico Model was badly flawed if not totally inoperative, and that the old order in Mexico was tottering.

In fact, a fossilized regime—created in 1922 for some 15 million Mexicans—no longer could cope with the growing sophistication and frustration of a population nearing 80 million. The regime's vaunted corporate state, in which the various groupings in the "revolutionary family" had pretensions to represent all the constituencies in the nation, was no longer working. A halting and insincere movement toward political pluralism by López Portillo was taken up briefly by De la Madrid in an attempt to prop up the system. But free elections for municipalities boomeranged when for the first time in the history of the country the PRI lost one election after another in the spring and summer of 1983. De la Madrid had to pull down the riot shutters with a resounding political thud to save the "face" and perhaps the future of the PRI when reformist critics within the PRI elite had to face the very real prospect of being voted out of power were elections to be fair.

This is the background that makes certain that the U.S. increasingly must look to the south with growing anxiety. A Mexican regime which continues to be unable to solve its domestic problems will become a major preoccupation of the U.S., dwarfing many other older concerns in Washington. It could fundamentally shift America's post-World War II concentration from Western Europe and East Asia to Latin America.

Among many old hands who have dealt with Mexico and Latin America, there is an abiding hope that the fatalism which permeates Mexican society, a heritage perhaps from its Indian origins, will somehow, along with the mystique of the PRI and its incredibly flexible and pragmatic system (a special product of the Mexican ethos), permit the regime to muddle through. But there is, realistically, less and less hope that it will.

What would the PRI's failure mean for the U.S.? One obvious and immediate concern is that destabilization, sporadic violence, and civil conflict in Mexico would within weeks send *millions* of refugees scurrying across the largely undefended 2,000-mile land border into the Southwest. The thought of moving across that frontier in the event of a breakdown in the country is ingrained in the Mexican psyche today as is another—if contradictory—belief, held by many of the middle class: that should the worst overtake their country, somehow or other, Uncle Sam would descend like the Virgin of Guadalupe and miraculously rescue them. Unfortunately, there is much more realism associated with the first concept than with the second.

Washington, notoriously unable to focus on any foreign policy issue until it is in full crisis, is still blithely able to avoid formulating a comprehensive policy toward Mexico. After the 1981–1982 financial crisis, because of domestic U.S. pressures stemming mainly from the banking community, Washington willy-nilly moved into a long-term strategy of massive support of the PRI regime.

The U.S. banking community has gone to great lengths, together with the Federal Reserve System and the international lending agencies, to try to prop up Mexico's shaky financial structure. That policy was reinforced when at the annual meeting of the International Monetary Fund and World Bank in Seoul in 1985, Secretary of

Treasury James J. Baker began a campaign to pressure U.S. banks to continue lending to Mexico and other debtors. The U.S. is pumping huge quantities of surplus food at bargain prices—not likely ever to be paid for—into the country to sustain its diet. Washington has also bought Mexican oil at generous prices for its strategic petroleum reserve even at the risk of alienating other suppliers in the Mideast. And, most of all, a Reagan administration firmly committed to a policy of halting Communist encroachment in Latin America, particularly in Central America, has turned the other cheek in the face of Mexican aid and comfort to regimes and clandestine groups allied to Havana and Moscow in the region.

There may have been no alternative to current U.S. policy, that is, no alternative but to wait and pray that somehow the PRI would weather this crisis as it has so many others. The Mexican moderate and conservative opposition is weak, fragmented, and unrealistic in its views of the current situation. The Mexican Left is dominated by a small but influential Communist movement, almost impervious to the disenchantment and a new sense of reality of some of the most devout fellow-travelers and even within the Communist parties of Western Europe.

Nor is there any hope that the present Mexican regime would permit a peaceful transfer of power to an opposition group, whatever its capabilities. What could well be in the offing is a new period of chaos in Mexico. That seems the likeliest scenario because of the weakness of both the Communist Left, despite its enormous inroads among intellectual elite, and the conservative Right. Neither seems able to build an alternative regime for the country. The question of whether the PRI has not outlived its time, of whether U.S. support, however extensive, and however well intentioned, will be enough to bolster it, has hardly been whispered. But in the months and years ahead, it will be asked, as it is in these pages, and asked increasingly.

Part I:
Los Estados Unidos Méxicanos

Chapter 1: The Myth of the Mexican Revolution

Every country lives by its myths. Or so I was reminded by a resident Belgian Jesuit—one of the new breed of Catholic priests who no longer perform "pastoral duties"—on my travels through Mexico. He warned me, somewhat pontifically, that "the United States, too, has its myths." I was tempted to reply that when national myths depart too far from reality, a society is likely to find itself in great jeopardy. (Nowhere in postwar Europe has that been more true than in his own Belgium and among his own Flemings.) And the problem in Mexico is just that: the myths (and attendant rhetoric) have moved so far away from reality that the yawning gap threatens to swallow the whole society into anarchy and violence.

What is the Mexico myth? It is a panoply of truths and half-truths and pure fiction about Mexico today which has been developed, especially since the 1940s, to justify an authoritarian rule of the society by a small elite wielding power through one political party. The myth is elaborate and sophisticated. Were it not so, the Partido Revolucionaria Institutional (PRI), the creature of that mythology, could not have given the country some sixty years of stability. The most significant aspect of this mythology is the indefinable mystique that surrounds the PRI, a faith in its powers and attributes which Mexicans and foreigners who attest to it find difficulty in defining in logical terms.

Perhaps the myth's most important article of faith is the claim that "Mexico has *had* its revolution." The implication in that oft-repeated cliché is that Mexico, because of the events of 1910–1922 known as the Mexican Revolution, is immune to the revolutionary outbursts that have dogged much of Latin America and the former Afro-Asian colonial world since the end of World War II. When Gen. Paul F. Gorman, then chief of the U.S. Southern Command (Panama), warned publicly that Mexico was "the most corrupt government and society in Central America" and that it would become a major security burden for the U.S.,[1] a spokesman of the Mexican Foreign Ministry responded through the press in Mexico City: "We must repeat that Mexico has already had its revolution in 1910, which it fought to change the economic and social structure of the country. Central America is fighting now for what Mexico has already fought for, and this is the difference between the Mexican reality and the Central American revolution."

The use of the word revolution presupposes that a premeditated and basic restructuring of Mexican society took place during the bloody years of civil strife which marked the almost two decades, that the regime which was inaugurated after the end of the troubles was essentially reformist and different from that which preceded it. And among American intellectuals, whose revolutionary rhetoric and left-of-center politics have become the conventional wisdom since the Korean War, the assumption is that because the Mexican Revolution promised fundamental social changes, it indeed left the country with a more-or-less democratic and progressive regime.

Such an interpretation of Mexican history flies in the face of the facts. The real story is far different. "The drama covers the years between 1905 and 1924," writes Professor Ramón Eduardo Ruíz. "However, it is not a simple chronology but an interpretation of events. It is my view of what took place, that Mexico underwent a cataclysmic rebellion but not a social 'Revolution.'"[2] Professor Ruíz proves his case several times over even though he puts the accent on the motives and the personalities of the individual leaders in the violence rather than on the changes they made (or did not make) in the fundamentals on which Mexican society was built.

After a long period of enormous if uneven progress, Mexico was in 1907 being ruled by a senile old dictator, Porfírio Díaz, surrounded by a brilliant but highly ideological and elitist group of advisers known as los científicos. They called themselves "the scientists" because they believed their social theories were based on scientific and therefore provable fact. They may have known more about the history of France and its political thought than about their own country, for they were infatuated with European positivism.[3] When a six-year drought brought hunger to the country and the panic of 1907 in the New York markets sent agriculture and mineral raw material prices crashing, an economic crisis struck the country and quickly devolved into a social and political crisis. A naive if idealistic political reformer, Francisco Madero, with both official and unofficial U.S. help, challenged the legitimacy of the regime, demanding that it give way to new political forces. The call for a new administration derived support inside the country and abroad, particularly in the U.S., from a campaign of propaganda and agitation that emphasized the evils of the *Porfiriato*, many of them the legacy of a Mexico that was just stepping into the modern world.[4]

But Madero, a scion of one of Mexico's richest families and an intimate of the old regime—two uncles were *científicos*—had no revolutionary program. He shunned any attempt at massive agrarian reform, for example, which was the only radical element introduced anywhere in the whole Mexican spectrum of political thought (with the possible exception of nineteeth-century European liberal and, less important, U.S. freemasonry anticlericalism).

Madero, with U.S. assistance (he operated his rebel movement from Texas and the border areas), successfully forced the tired old dictator to withdraw to Europe. A struggle for power ensued, marked by Madero's martyrdom at the hands of a typical *caudillo*, Victoriano Huerta, a charismatic military-political figure of the Ibero-American type. For close to twenty years, Mexico almost reveled in bloody chaos. *Caciques*—feudal leaders whose power dated from the Spanish conquest in the early sixteenth century although rooted in earlier Indian forms—fought sporadically for local control. Alliances were opportunistically formed and broken and reformed at the national level. They were not ideological, although there was a great deal of Latin rhetoric used in the attempt to enhance the opportunism of the leaders, mainly from the middle-class, who sought control. Even in the state of Morelos, where a poor and dedicated Indian and local leader named Emiliano Zapata waged a somewhat successful campaign for "land to the tillers," the intellectual base was extremely shallow. After Zapata's assassination, his movement died without leaving any ideological legacy, nor, in fact, much else except a romantic legend that latter-day pseudo-Marxists and populists would try to exploit.

The romantic bent of many of those who have examined the period is epitomized in these words from the preface to one of the best-known recent books from the U.S.: "What follows is a story, not an analysis, of how the experience of Morelos villagers came to pass—how their longing to lead a settled life in a familiar place developed into a violent struggle; how they managed their operations; how they behaved in control of their territory and in subjection; how they finally returned to peace; and how they then fared. Zapata is most prominent in these pages not because he himself begged attention but because the villagers of Morelos put him in charge and persistently looked to him for guidance, and because other villagers around the Republic took him for their champion. Through him the country people worked their way into the Mexican Revolution. If theirs was not the only kind of revolutionary experience, it was still, I think, the most significant."[5] The author, who now heads the history department at Harvard University, has called himself "a communist with a small c." Had his investigation had a more forthright analytical and less ideological approach, it might have led him to another conclusion: i.e., that Zapata represented largely a local phenomenon without ideological underpinnings, which was later capitalized on by propagandists and ideologues who made use of him as a nativist symbol for a kind of revolt other than that in which the Mexican had engaged.

When finally, this sporadic, regional violence ended its slaughter —perhaps as many as a million Mexican soldiers and civilians died —and its nihilism exhausted the country, the factional leaders came together to reestablish the Mexican state. But when peace descended in fitful stages in the early 1920s, the accommodation was among regional leaders who paid only lip service to the revolutionary slogans. The result was a return to an omnipotent executive, more powerful in the history of Mexico than any leader in any Western country, a return to the dictatorship of the *Porfiriato*.

There was almost universal agreement among the new leaders that the cardinal sin of the *Porfiriato* was that the reign of old Díaz had lasted too long—35 years. Thus a proviso that a president could serve only one six-year term was enshrined—but nothing was done to inhibit the virtually absolute powers of the presidency. It was an implied assumption that Mexico knew no other political institution than autocratic rule from either its Spanish or its Indian heritage and that it could only function with that kind of system.

Lorenzo Meyer, a prominent Mexican political scientist, although he rejects this overall interpretation, nevertheless concludes: "The liberal institutions created by Juarez and his followers in the second half of the nineteenth century had no citizens to give them flesh and blood. The Porfirian dictatorship signified the recognition of this fact. Institutional exclusion was again accepted as the main ingredient of political control. The Mexican Revolution confronted this situation and, in 1917, Mexico gave itself one of the most advanced sets of political rules at that time, but the raw material for democracy was absent. Perhaps the time lost could not be regained. The Revolution, struggling for survival, had no time to create the necessary social and political preconditions for democracy. Expediency and social inertia led to the adaptation of the authoritarian system of the past to the conditions of the present. President Calles made the crucial decision in this respect. After a while, privilege and a powerful set of vested interests flourished in a system hostile to democracy, and the beneficiaries are now its most dedicated supporters."[6]

It was years later, especially during the administration of President Lázaro Cárdenas (1934–1940) with his heavy personal and emotional commitment to the Indian population of his native Michoacan state and the poor of the country, that the events of the period were mythologized and the bloody period given a form and a substance it never had. Octavio Paz, Mexico's foremost poet and a historian and social critic described the Mexican Revolution, when he still held to many myths that he has since discarded, thus: "The Revolution has hardly any ideas. It is an explosion of reality: a return and a communion, an upsetting of old institutions, a releasing of many ferocious, tender and noble feelings that had been hidden by our fear of being. And with whom does Mexico commune in this bloody fiesta? With herself, with her own being. Mexico dares to exist, to be. The revolutionary explosion is a prodigious fiesta in which the Mexican, drunk with his own self, is aware at last, in a mortal embrace, of his fellow Mexican."[7]

It was fashionable when Paz wrote that essay for Mexico's writers and artists to endorse the Revolution as the expression of their genius as well as of the people of Mexico. Slowly but surely, that radical chic aspect of the events of 1910–1922, which has lent so much to its mythical aspects, is eroding among the artistic elite in the country. Jonathan Kandell, writing on the mood among young writers in Mexico in 1984, says: "Through a sophisticated policy of financial inducements and prestigious awards, writers, painters, and film directors were encouraged to deal with the Revolution, the pre-Columbian Indian heritage, populism, the countryside, nationalism, and related themes that had official approval. . . . [Y]ou have a kind of yawning gulf between Government and the intellectual community that has not been seen in Mexico since the first decade of this century."[8]

From the 1920s onward, Communists inside Mexico and abroad attempted to link the events in Mexico with the Bolshevik Revolution and the worldwide Communist movement. Especially in the Mexican artistic community, where Stalinists made such converts as the muralist Diego Rivera and David Siquieros, they sought to lace Mexican events into "the world struggle of the proletariat." The Soviet filmmaker Sergei Mikhailovich Eisenstein made a series of films on Mexico, *Que Viva México*, which Soviet propagandists emasculated and turned into a melodramatic presentation on the *Porfiriato*, drawing absurd analogies to the Russian peasant and the Soviet Revolution.[9]

In one of the most significant if least chronicled events in Mexican history, Cárdenas welcomed a Spanish Republican emigration—the estimate of the total varies but they may have numbered as many as 75,000—after the defeat of the Republic in 1939. In Mexico these emigrants—ethnic Spaniards, a relatively large contingent of German Communists, and other European revolutionaries—were considered martyrs to what was *the* cause of the Left in the pre-World War II period. Mostly professionals, they had an incalculable influence on Mexican intellectual life from the 1940s onwards through their domination of the universities and their preponderance in the professions.[10]

That influence continues to the present. An example is El Colegio de México, Mexico's leading think tank and graduate faculty, which was originally founded by Mexican intellectuals to house a group of Spanish émigré professors as *La Casa de España*.[11] Even today prominent members of the Colegio are sons and daughters of Spanish émigrés, although it is generally played down by them and others working with the faculty—perhaps because of the traditional antagonism toward *gachupines*, the pejorative term commonly used for Spanish emigrants to Mexico. Writers and observers, such as Patricia W. Fagen, are either disingenuous or naive in their appraisal of the Spanish Communist party's activities in Spain and in Mexico within such cultural organizations as the Colegio. Members of the Spanish Communist exile apparat have been prominent in the whole Mexican Communist world, especially among the European expatriate community in Cuernavaca, near Mexico City. Fagen does point out that "During the student demonstrations and strikes of June-October 1968, which culminated in the bloody confrontation in the Plaza of the Three Cultures at Tlatelolco, the sons and daughters of Spanish refugees were found not only participating in the ranks of the protesters but serving in the leadership positions as well. . . . [T]hey were impervious to criticism from older Mexicans who sought to blame Mexico's difficulties on the influence of foreign radicals, and who counted the refugees' children among them."[12]

Coming as they did from a highly politicized environment—many of the Spaniards and their fellow-traveling Europeans were Stalinists and other vintage Marxists and anarchists—the leftists among them helped to link the Mexican Revolution to the Soviet Revolution, building the legend over the chaotic earlier events in Mexico. The Stalinists among the Spanish emigrants, as so often was the case during the 1930s, were the best organized and the most effective in delivering their message.[13]

A former U.S. Communist, actively working under cover in Mexico for the Communist cause in 1938-1939, reports an encounter with the notorious Carlos Contreras or Comandante Carlos (Vittorio Vidali). Vidali was a Comintern agent, chief political comissar for the Fifth Regiment, the most successful of the Communist-led military groups in the Republican army during the Spanish Civil War.[14] Vidali was a brutal executioner for Moscow in the bitter internecine war on the left during the Spanish conflict. Contreras (Vidali) told our interlocutor at that time that the war was all but over in Spain and that the only remaining question was what would happen to the Communist cadres (under Soviet discipline). Contreras said the most important would be sent to the Soviet Union and the rest to Mexico. The source also suggests that, in retrospect, he now believes that Contreras was in Mexico to help arrange the murder of Trotsky which took place the next year.[15] Isaac Don Levine has told the incredible story of how a battalion of Stalinist killers was recruited by Moscow and sent into Mexico for the murder of its arch ideological enemy.[16]

The Communists dominated several cultural institutions and such supposedly all-embracing political organizations as the Union Democrática Española and the Ateneo Español de México. Modeled after a Spanish cultural institution, and intended to represent all the Spanish émigré political factions, the *Ateneo* was in fact heavily influenced by the pro-Moscow faction of the Socialists under the former Spanish Republican Prime Minister Juan Negrín. It also developed into an important center for Latin American dissidents and exiles—Colombians, Nicaraguans, and Cubans. And later it became the partial cover for guerrilla training activities of Fidel Castro by Alberto Bayo, a former commander of the Spanish Republican army.[17]

The Spanish Republicans' intellectual concerns helped to pull what had been generally perceived as essentially isolated Mexican events largely without ideological character into the net of world revolution being preached out of Moscow through the Cominterm with its claque around the world. It was as though, having failed in their own revolution, the Spanish Republican Communists were determined to give shape to the bloody and nihilistic Mexican events. They and other foreign friends, many of them American leftists, were able to persuade the more rustic Mexicans—and the world—that such regional bandit-populists as the colorful Pancho Villa were, deep down, revolutionaries, complete with plans for social engineering.[18]

Some Mexican intellectuals—like Jesús Silva Hérzog, father of the finance minister in the De la Madrid government, patron of the Mexican Left, and former Mexican ambassador to Moscow—try to have it both ways. They claim ties for their revolution to a worldwide movement but argue in the same breath that it did not have an historic Marxist blueprint but was native grown. The real question, of course, is how much Mexican society and its governance were changed by the events of 1910–1922. Just as the breakaway from Spain in the early nineteenth century was more a product of events in Europe—the decline of Madrid and its occupation during the Napoleonic Wars[19]—than the growth and victory of an indigenous independence movement, so the bloody events of 1910–1922 were a breakdown of the status quo largely brought on by external forces. There is abundant evidence that, contrary to the conventional interpretation of the three hundred years of Spanish colonial rule in Mexico as a period of decline and stagnation, Spain built enormously successful and flexible institutions.

There were, of course, two great faults built into the Spanish colonial system: the overwhelming centralism, a product of Spain's own regional woes and the piecemeal *reconquista* that drove its Moorish conquerors and the Jews from the country over a period of two hundred years; and the reluctance of Madrid to permit America-born Spaniards, the *criollos* (*criollo* = cradle, thus those who were infants in the New World), to participate in local government. These and other faults—including Spain's long and largely unsuccessful attempt to keep British and other European commerce out of its colonies—created the basis for independence when Napoleon occupied the Iberian peninsula and the orders no longer came from Sevilla. But the institutions of Spanish colonialism were enormously powerful, despite the strains that Mexico placed on the declining power of the metropolitan center.

"Governing Mexico's complex society presented a great challenge to authorities," writes Professors Colin M. MacLachlan and James E. Rodríguez O.[20] "The establishment of an institutional structure sufficiently flexible, yet strong enough to permit the evolution of an orderly society, represented a major achievement. Although Mexicans still fondly recall certain astute colonial administrators, the political structure itself deserves credit both for producing effective officials and for surviving the incompetent. New Spain [Mexico] accommodated varied and often antagonistic interests, which sometimes resorted to violence, without endangering either the continuity or the legitimacy of colonial government." The authors have presented sufficient evidence to launch a continuing study which, as their publishers say on a jacket blurb, "challenges the widely held notion that Mexico's colonial period is the source of many of the country's ills."

In the end, Spanish rule in *Nueva España* fell apart. But it was not dynamited from the Western Hemisphere by a highly motivated, ideological independence movement such as came together in Philadelphia in the summer of 1776, colonials asserting their rights as Englishmen.

In the same manner, the events of what is called the Mexican Revolution were more a matter of erosion, an implosion rather than an explosion. It is true that the subsequent policies and the ensuing troubled decades wiped out much of the pattern of the huge landowning latifundio which had existed before 1910. But that system of the *haciendas* was on its way to being destroyed by the *Porfiriato* which, while it had created a new class of *hacendados* among loyal Díaz followers, undermined the concept of the old self-contained, Spanish colonial *hacienda* by introducing the idea of accumulating land for profit-incentive enterprises, cash crops—in sum, the beginnings of modern capitalism.

In any case, the fighting and its political outcome did not produce a new consistent pattern of land ownership. Land tenure remains chaotic today despite all the attention it gets from official propaganda. It is a victim of the constant outbreaks of civil strife over the inability of the government to make the system of common-held lands produce. The most important piece of continuity between the *Porfiriato* and its successor regimes was the maintenance of an all-powerful elite, including most of the leading families before 1910. But this, along with the continuing strong racist undercurrent, is one of the taboo subjects of contemporary Mexico—caste is to be inferred rather than deliniated in the enormous number of studies of the Mexican elite by Mexican and U.S. academics.[21]

That leads us to another part of today's Mexican myth, which holds that the country, with its great social mobility, is an integrated nation of mestizos—people of mixed Indian and European blood, the so-called "cosmic race" of the famous Mexican historian, José Vasconcelos. Mexican government propaganda and the intellectual community idealize the Mexican Indian, the Indian heritage of modern Mexico, and the role it plays in today's Mexican culture. The poet and political commentator, Octavio Paz, dean of Mexican intellectuals, has written " . . . and [Mexican] political construction, if it is to be truly productive, must derive from the most ancient, stable and lasting part of our national being: the indigenous past."[22]

But the anomalies are everywhere apparent. While the Indian is romanticized and his history and suffering have become the major subject of the art of Mexico's famous muralists, discussion and serious study of race is taboo in Mexico (except for the generally Marxist-dominated anthropological studies of the Indians themselves). Racial prejudices, animosities, and discrimination lie just under the surface.[23] The elite, while largely of mixed bloodlines, nevertheless favor those of light complexion, of European appearance, and form a definite if amorphous caste largely based on race and color. The Mexican government hierarchy is in the main, chosen from this elite, although, paradoxically, individuals in politics may from time to time attempt to exploit the national myth by boasting of their Indian ancestry. And to an even greater extent, the leaders of Mexico's private sector, or what is left of it after the bank nationalization of 1982, come from this same group.[24]

Just as the myth pretends that the revolution solved the problem of race—the Indian, social mobility—so it affects to have answered the country's economic problems. There is mounting evidence that it, too, is untrue—with abundant evidence long before the crisis dramatized by the highly publicized international debt problem.

Mexico did have a highly touted period of fast economic growth in the 1950s and 1960s. Indeed, throughout its post-Conquest history, Mexico has been unique in its high savings rate—in the Spanish colonial period Mexico exported capital to Spain and was probably largely responsible for the growth and development of other Spanish dependencies, such as Cuba and the Philippines. And there are scholars who believe that much of the celebrated high growth rates which began in the 1950s is simply a function of the fact that for the first time statistical information dating from the post-World War II period became acceptable to non-Mexican scholars.[25]

The results of the 1980 census—under the direction of De la Madrid, who then headed the Ministry of Planning and Budgeting—have only partially been released. There is speculation that one reason for the delay is that they would prove that per capita incomes were falling even before the onset of the financial crisis in 1981. Some statistics have been leaked, however, and suggest that most of the worsening trends laid out here continued or accelerated. The rapidly growing population—the pre-World War II population figure has doubled and will probably do so again well before the turn of the century—has been both a generator for economic development and a damper on per capita income.[26] Mexico has also failed to solve its agricultural problems which have limited its internal markets, while all the time pursuing a program of high-cost, highly protected, import-substitution industrialization.

While this kind of industrialization has benefited a small elite of entrepreneurs and industrial workers, it has kept many goods beyond the means of a great part of the population. Raymond Vernon foresaw the dilemma of highly protected production facilities and narrow markets as early as the 1960s. "By the late 1950s, the easy opportunities for domestic investment in import-substituting manufactures seemed to be reaching an end. Consumer goods were no longer being imported into Mexico in very large amounts; less than one-fifth of all

Mexican imports fell in the consumer category. Substitution from this point forward would have to take place mostly in intermediate goods —in steel instead of bedsprings, in aluminum instead of kitchen pans, in engine blocks instead of assembled cars, and so on. Such substitutions usually involved larger investment, more difficult technology, and a more difficult market structure; from all points of view, therefore, it represented a forbidding terrain."[27]

The undervaluation of the dollar against the peso somewhat obscured this phenomenon in the late 1970s, but Vernon's prophecy was fulfilled. Meanwhile, the level of the *campesino* in the countryside changed little and then only because of massive technological breakthroughs in the country as a whole in which he was an accidental participant, i.e., the introduction of mass communications and national markets in a small number of important products. For example, Mexicans consume one-sixth of Coca Cola's worldwide output and one-fourth of all Pepsi Cola produced, according to a 1985 study by the National Consumer Institute in Mexico City.[28]

Nowhere, however, does the mythology of the modern Mexican state depart from reality more than in the realm of freedom and the rule of law for all its citizens. The constitutional structure of the state itself—"Los Estados Unidos Méxicanos," the United States of Mexico—is a lie. No more highly centralized system exists anywhere in the world outside the Communist bloc than in Mexico, despite official professions to the contrary. The thirty-one states (plus the federal district of Mexico City) are simply administrative units of the central government. Their governors—chosen through the PRI party machinery as personally dictated by the president—are only agents of the chief executive. The presidency is all powerful. Neither the courts nor the parliament constitutes anything more than a rubber stamp on that power. Recently, some *PRI* ideologues have tried to make a virtue of what they call "presidentialismo." (A typical example was the passage by the Mexican Congress in the first days of the De la Madrid administration of two new amendments to the constitution, originally proposed by López Portillo, which *ex post facto* "legalized" the nationalization of the private banks which had taken place some six months earlier. The absurdity of the legal fiction was underscored by the fact that during the nationalization, in answer to a protest from the bankers, the chief justice of the Supreme Court declared the nationalization legal without the need for a change in the fundamental law.)

An American lawyer long resident in Mexico, somewhat protectively and supportively, explains that in Mexico legislation by the Congress has little significance compared to the executive decree. If, for example, he explains, the government permits a foreign corporation to invest in a certain manner, it does not constitute a precedent for another corporation seeking to do the same thing. He says, ruefully, that he has great difficulty explaining this to "the typical Wall Street lawyer" with whom he must deal. That is understandable. Equality under the law is not a peculiarly Wall Street concept, nor for that matter a specialty of Anglo-Saxon law, but rather the basis for equity under any system of beneficial law. And it is a fragile legal commodity in Mexico.

This arbitrary rule by the president of the republic is, perhaps, a greater refutation of the "progressive" character of the regime than the more publicized corruption that makes the life of the ordinary Mexican so capricious. It is certainly at the base of many of Mexico's current problems. For example, the land tenure law is so chaotic that it inhibits any investor—the lowly tiller who has to count every centavo or the millionaire on his vast acreage. When the Mexican government seized the dollar bank holdings of its own and foreign citizens in the bank nationalization of 1982 and replaced them with devalued pesos, it was only another example of this arbitrariness.

Intimidation of the media has reached the state of an art, although as the crisis deepens for the regime, it is becoming less subtle and less effective. In the past, very little was printed in the Mexican press or heard over its radio or seen on its television which did not have the official stamp of approval. In November 1983, for example, during the annual convocation of the ninety-odd bishops of the Mexican Catholic hierarchy in Mexico City, De la Madrid, the new president, invited a group of representatives of the hierarchy to the presidential palace, Los Piños, for dinner and an extended exchange of views about Mexico's current problems. The history of troubled relations between Mexico's post-1910 government and the Church would make any signals of changes in that relationship, especially with the relatively new president, of prime importance. That was doubly so in the case of De la Madrid since he is known to be a Mass-going Catholic before he entered the presidency—with the exception of Echeverría, the first since Madero. And his wife is a fervent Catholic, it is said, with connections in the semiclandestine Opus Dei, a social and political Catholic lay movement.[29]

Yet not one word appeared about the meeting between the president and the hierarchy, neither in newspapers of the left wing, like the PRI's anticlerical *El Día*, nor in the conservative, proto-Catholic opposition's *El Heraldo*. A church spokesman pointed out this episode, knowingly, to the author, suggesting in effect that in this instance all parties deemed that it was better that the whole subject not be discussed. This was a rather benign example of how the Mexican government has in the past manipulated the press, through the distribution of newsprint via a monopoly, a government-owned corporation.

In late 1983, when *El Heraldo* published detailed news reports and photographs of fraud in municipal elections in Mexico's fourth largest city, Puebla, indicating that the opposition had won a sweeping victory, a telephone call from Los Piños was enough to have the editor fired in twenty-four hours. The press had virtually ignored a similar situation which had occurred somewhat earlier in Mazatlán, the West Coast port and tourist resort in Sinaloa State, where, it was generally agreed, the elections had been fraudulent—and admittedly so, according to junior government officials. That communications were broken off between Mazatlán and Mexico City during and immediately after the elections may have helped the news blackout.

In early 1984 it was announced that the newsprint monopoly, PIPSA, would be transferred from the Ministerio de Hacienda (roughly equivalent to the U.S. Department of the Treasury) to the Ministerio de Gobernación (home of the judicial police including the secret services)—a not very subtle hint of growing pressures. Where free expression has existed in the Mexican press, it has been the result of internal bickering within the administration, particularly the influence of the rambunctious Left inside the PRI and the overwhelming domination of the media by left-wing journalists.

Such cooption and collaboration is the rationale for the system and for the effectiveness of the Mexico Model. Yet the most cursory examination of it today suggests that it may no longer be effective. And the growing independence of the Mexican press since the earthquakes may be one more telltale sign of the erosion of PRI power.

Here as elsewhere, the Mexico that has developed in the past few decades intrudes, and the new Mexico with its exposure to modern technology and world standards is making the old methods of compliance more difficult to enforce. Foreign reporting on Mexico on cable television is being blocked out to half a million viewers in Mexico City. As Cablevision S.A. reported this year, "The expanding penetration of American television here [in Mexico] has made U.S. network treatment of Mexico a new irritant to Mexican authorities, who appear increasingly concerned about the domestic and international impact of such accounts. . . . Failure to screen out news reports about Mexico that the government deems inaccurate or derogatory has led officials to levy a 50,000 peso fine on the cable transmission company's owners."[30] Although the fine is small, the owners of the cable company do not like to be at odds with government officials—especially since there is constant and vituperative pressure from the Left, within and outside the PRI, to nationalize all electronic media.

Fraudulent elections in this kind of environment become not only the norm but almost irrelevant. However, the growing depth of the economic and political crisis has given pragmatic substance to the argument for reform and greater freedom; i.e., the depth of the crisis demands the wholehearted participation of all the people, especially of the new and growing middle class, if it is to be solved. There was, therefore, some hope that the elections for the lower house of Congress, seven governorships, and some two hundred municipalities in the summer of 1985 might be the occasion for a new era in Mexican politics. Voices in liberal Mexican quarters anticipated that De la Madrid's promise of "moral rejuvenation" would permit fair elections, as for example, Octavio Paz, who called for them in a two-part television interview on Mexican history.[31]

And there were also growing indications that a powerful new moderate and conservative sympathy existed in the country and should have the right of expression through PAN, the National Action Party, which included important elements of the private sector business community and the Catholic church. PAN's executive committee chairman was Pablo Emilio Madero, nephew of the initiator of the Mexican Revolution, a politician whom the PRI found it hard to dismiss as reactionary and counterrevolutionary—the standard ploy used against PAN during the thirty-five years of its existence. More than a few Mexican scholars and thinkers hoped to see the development of a multiparty system, however slowly, and however much it would differ from those in other democratic countries. The Church, braving the criticism of the government, had made appeals through individual churchmen and a pastoral letter from the hierarchy for everyone to vote whatever his choice.

But efforts before the contest by the infant human rights organizations in Mexico[32] to insure fairer elections by having foreign observers were met by an aggressive statement by Manual Bartlett Díaz, minister of Gobernación, that Mexico had "its own particular system" and that "no one could give us lessons in democracy." The primitiveness of the electoral corruption was illustrated in an episode when the PAN offered to pay for transparent ballot receptacles in all the elections (used only in the state of Morelos). It temporarily won a fight for them before the National Elections Commission, but was finally overruled. In Sonora, birthplace of the Mexican Revolution in 1910, the popular former mayor of Ciudad Obregón, Adalberto Rosas

López, told newsmen just before the election that despite a powerful PAN surge which he believed would net a four-to-one victory if there were a fair poll, "we have been told we're playing in the major league and that there is no way [the PRI] is going to cede power."[33]

The 1985 elections were in reality a disaster, viewed from the standpoint of the growth of representative government in Mexico. Within the government a debate over how to handle the elections had been won by the "hardliners," which would give "total" victory to the PRI in all districts, states, and municipalities.[34] PAN was to be humiliated and forced to retreat to its "assigned role" in the managed regime. Everything was to be done to encourage the minor parties on the Left, who work as appendages of the PRI, in order to discourage what seemed to be a bipartisan trend with PRI on the Left and the PAN on the right from emerging. And, finally, the elections were to demonstrate, especially to investors and foreign observers, that the magic of the PRI still made the Mexico Model viable.[35]

There was another minor cloud on the horizon no larger than a man's hand. The growing public perception of PAN as a party of the middle class combined with the continuing left-wing rhetoric and revolutionary pretensions of the PRI risked that should Mexico move toward a multiparty system, there would be "a real danger for today's political class in that the following step would be the conversion of the PRI into a party for the workers."[36] The threat was that the government party would move radically even further left.

There was a massive government propaganda campaign aimed at tarring the conservative opposition with promoting violence, a grim warning among Mexicans who can still remember more than fifty years later the killings and brutality of 1910–1922. Unfortunately, there were just enough minor outbreaks among young, frustrated Panistas to make the threat credible—or riots by the so-called, "porros," the PRI's hired thugs. (On Jan. 1, 1986, they burned the city hall in San Luis Potosi after a riot which the Government blamed on the PAN.)

In fact, the PAN leadership accused the government of deliberately provoking violence in some situations, a not wholly un-warranted charge.

Earlier, for example, in January, after an election fiasco in the city of Piedras Negras just across the border on the Rio Grande from Eagle Pass, Texas, PAN demonstrators had closed the international bridge with civil disobedience demonstrations after they charged the election for mayor had been stolen by the PRI. Public buildings were burned, and Mexico City brought in the army. During the campaign a spokesman in the president's office had charged PAN with seeking to "destabilize our country"—a phrase used in the worldwide jargon of the intelligence community to describe violent plots to overthrow the regime.[37] The government was only slightly embarrassed over the fact that the PRI had had to withdraw a candidate for Congress, José Antonio Zorilla, until March 1985 head of the Mexican Departmento Federal de Securidad (DFS), Mexico's secret police. Zorilla had been linked publicly with the kidnapping and murder of an American anti-narcotics agent in February and was the subject of court action in California concerning the "laundering" of drug funds through Mexican and American banks.

The campaign waged by the government party made it quite clear that nothing had changed, that elections would be stolen in the good old-fashioned Mexican way. And the public responded, not as many had anticipated, with widespread violence, although there was enough to create anxieties, but with abstention. In the Mexico City federal district where political activity is obviously at its highest, less than half the registered electorate bothered to go to the polls. Overall participation in the elections dropped from 50 percent in 1982 to 20 percent three years later in 1985—and that is the official figure, which is probably inflated. More than any other criteria, these abstention figures proved that the PRI's managed elections had lost public confidence, even as a *fiesta* celebrating the control of the party of the Revolution.

On the day after the elections—six days before the official returns were in—the government claimed it had won all seven gover-norships and 292 of the three hundred seats up for election in the lower house. That was later modified slightly, but the announcement of victory, coming only hours after the polls closed, cast grave doubts on government claims. "Opinion in Mexico City found such across-the-board victories scarcely credible after three years of economic aus-terity and corruption scandals. . . . Furthermore, the premature an-nouncement seemed to reinforce the opposition's argument that the election results had been decided in advance."[38]

All kinds of electoral chicanery was used—some of it the "legitimate" sort, such as the use of office and government funds, that occurs in any voting democracy, but the many activities were de-signed to deliver Mexico City the victory at any cost.[39] There was cer-tainly considerable evidence that it was, as the conservative opposi-tion claimed, the most corrupt election in Mexico's history: hundreds of opposition poll watchers were disqualified the night before the elec-tions; ballot boxes disappeared on election day, carried away by police and agents of the secret services; voters were turned away from polls where the opposition was expected to do well.[40] More than ever before, foreign journalists were on hand to see the voting and they repeatedly reported local instances of irregularities. Some invidiously compared the Mexican elections with those recently held in El Salvador and in Sandinista-controlled Nicaragua.[41]

The government answered with charges of a foreign press campaign against Mexico, a part of its repeated accusations that PAN has close connections with Americans, most particularly the Republican party (some Panistas as well as PRI leaders were invited to the 1980 GOP convention which PAN members attended), and was therefore treasonable.[42]

Ironically, the PRI would in any case probably have won a fair election with large majorities, but by abusing every electoral rule it put into question individual contests all over the country for observers inside and outside of Mexico; and as *The Washington Post* said in an editorial,[43] no one would ever know what really happened in the gubernatorial elections in Sonora and Nuevo Leon. "The Party of the Institutionalized Revolution," said the *Economist* of London, has killed the hope that pluralism might at last be coming to the largest country in the West that still forbids any real opposition. . . . Mexico, potentially the most prosperous economy in the Spanish-speaking world, will remain for the rest of this decade with a political system 50 years out of date even by Latin standards. Mr. De la Madrid's presidency, now over the halfway mark, will be increasingly hamstrung by the political system he has refused to reform."[44]

Both of the major contenders against the government, those on the Left and on the Right, lost seats in the final tally. PAN lost thirteen seats in the four-hundred-member chamber. (One hundred seats are distributed on a proportional basis to the minority parties.) The Partido Socialista Unificado Mexicana (PSUM), the Communists, and four other left-wing groups lost five seats to the PRI.

Nevertheless, a government spokesman wrote for external consumption in the U.S. that "Recent elections have been characterized by greater competition and the appearance of new forces that seek representation. The Mexican political system has been successful because it has the ability to regulate conflict and promote institutional reforms in the context of public loyalty to historical values."[45] Thus the sophistry of spokesmen for the regime continued to espouse the efficacy of the Mexico Model and Mexico approached a new electoral round of state and municipal elections in 1986 with no more hope of fairness—but even greater expectations of violence.

Internally, the admission of fraudulent elections is more honest, even if the rationalization much more complicated. Arguing that the legitimacy of the regime and the ruling party arises from the Revolution, an official PRI publication argued: "Elections in consequence in Mexico do not grant legitimacy [to the regime], give sanction to a renovation or [its] exercise [of] power. Electoral processes cannot have in the country [Mexico] the same definite character that they give to liberal democratic regimes. The Mexican state is not a state in debt to the people. It does not have to have a recurring secondary procedure to legitimitize itself. It gives itself its own legitimacy and it is renewed by the people of Mexico through its organic bonding with the same [people of Mexico]. [It is an] organic bonding that is expressed in social conquests."[46]

Perhaps no spokesmen for a regime have deluded themselves more about their naked manipulation of power in a major country since tsarist Russia. This kind of rationalization was possible in the 1930s, the 1940s and the 1950s, perhaps even into the 1960s, when the idea of a Mexico Model was in vogue. But that time has passed. As one American observer examining the elections put it, "Mexico has little else to offer its fast-growing population but a chance to speak out and share in the country's future. . . . If a country is so unwilling to accept political change, can it carry out the tough economic reforms necessary to solve the long-running economic crisis?"[47]

Chapter 2: The Mexico Model

The concept of the Mexico Model—a formula for economic and political development in the nonindustrialized world—became an attractive one for many political scientists and economists in the post-World War II period. For many students of economic growth in the so-called developing countries, it seemed to provide a recipe for stability and growth in the exploding muddle of economic deprivation and political ferment that overtook the Afro-Asian world after the decolonization process of the 1950s, and which had earlier on plagued—and continues to bedevil—Latin America.

Frank Brandenburg, who wrote the most popular general book on Mexico in the post-World War II period, summed it up this way: "With underdeveloped countries everywhere pushed by their masses into modernization schemes that promise the arrival of tomorrow today, recent Mexican experiences have much to offer the world. The legacies that form the issues in today's freedom struggles in Africa, Asia, and Latin America have striking counterparts in the Mexican record: brutality, militarism, racism, poverty, privileged foreigners, feudalism, ignorance. A half-century before President Kennedy launched his Alliance for Progress, a bearded mystic [Madero] from the northern plains of Mexico led his compatriots against the invincible dictator Porfírio Díaz and unleashed forces that would make Mexico one of the first nations to undergo a national social revolution. Transforming Mexico into a modern nation meant undertaking a permanent revolution—the most sweeping transformation of Mexican life since the impact of Cortes and the Spaniards that followed him. This book is an interpretation of the causes and effects of this revolution, the Mexican Revolution . . . It is a timely reminder of the urgency of discovering practical solutions to the problems imposed on the emerging nations by economic backwardness, social estrangement, and authoritarianism." [1]

Indeed, Mexico in the 1950s and early 1960s did appear to be a model of economic progress and development. That period of prosperity had been laid during World War II, when Mexico had enjoyed an unprecedented boom. On the eve of the war, President Lázaro Cárdenas had made sure, as the European conflict drew nearer and nearer to the Western Hemisphere in the late 1930s, that Mexico would not repeat the experience of World War I, when flirtation with the Germans had almost caused a second U.S.-Mexican War. At that time, German maneuverings in Mexico probably had more to do with Woodrow Wilson's decision to enter the European conflagration than most historians concede.[2] They were probably the last straw which caused Wilson to renounce his pacifist sympathies and put the U.S. into the war on the Allied side. And there may also be something to the theory that Wilson felt the revolutionary events in Mexico might be jeopardized by the old-diplomacy type maneuvers of the major powers.[3]

In any case, the world had come a long way since World War I even if the players seemed to be, alas, very much the same. In Cárdenas Mexico had a president with strong antifascist sentiments— despite the fact that Nazi Germany and fascist Italy had been among Mexico's best customers after the expropriation of foreign-owned oil companies. And, secretly, he proposed to President Franklin D. Roosevelt a hemisphere-wide boycott of the Nazis after Roosevelt made it clear he would not intervene in Mexican internal affairs to protect U.S. investments there.

By November 1941, Mexico and the U.S. had worked out a series of economic and political agreements that made Mexico a loyal ally during the war. The war provided opportunities for Mexico to sell its mineral resources to the U.S. at excellent prices, and also to send contract laborers into the U.S. to help harvest American crops, whose salaries were sent back to the workers' villages in Mexico. It was this fillip that pushed the Mexican economy with a roar into the 1950s when it attained an average real growth rate of better than 6 percent per year. Mexican agriculture experienced the world's first taste of "the green revolution" with experimentation in new seed varieties of corn largely developed by foreign scientists in Mexico. Grain production was so boosted that for a short time the country even became a net exporter.

Meanwhile, industrialization began to give the country the attributes of modern economy. Major new industries were launched by aggressive entrepreneurs, even if many of the entrepreneurs were— as they have always tended to be in Mexico—recent arrivals from Europe or the U.S. The war years gave Mexico tens of thousands of European refugees in addition to the earlier Spanish Republican emigration. These new arrivals fired the whole intellectual, economic, and, to some extent, social scene. The discovery by this elite of the richness of Mexico's Indian plastic arts heritage—however much it was cheapened by crude Marxist propaganda—along with these new, imported talents turned Mexico City into a glittering and increasingly cultured world capital. The plastic arts, experimental architecture, world-class music, good restaurants, and general internationalization led to a new elan among Mexico's elite. It was Mexico City's finest hour, living up to the dreams of that doomed royal couple, Maximillian and Carlotta, who during their bizarre attempt to establish a European-backed empire in Mexico a century before, had planned a second Paris down to copying Napoleon III's broad boulevards and luxurious parks.

Yet it was clear that whatever had developed in Mexico was less a planned political scenario than the accretion of history. In the 1920s, the regional leaders, who had put Mexico back together after almost twenty years of chaos, rejected the recommendations of the 1917 constitutional convention. It had been dominated by intellectuals and ideologues who sought a continuation of the Reforma of President Benito Juárez, that strange, Lincolnesque figure of Mexican history, an Indian who in the 1800s, while exiled in New Orleans, had imbibed deeply of U.S. liberal political theory mixed with large doses of Freemasonry. Juárez not only wanted a Mexico committed to the separation of church and state and dedicated to befriending the underprivileged, he also wanted, at least theoretically, to turn his back on the Spanish heritage of government intervention in economics in favor of the Anglo-Saxon doctrine of laissez-faire. The political experience of the "generals" during the bad times, however, led to the reconstitution in the 1920s of a strong executive and a highly centralized government with a strong hand in economic policymaking. Although the strongest plank in Madero's revolt against Díaz centered on multiple terms in office, the attempt of one of the leading general-presidents of the period, Plutarco Calles, to continue to dominate the executive from behind the scenes after his term of office had expired, was what most probably led to the establishment of the sanctity in the new regime of one six-year term for the chief executive.

At first, the new chief executive was held in rein by a dispersal of real power. There were the surviving generals of the guerrilla campaigns, who took on more and more prestige as the "revolution" was enshrined. Some of them had large and important regional followings, and in some instances defied the central government in pursuit of their own policies as regional warlords. The radicals of the Left, a tiny group before the chaos, became the nucleus of a trade union movement, which although it quickly became part of the power structure, and gradually an instrument of control rather than of agitation against the government or employers, did share power in the early days with the other political entities. The remnants of the agrarian reformers—particularly those calling on the ghost of Zapata—became bureaucratized spokesmen for the *campesino*, the traditional peasant in the countryside. But, increasingly, as the government bureaucracy grew and the stability of the regime lengthened, a formalized representation of these classes was folded into the ruling structure.

By the presidency of Lázaro Cárdenas (1934–1940), an official "revolutionary family" had evolved of organizations around the ruling party which were the apotheosis, ironically, of the corporate state that both Benito Mussolini and Francisco Franco attempted to establish in the 1930s in Italy and Spain, respectively, with such disastrous consequences. Although the phrase, "the revolutionary family," began to be used as early as the Calles administration (1924 –1928) to refer to the officials around the president, it later came to mean those organizations acceptable to the regime as well as individual members of the elite acceptable to the presidency. It would not be untoward to make a comparison between the Mexican revolutionary family and the *nomenklatura*, the elite of the Soviet system.[4]

In theory, the interests of all the national constituencies were served by these groups representing the major sectors of the society. Even the business community—generally antagonistic to the monopoly party ruling in the name of the "revolution"—was represented through the old Spanish-style chambers of commerce, industrial chambers, and trades associations. If major policy decisions were to be effected, theoretically there was a give-and-take within these groups inside "the revolutionary family" and a compromise was hassled out. The proof of this, it was argued, was that left-wing presidents were followed by conservative chief executives and vice versa; it was argued that democracy inside the ruling party not only sorted out the issues, but tended to adjust for excesses by one side or another.[5]

Thus, Cárdenas and his left-wing administration that nationalized the foreign-owned oil industry was followed by Avila Camacho (1940 –1946), the "great pacifier" of the Catholic opposition, and Camacho by Miguel Alemán (1945–1952), the proponent not only of the private sector in the Mexican economy but a successful suitor of foreign capital investment. The system, it was argued, provided through the one-party structure a process of discovering and training young executives, and even young *técnicos*, who could efficiently direct the growing bureaucracy in its state intervention. Many were prepared to argue that it was in essence a democratic system, a far better one for the preindustrial societies than representative government. And later, when many of the newly independent Afro-Asian regimes fell victim to demagoguery and corruption of the one-man, one-vote regimes, some Western theorists were prepared to argue that the Mexican PRI system was better with its "internal party democracy" than soiled copies of Westminister hypocritically manipulated by WOG's (Western Oriental Gentlemen).[6]

Yet, it is now clear, three major currents were eroding the Mexico Model and giving it a new and very different character, setting the stage for the present crisis, even as it was being lauded as the prescription for the ailments of an underdeveloped country. They were:

1. The growing centralization of power in the presidency at a time when intellectual currents, the economy, and the social structure in the country were necessitating more and more pluralism.

2. The bureaucratization of the economy with more and more state intervention, inefficiency, corruption and disparity of income.

3. The demographic explosion that was eroding all progress with a population fighting for smaller and smaller pieces of the pie and presenting the country with incalculable social pressures.

The discordant voices that had emerged from the period of chaos in the 1920s had, paradoxically, profited the regime and the people of Mexico by their very diversity. Perhaps for the first time since the Spanish Conquest, the varied geographical regions of the country with their different social settings were being represented at the center and permitted, in some cases, a certain amount of autonomy. But as the years passed, and the military heroes of the war died off, the Mexican political stage had fewer and fewer stars and fewer and fewer voices which could stand up to the powerful centralizing forces that the country had inherited from both Spain and its Indian past and which were concentrated in the president-emperor. The military, formerly part of the revolutionary family, was virtually gone by 1941 when Camacho, the last of the generals-presidents came to office. Camacho's successor, Alemán, wound up the military's membership in the revolutionary family. He set up the Guardias Presidenciales, a single, elite, armored unit of the armed forces placed directly under the command of his uncle, a general. At the same time, he inflated the ranks of generals to such outrageous proportions that they no longer had prestige or influence.

The selection of the president, which had once been an intricate, collective compromise involving many elements—the wishes of the incumbent, the demands of the military, the threats of labor radicals turned bureaucrats, the blackmail of the agrarian radicals turned technocrats, the persuasion of the intellectuals, the government bureaucracy itself—increasingly became a unilateral decision of the all-powerful chief executive who simply tapped his successor while everyone else fell into line.

Gradually, too, the initial attempt to give the country a mixed economy was overwhelmed by two tendencies—the xenophobia which led to the nationalization of foreign private ownership started with Cárdenas' widely acclaimed expropriation of oil in 1938, and the acceptance of the prophetic pronouncements of Raul Prebisch's and his gospel of import substitution. Prebisch, an Argentine economist with wide influence not only in Latin America, but through his chairmanship of the United Nations Economic Commission for Latin America (ECLA), to the whole of the underdeveloped world, preached the concept that the continuing deterioration of the terms of worldwide trade had made manufactures permanently more expensive relative to raw materials. Raw material producers like Mexico—and the other Latin American exporters—had thus become the hewers of wood and the drawers of water for the world economy, the Argentine economist argued. To improve their position, Prebisch preached, only an "import-substitution" strategy could be successful. It called for imported manufactures to be replaced by production inside the country, an essential industrialization to be undertaken in effect at any price.

That price turned out to be the creation of highly protected industries giving monopolies to domestic and foreign producers who would fashion the new industries in Mexico irrespective of "world economics," that is, however much their costs and prices were above world prices, with competition kept out of the local market by tariffs and other restrictions. Not only did it make efficiency and productivity a relatively low priority for the developing Mexican industrial sector, but it created a group of industries highly dependent on imported spare parts and raw materials, linking these local industries to the world market for components. At the same time, it created industries which were not competitive in world markets and thus created a demand for foreign exchange that they could not earn and, increasingly, that the traditional Mexican exports could not supply in sufficient quantity. To top if off, these new industries were often politically arranged deals in which individual investors got protection not only from foreign competition but from other potential Mexican producers. These deals not only enhanced the outrageous corruption that had characterized Mexican governments since the Conquest, but they increasingly wedded the private industrial and mercantile sector to a mushrooming government bureaucracy.

Meanwhile, the demographic explosion taking place in the countryside aggravated every Mexican problem. Attempts to feed the population, which appeared to have growing success in the 1950s, failed as a combination of the snowballing population and a growing feud with foreign geneticists carrying on experimentation in the country turned the international spotlight away from Mexican food problems, and the continuing muddle of land ownership. As agricultural productivity refused to rise to meet the increasing demand for livelihood from the agricultural sector, there was more and more agitation for new land distribution—inflamed by the revolutionary rhetoric demagogic politicians often based on total ignorance of the real agricultural problems—thereby further limiting investment in the agricultural sector as the land tenure question grew in complexity.

Antonio Ortiz Mena, head of the Interamerican Development Bank since being politely pushed out of the Mexican government in 1969, in a series of detailed interviews criticizing the Mexican government's economic policy, argues that what he calls the evolutionary program of the Revolution took a sharp turn in 1970, breaking with its past during the Echeverría and López Portillo administrations. Those changes, he contends, brought on bankruptcy and a flight of capital. "The one thing we were able to do was to destroy production, above all in the countryside where it ruined us. How can you explain [the case of] sugar? In 1970, we exported 500,000 tons to the U.S., today we import a million tons. And we nationalized almost all the industry. And we wasted money on more workhands in the industry. And we raised the price of sugar. This is another phenomenon that reveals the total mixup."[7]

On the problem of land tenure, Ortiz Mena says that "in the last period of the Mexican Revolution, with its traditional evolution until 1970, there had been a dimmunization of the workforce in the fields, which would have been expected; to reduce the people which weighed heavily on the countryside, so that those who remained would live better, would be possible only with the augmentation of the wealth of agriculture through augmented productivity of the arable land, a given factor without which nothing can be done. But if the number of persons maintaining the same level of productivity grows, the totality receives less. What caused the collapse [of agricultural development] was the abandonment of the tradition of the Mexican Revolution: [the] launching [of] three million people without land against those who occupied the land, and these were *ejidatarios* [members of communal holdings, members of] cooperatives, and small proprietors."

Certainly, the attempt to reconstruct the primitive communal holdings of the pre-Conquest Indian villages, *ejidos*, neither satisfied the demand for holdings nor raised productivity. The government it-self continued to hold title to the land, undercutting the possibility of investment by the tillers. Land in the *ejidos* is theoretically redistributed from time to time so that no member tills the same plots indefinitely. But that has the effect of penalizing those who produce more, and discourages any kind of soil shepherding. All this has meant that when *ejidatarios* have found their holdings too small or water or financing for seeds and fertilizer not available, they have fled to the cities. Unemployment was rising in a country which tradi-tionally had had large reservoirs of underemployed and unemployed. Income distribution became even more skewed as the narrow in-dustrialization set up a "modern" priviledged caste in the new highly protected industries who lived and worked in a totally different style from the bulk of the population. Even the workers in these new in-dustries were set apart as Western-style social welfare benefits devel-oped under government-sponsored union control which were unavail-able to the mass of the *campesinos* living in the rural areas.

Attempts at social progress were also being eroded by the population explosion. Education, for example, enhanced by the road-building program and the enormous growth in communications, nevertheless failed, for propaganda, directed by the highly politicized teachers' union (with 800,000 members the largest "union" in Latin America) took the place of real education. The organization resembles no union in the democratic West but rather is a paid, government claque, supporting an enormous hierarchy paid for by the Ministry of Education.

Today, although the educational system does reach out to vir-tually all of Mexico, dropout rates among first-year entrants to the public education system are over 50 percent—that in a country where at least half the population is under fifteen years of age. The absolute numbers of illiterates are growing; the percentage of the population which is illiterate has not improved in decades.

Nor are other social services in better shape. In a country with almost unlimited problems of public health, José Kuthy Porter, presi-dent of the National Academy of Medicine, reported in June 1984 that some 15,000 Mexican doctors were without work and called on the government to reduce the numbers entering medical schools.

The final disintegration of the Mexico Model took place politi-cally as power continued to concentrate in the presidency, resulting in the two failed presidencies of the administrations of Luis Echeverría, from 1970 to 1976, and of José López Portillo, from 1976 to 1982. Even were the other attributes of the system as meritorious as its proponents contend, this failure to permit a democratic selection of the presidency would reveal the bankruptcy of the system. For even more today than earlier the Mexican system is ruled by a chief executive who carries overwhelming responsibility and power.

In 1969 the outgoing president, Gustavo Díaz Ordaz, in a decision he afterward is reported to have regretted, chose the first president of Mexico since the 1920s who had no experience either in elective office or in the military structure. Luis Echeverría had served in the swelling bureaucracy and made his way up to the highest levels as a consummate bureaucrat. But Echeverría's main claim to the presidency when Díaz Ordaz chose him was as head of Gobernación —a post occupied by the three presidents who preceded him in office. It could be argued that the route through Gobernación to the highest office was evidence of the increasing authoritarian nature of the regime.

Echeverría was as far from the stereotype of the ordinary Mexican as can be imagined: cool, obviously ambitious, energetic, impatient, even volatile, verbose, thin, balding, spectacled, nonsmoking, nondrinking. He was the quintessential product of the new Mexican, post-World War II elite, a product of what was—in his time —the elitist of the country's institutions, the Universidad Nacional Autónoma de Mexico (UNAM), the national university in Mexico City, now a sprawling megauniversity of 375,000 students. It was this association of UNAM friends that was to dictate much of what happened in the next decade in Mexico.

Echeverría considered himself a populist, and although not a professed Marxist, he flirted with the extreme Left inside and outside Mexico. There is some evidence that he encouraged the young student radicals at UNAM who, in 1968, attempted the same sort of insurrection that took place in Paris that summer and was reflected in other Western capitals. But he was, nevertheless, still the *Ministro de Gobernación*, the minister in Mexican government charged with the public order, who brutally suppressed the demonstrations.

Díaz Ordaz was absent from the capital when the student crisis blew up. Whatever Echeverría's role in the bloody affair, when he himself reached the presidency he appointed a government dominated at least in its second echelon—by young technocrats of the farthermost left wing of the PRI, some of them involved in the revolt's leadership. He proceeded posthaste to make radical changes in the Mexico Model. He purged the right wing of the PRI from power: Alfonso Corona del Rosal, the party's right-wing leader, got no government post although it had been the custom to reward all elements of the party in a new government.

In 1971, Echeverría used a riot, in which paramilitary government agents were employed against student radicals at UNAM, as a pretext to purge Alfonso Martínez Dominguez, then regent (appointed governor) of the federal district (Mexico City). There is considerable evidence that in this instance the Soviet Union, using North Koreans as surrogates, was directly involved since they had recruited young student activists who were transferred from Moscow to North Korea where they received training as terrorists and guerrillas.[8]

Echeverría moved decisively to expand the role of the presidency in the revolutionary family. He was able to oust five governors during his incumbency in the hope that his followers would still be around at these regional posts when his successor came in. And his almost constant changes in the cabinet emphasized the all-powerful role of the president. The more conservative Antonio Ortiz Mena, who had guided a noninflationary economic program for a decade, found refuge in a "golden exile" as head of the Interamerican Development Bank in Washington.

Echeverría became, uncharacteristically for Mexico which had so often tried to keep its distance from world controversies, a major player in the United Nations debate over "a new economic world order." He moved rapidly toward more statist solutions for economic problems at home while advocating them on the international scene. Public spending poured into housing, schools, and agricultural credits. As the economic problems increased, despite an annual average growth rate which the government claimed was 5.6 percent, the government bought out bankrupt companies—state-owned corporations increased from eighty-six to 740 during his sexenium. Government attempts to enhance revenue to pay for these operations drove taxes up from 8 percent of the gross domestic product in 1970 to more than twice that by 1975. In six years, from 1970 to 1976, the money supply increased by an average of 18 percent a year, 50 percent over the previous administration's record. The inflationary spiral grew to an average of 23 percent annually against the peso that had been kept almost stable for the two previous decades. And the deficit in the balance of payments tripled between 1973 and 1975 with the increasing demand for imports and the gradual flight of capital abroad.

Inevitably, this led to pressure on the peso, and the first massive devaluation of 1976.

The growing economic difficulties, however, were only a complement to the basic political ineptitude of the regime. Echeverría was running a campaign to make himself secretary-general of the United Nations simultaneously with his role as Mexican president. The young leftists around him believed that he could put together a coalition of Third Worlders with Moscow's blessing. In pursuit of this strategy which predated Echeverría's tenure as president, he had in 1975 during a trip to the Middle East, exasperated his Israeli hosts by meeting Yasser Arafat of the Palestine Liberation Organization (PLO) during a visit to Cairo and endorsing the PLO's claims.

The whole strategy fell apart during a United Nations Economic and Social Council (UNESCO) conference in Mexico City in 1972, when Mexico endorsed the "Zionism is racism" resolution—apparently because Mrs. Echeverría, a delegate, was led astray by the young *técnicos* of the Ministry of Foreign Affairs who dominated the government. Echeverría had to recant ignominiously when Jewish groups in the U.S. imposed an effective boycott of Mexican tourism. The Secretary for Tourism of the Mexican government came cap-in-hand to the American Jewish Committee (AJC) and other organizations in New York to apologize, a performance which, because of its obsequiousness and general boorishness, embarrassed the Americans present.

In another attempt at high diplomacy, Echeverría built an elaborate embassy for Fidel Castro's Cuba as "a gift from the Mexican people." Pressure was put on high Mexican army officers to visit Cuba and the Soviet Union, the latter of which they point blank refused. Mexico's increasing role as the center of pro-Moscow, pro-Havana intrigue in the hemisphere was leading to more behind-the-scenes difficulties with the U.S.

Toward the middle of the six-year administration, it became apparent that Echeverría also was trying to thwart the cardinal rule of the Mexican political process by dictating the policies of his successor. He attempted to make the selection process a pseudo-public affair, and thereby to commit the next president to an Echeverría program, a plan drafted by Jesús Reyes Heroles, the leading left-wing politician-ideologue in the PRI. Echeverría refused to take a back seat during the campaign for the next presidency, normally a cut-and-dried affair in which the PRI candidate, who is certain to win, tours every part of the country and quietly relegates the outgoing president to the background. On the contrary, Echeverría was determined to overshadow his successor, José López Portillo, in an effort so flagrant that even the international press began to publicize it.

To add to the failing PRI theatricals, the conservative Partido Acción Nacional (PAN), the main opposition party, had great difficulty in nominating a candidate because of its own internal problems. The charade of Mexican elections was revealed as more bogus than ever before. In the final months of his administration, Echeverría's confrontation with the private sector reached a fever pitch with more than the usual rumors of a military coup said to be backed by the then powerful industrial community of Monterrey. And then, in the north, there was an epidemic of agrarian agitation over land, a problem which Echeverría "solved" by a massive expropriation only ten days before he was to leave office.

Echeverría introduced an air of crisis and lack of confidence that Mexico had not felt since the early 1930s. Further adding to the tension was an attack by an unidentified terrorist organization on the car of the sister of the president-nominee in August 1976. She was unhurt, but one of her bodyguards was killed. And then, on August 31, a final blow to Echevería's prestige: the government had to devalue the peso for the first time in twenty-two years by a massive 37 percent to the dollar. Furthermore, when it was refloated, a second devaluation occurred that brought its value to half what it had been only two months earlier.

It was the end of the post-World War II bubble of prosperity —and confidence. And it was with a sign of relief that the country (and Washington) welcomed Echeverría's successor, again a *técnico* without experience in elective office or the military, but an ebullient, charismatic figure, who was believed in conservative circles in Mexico and Washington and New York to be a solid, moderate, politican of the traditional Mexican variety.

López Portillo was the scion of an old political family from the wealthy and semiautonomous state of Jalisco (Guadalajara)—his uncle had negotiated with Wilson in Washington to end the Tampico Incident in 1914. But, nevertheless, López Portillo had virtually no political base except among the bureaucrats in the government offices where he had served. His opening gambit was to try to heal the wounds that Echeverría had created. In his inaugural, he made it clear that he was his own man, not Echeverría's, thus igniting one of the bitterest feuds in contemporary Mexican political history. He offered an olive branch to the private sector, promising to live up to their legitimate demands in a mixed economy. And he asked for help in putting together a new program, with the slogan, *La solución somos todos* (We are all part of the solution).

His appointments were supposedly pragmatic bureaucrats, some of whom he had known from his days at UNAM or even earlier in secondary school, or even the sons and daughters of his classmates. Spoils were spread among the various ideological factions of the PRI, among the followers of former presidents—including *Echeverrístas*— and among the defeated candidates for the presidency. According to one prominent student of Mexican elite power politics, he adhered almost religiously to the most traditional kind of balance of forces—social as well as political—as evidenced by his including in government those family connections that dictate so much of the Mexican power elite's composition.[9]

Most Mexicans were encouraged. And as Allan Riding, no friend of the Mexican moderates, wrote in *The New York Times* in November 1976, "After being on the defensive for the last six years under President Luis Echeverría Alvarez, Mexico's conservative middle and upper classes are now confident that the country's current economic troubles will force President-elect José López Portillo to move sharply and rapidly to the right." Or as another old journalistic hand on the Mexican scene put it in a paid advertisement for the Mexican government, "López Portillo, despite the exhausting pace of his long campaign, seems to have convinced his fellow Mexicans of the necessity of bringing into reality a model for development consistent with the needs of the country in order to move steadily forward toward a vast future, as the most outstanding Mexican and foreign observers have indicated. . . . López Portillo's position has been strengthened by his identification with the aspirations of his people and he is, therefore, assured of being at the top of the public's awareness and the collective will."[10]

Rarely have political expectations and prognosticators been so wrong. The catastrophe that was to overtake the López Portillo administration would dwarf the misfortunes that had dogged Echeverría's six years. And the single catalyst was oil.

The price coup of the Organization of Petroleum Exporting Countries (OPEC) in the Middle East and the intoxication of the oil exporting countries with their new found power were nowhere more dramatically reflected than in Mexico. Three years after his hangdog official visit to the U.S. as president Jimmy Carter's guest in the White House following the debacle of Echeverría's devaluation, López Portillo returned to Washington in September 1979 with an altogether different mien. Allan Riding, again writing in *The New York Times Sunday Magazine* on the eve of the visit, characterized López Portillo as "president of a Mexico now swelling its chest, confident enough at last to look Washington in the eye."[11] Gone were the attempts to curb the growth of overambitious projects of the Echeverría administration, and in its place there was the full-scale launching of the state into all manufacturing fields, and the growth of bureaucracy. Government employment grew from around 600,000 at the beginning of the administration to nearly 1.5 million when López Portillo left office in 1982. The irony is that Mexican authorities had repeatedly emphasized the need for Mexico to avoid the "Venezuela syndrome," —the use of oil revenues to support inefficient government spending on unneeded, long-term development programs.

López Portillo had promised two years of stabilization to recover from the Echeverría devaluation, two years of moderate growth, and then, finally, two years of close to the 6 percent annual average growth rate of earlier days. But the oil windfall after the initial raising of OPEC prices in 1979 unleashed political pressures that overcame wiser counsel. The Global Development Plan of 1979 laid plans for spending that far exceeded surplus oil revenues. Economist Victor Urquidi, leftist head of the prestigious Colegio de México which played a large role in encouraging Mexican excesses, now sums it up like this: "All pretense of scarcity and rationality in expenditure was thrown to the winds. Mexico, the president said publicly, was now going to manage abundance. Many optimists envisaged a surplus that would enable Mexico to repay its foreign debt which earlier had been judged to be rather high. Real investment by both the public and the private sector—the latter engaging in its own reckless expansion—was increasing by 15 percent to 20 percent per year . . . In the end the external debt had risen to close to $80 billion by the end of 1981 (of which $20 billion was owed by private corporations in banks). . . . It is too easy as many have done to blame the world economic crisis on the oil glut—plus the voracious appetite for profit of the international banking system—for Mexico's recent and current economic and financial ills. The blame lies squarely on poor policy formulation and on overoptimistic expectations, with no contingency planning."[12]

Of course, it is equally clear that the U.S. and European and Japanese banks, under pressure to farm out their own incoming petrodollars from the Middle East, were anxious to lend whatever Mexico was willing to borrow. The banks were impressed with Mexico's reputation in the past as a good risk and by her adherence to the 1978 International Monetary Fund (IMF) programs after Echeverría's massive devaluation. The banks were as optimistic about Mexico's oil reserves as the Mexicans and in the headlong race to lend, they even foresaw the time when the country would become a net capital exporter. But had they examined some of their own barometers—the debt-export ratio even in the golden years of highest expectations violated the old rule of thumb that if short-term debt exceeds 50 percent of exports, the country is in trouble—they would have foreseen the disaster.

But beyond the bankers' books were far deeper problems. López Portillo, despite his own former experience as secretary of finance in the Echeverría government, was looking for magic solutions. He postponed devaluation arguing that "when a president devalues, he devalues himself"—an obvious reference to the experience of his predecessor, Echeverría. Finally, when a long overdelayed devaluation in February 1982 failed to halt the flight of capital, López Portillo reached for the magic elixir of more government intervention; he appointed Carlos Tello, a *técnico* and avowed Marxist with a following among American academics, as governor of the central bank to replace Miguel Mancera. Mancera had earlier written a paper on why Mexico could not implement effective exchange controls, living as it does side-by-side with the U.S. and the greatest free money markets in the world.

But López Portillo—with Tello's advice—froze $12 billion in foreign currency held by Mexican residents (not a few were retired U.S. citizens lured to Mexico by low living costs and high interests for dollar bank accounts). And then on September 1, 1982, in a move of sheer desperation, he nationalized the fifty-nine Mexican private banks with their 4,378 branches (excluding Citibank, the only U.S. retail bank in Mexico), and slapped on exchange controls. Another 30 percent devaluation of the Mexican peso and the institution of a two-tier exchange control were aimed at halting the continuing outflow of capital.

There was no disguising that the nationalization was a political act rather than an economic solution to Mexico's problems. The Mexican government already had control of its banks through a National banking Commission, and interest rates were set weekly by the government. International transactions were controlled, and the government took 70 percent of all dollar account deposits with a requirement that some 40 percent of all peso deposits go immediately into the Central Bank. But López Portillo was looking for a scapegoat, playing to the left-wing galleries; he hoped that the nationalization would end his tenure as president in a burst of nationalist fervor such as had met Cárdenas' government takeover of foreign oil fifty years earlier. His public speeches talked of the betrayal of the country by the bankers and businessmen—forgetting that it had been his refusal to face up to the question of the overvalued peso that had made dollars, as the wags had it, the only cheap thing in Mexico.

"I can testify," he said, "that in recent years a group of Mexicans, led, counseled and supported by private banks, have taken more money out of the country than all the empires that have exploited us since the beginning of our history."[13] The controlled press of course cast López Portillo as a hero, and the left-wing groups rallied around him. But along with the downward spiral of the peso the flight of capital continued, and the declining confidence in the future of the country.

Before he flew off to self-imposed exile in Europe, López Portillo had broken the bank. Not only had he left chaos and a decimated

Mexican economy, but he had left a record of rapacious greed seldom seen since Nero. Washington intelligence sources estimate that he personally stole as much as $3.5 billion from the national treasury. That is probably no exaggeration, as some knowledgeable observers say that López Portillo, himself, does not know how much he stole. Well-founded reports in PEMEX and government circles claim that he accumulated foreign accounts at the rate of 90,000 bbls./da. of exported petroleum at a time when the price was $30 a barrel.

Whatever the actual sum, López Portillo fled the country with an enormous fortune. Mexico had experienced nothing like it since Cortes and his conquistadores had melted down the golden religious treasure of the Aztecs to carry off to Spain. For those conservatives in the international development community who had for years argued that corruption was not the issue in the nonindustrial countries, that high rates of growth in all societies in all periods of world history produced enormous corruption but also built those societies, the phenomenon of López Portillo was puzzling, not to say deflating. Corruption at this level might, indeed, have to be considered an economic phenomenon that had to be taken into account in any future study of economic development prospects.

The public was also treated to the spectacle of a totally demoralized man, his family life in shreds. One of the most bizarre acts that followed was a semipublic debate via the newspapers between the past president and one of his mistresses, former minister of tourism in his government and the divorced former wife of Echeverría's son, a beautiful young leader of the 1968 left-wing UNAM students. Mexican cynicism and bitter humor flowered in the aftermath of this total demoralization. López Portillo had built himself a forty-four bedroom house in suburban Mexico City (as well as two homes for his lady friends on government land abutting Chapultepec Park). So when only a few weeks before the devaluation he told the country in a speech defending his economic policies that sacrifice was necessary, that he would fight like a dog for the peso before he would submit to the dictates of foreign capitalists, the mansion immediately was dubbed "casa del perro" (the dog house). Suddenly the idea of living like a dog took on the ironic connotation of living luxuriously. Peddlers in the chic Zona Rosa nightclub and tourist area began selling pesos with a small plastic dog attached. And when the ex-president appeared publicly in retirement in Rome, he was followed by a group of young Mexican tourists, barking away.

If *dignidad* was as important an ingredient of the Mexican personality and character as generations of Mexicans have told their rustic northern neighbors, López Portillo had abandoned it on a national scale that seemed to call into question the values of the whole society —and certainly of the Mexico Model.

Chapter 3: Los Neo-Científicos

True to the traditions of the Mexico Model, López Portillo's chosen successor could not have been more different from both his two immediate predecessors. He appeared to be an antidote to the two previous administrations—a quiet, introspective man, who, moderates hoped, might even be a "conservative" by PRI standards. A Mass-going Catholic, rumor had it that Miguel De la Madrid Hurtado was not even a member of the Masonic lodges. Freemasonry in Mexico, long since shorn of much of its European and U.S. heritage, provides a vague, anticlerical, leftist environment for the inner plottings of the PRI.[1] De la Madrid was also a devoted family man and his wife was said to be not only a fervent Catholic but a political conservative with ties to Mexico's Opus Dei, a Catholic lay movement which operates a business school and a liberal arts university in Mexico. He would move the PRI back toward the center, the optimists confidently predicted.

But it would have been equally easy to predict that De La Madrid would be forced, given the enormity of the crisis he had inherited, and his own deep involvement in the PRI establishment, to follow the pattern of the two failed presidencies before him. Professor Roderic A. Camp, a scholar of the Mexican elite, called De la Madrid quintessential. "De la Madrid symbolizes the control of the new administrative elite, the *political technician*, in Mexico. The data show . . . that ever since the 1930s, few cabinet members and their immediate subordinates have been political militants or have used political party posts to rise to the top. Although traditionally a fifth of Mexico's cabinet secretaries also were high party officials, that figure should have increased as the party increased in strength and became integral to the government. Instead, however, the number of politicians holding high party posts has stabilized at about one-seventh, and this has been equally true in the careers of secretaries. For the first time in recent political history, cabinet secretaries, who are the most prestigious group within the Mexican political system, have held high party posts in numbers *fewer* than all other politicians."[2]

While a conservative, if again only by PRI standards—or as moderates and conservatives in Mexico would say, not a Jacobin— De la Madrid was nevertheless a child of the left-leaning Mexican bureaucracy. His American exposure as a Harvard graduate student only intensified his tendency to see government intervention as the indispensable medicine for Mexico's ills. And when he made his first visit to the Supreme Court after his inauguration, it was to present the Mexican judges with two amendments to the Mexican constitution. These not only legalized *ex post facto* the nationalization of the country's private banks carried out by his predecessor, but they completely changed the rules of the political-economic game in Mexico. It could be argued that since López Portillo did not need constitutional authorization for the nationalization, the new amendments did little beyond tidying up one corner of Mexico's somewhat crowded legal closet. The lack of judicial propriety was clear when the president of the Supreme Court proclaimed the nationalization constitutional after the bank owners had instituted a legal action challenging it.

But on second examination, the De la Madrid administration decided on the necessity of the constitutional amendments. For the amendments did more than just plaster over the bank nationalization in the hodgepodge of the Mexican legal system. They laid out a completely new philosophical basis for the political economy. The new statutes further reduced the sanctity of private property and individual property rights and announced that henceforth the government would be the sole arbiter of economic matters. Few in the country, concerned as most were with the horrendous immediate implications of the massive devaluations, the confiscation of dollars, and the nationalization of the private banks, were aware of the fundamental change. The concept of a mixed economy, enshrined as the economic philosophy of government since the 1920s, was gone.

Perhaps even more important as an indicator of where De la Madrid would take the country were his choices for the cabinet and other positions in the new administration. If one were to examine the background of the eighteen top officials in the administration—ministers of state, attorney general of the republic, the appointive regent of the federal district of Mexico City, governor of the central bank, the district attorney for the federal district—a very clear picture emerges. They were, almost without exception, *técnicos* with outstanding technocratic qualifications—eight lawyers, four economists, twelve postgraduates with degrees earned abroad, six former members of the staff of the highly respected Banco de México (the central bank), and all but two graduates of UNAM. While the theme of the De la Madrid presidential campaign was decentralization of power, nine came from the federal district, which, with the large contingency of UNAM graduates, was a clear indication that the centralizing movement was destined to continue.

But the De la Madrid's choice of cabinet also intensified the trend toward political inexperience. Only one member of the whole team had ever served in an elective office, and that only as a *diputado* (representative) in the lower house, not as a governor or a senator. Two had been presidents of the PRI, but one for a very short time. (One of these, probably the strongest member of the cabinet and the leader of the left wing, was Reyes Heroles, who died in March 1985, to be replaced by another less-known *técnico*.) Only three members of the group had served in the government political party for more than ten years—six less than five. Half of the members of the governing group were under fifty. In other words, one sees a president—himself a *técnico* with no grassroots political experience—surrounding himself with similar products of Mexico City's bureaucratic hothouse.

If, as most observers believed, the system was entering its greatest political test since the 1920s, it was doing so with a group of political novices. One admittedly right-wing leader of the PRI made this judgement to the author when De la Madrid was "tapped" by López Portillo in 1982. "I would rather have seen a left-wing demagogue than this man," he said. "Mexico is going into the greatest crisis in its history and when De la Madrid finds out that all his computer models and statistics don't mean anything, he will be absolutely naked. He cannot even talk to the Indians." The old reactionary was reflecting a generally held view that came out of the election campaign, a view shared even by the new president's friends concerning his political talents.

De la Madrid combined Tom Dewey's coldness and lack of charisma with Jerry Ford's clumsiness as a candidate. He had a knack for falling all over himself, and the Mexican version of donning an Indian war bonnet was not his style. (A photograph of the new president in the garb of *los indígenas* of Chiapas looks like a burlesque.) When the two massive earthquakes struck Mexico City in September 1985, De la Madrid found it impossible to assume the role of the charismatic leader of the Mexico people during their hour of adversity. Instead of using television to address the nation, he donned a leather jacket and toured the destruction like the technocrat he is. When the second quake struck and a group of the city's frightened homeless instinctively gravitated to the presidential quarters for reassurance, the president failed to appear. This total lack of public relations sensibility is seen by his friends and supporters as his refusal to use the traditional populist and demagogic appeals of the office of the Mexican president. But it is typical of the man. Paradoxically, the reason De la Madrid has in the past reassured New York bankers and Washington State Department career officers is precisely that which makes it seem unlikely he can pull off the kind of miracle that is necessary to save the Mexico Model. His Harvard studies in public administration and his easy command of English might endear him to U.S. bureaucrats and investors, hoping against hope that somehow he might pull another rabbit out of the hat and save their $100-billion Mexican debt commitment. But it is just this kind of dedication to American "social science voodoo," the pseudoscientific attempt to explain life's phenomena in statistical and scientifical terms, which is most alarming.

Typical of this *weltanschauung* is this curious relationship drawn by De la Madrid between Mexico and the world: "On the one hand, the extreme left [in Mexico] wants a complete change of system in Mexico, basically a socialist system. On the other hand, we have extreme conservative parties who even think that many of the things done by the Mexican Revolution should be undone. *They think more in terms of Western democracy, in terms of a basically capitalistic system.* And these two options are not accepted by the majority of the Mexican people"[3] (emphasis added). Thus, in what can only be assumed to be ideological confusion or a commitment to a set of values different from the West, De la Madrid rules Mexico—with its humanist and Catholic ethos—out of the West.

De la Madrid and his young crew resemble nothing so much as a new group of *científicos*, a new group of brilliant, educated government bureaucrat-advisors with little in common with the great majority of their countrymen, with the ordinary man, and indeed, with little knowledge of the practicalities of daily life in Mexico. Just as Díaz's advisers at the turn of the century tried to use French positivism to order the Mexican transformation to a modern state, De la Madrid's *neo-científicos* appear to be trying this time to use American scientism—the view that the world is a logical place in which everything can be deduced and "solved" if there are enough systems and dedication (paging Robert P. McNamara).

An example: In November 1982, Stafford Beer, a British cybernetics expert and professor at Manchester University Business School and the University of Pennsylvania Wharton School of Business Administration, approached the president-elect through a Mexican intermediary with a project to investigate and redesign the Mexican bureaucracy based on an analysis of De la Madrid's own campaign book, *The Great National Problems of Today*. After a frustrating year working with the Mexican bureaucracy and the president's staff, Beer resigned his commission and wrote De la Madrid a scathing letter warning him that while the British cyberneticist had the time to wait, "it is my considered opinion that Mexico does not have the time."[4] Beer warned that Mexico had developed "a bureaucracy which had almost no purpose but self-aggrandizement." And while he said he believed that De la Madrid had identified a structural reform that had to be made, he saw no means to make it unless the president himself became directly involved. Beer gave examples of bureaucratic inefficiency and corruption which he had encountered and suggested that the attempt to hold on to a monopoly of political power for one party and one group might be at the root of the problem.

But what is more basic to the whole episode than Beer's analysis —however correct and cogent—was De la Madrid's belief that Mexico's problems which are essentially political could be solved by the introduction of computer systems. Responding to an inquiry from this author in a personal letter,[5] Beer writes: "There is no doubt of the 'scientistic' tendency of the government. Of course, I am a management scientist. But how often I wished I was selling proper science to men with *sombreros* and Zapata mustaches! That is a viable proposition as I have demonstrated elsewhere. [Beer has consulted in some sixteen other countries besides Mexico.] Instead, one is confronted by suave products of American business schools, whose only wish is that you read and applaud their Ph.D. theses."[6]

By midsummer of 1984, the character of the De la Madrid administration had become clear. The new president heads a government of sophisticated experts who can talk the gobbledygook of the international financial community, so attractive to foreigners, but there is little hope that they will arrive at political solutions to the fundamental crisis that has overtaken the Mexican state. The scientistic treatment of economic problems, for example, originally inspired confidence in some banking circles—although the regional bankers in the U.S. southwest attempted to unload their debt on the New York banks from the beginning of the crisis. Some observers in the banking community privately did not believe that Mexico would—in the long run—be able to maintain the servicing of the loans, much less repay the principal. A look at the 1984 restructuring of the debt indicated why: The amortization program of the Mexican debt required that Mexico repay $9.672 billion in 1985, up from $1.305 billion in 1984. Obviously, those figures were arrived at with the idea that a new and major restructuring would take place before the 1985 bill came due. That was undertaken in the summer of 1984, although a final settlement was not achieved until late summer 1985 because of the resistance of the U.S. regional banks in the Southwest who have from the beginning been skeptical of the ability of the Mexicans to pay.

The major New York banks succumbed to the logic of the situation. Under the former debt schedule for repayment, the Mexicans would have had to have come up with more than $9.7 billion in 1985 and an additional $9 billion plus in 1986. That was obviously impossible. The banks, led by the major New York creditors, acceded to the Mexican request for a fourteen-year stretch-out of $48.5 billion of the $66 billion public sector (government) debt. Mexico was given a year of grace and would not have to begin to repay principal until 1986. The new agreement also considerably lowered the interest rate level on the debt and thereby reduced debt servicing charges alone by $10 million to $12 million annually. Another part of the legerdemain of the new agreement was permission by the non-U.S. banks to convert their debt into their own currencies rather to have to repay in dollars with the continuing prospect of a strong dollar for the next few years.

Finance Minister Silva Herzog reckoned that the new arrangement would save Mexico something like $350 million a year over the whole fourteen-year period of the restructuring. The Mexicans talked of their need for at least another $16 billion in "new money," that is, capital to get on with the financing of growth of the economy. In fact, they went away without any promise from the 550 foreign commercial banks that there would be such infusions of new money. A few days after the announcement of the restructuring of the loan, De la Madrid announced that Mexico needed $20 billion to finance its development in the next six years. And he added that, in the main, Mexico would not go to the commercial banks for such financing—as well he might, with no encouragement at all from the banks—but would seek these new funds from exports credits from the lending countries and in government-to-government transfers.

It was also significant that shortly after the signing of the new rescheduling agreement Citicorp, one of the principal New York lenders, purchased insurance from Cigna Insurance at a price of $900 million to cover a portion of the estimated $12 billion which Mexico, Brazil, Argentina, and other Latin American countries owed it. It may have been, as some observers said, prudent policy but it also suggested a lack of confidence that the major borrowers—including Mexico—would repay their debts.

Perhaps the most important aspect of the new stretch-out agreement, however, was that the Mexicans had rejected all "conditionality"—that is, any quid pro quo with the banks as to how they would run their economy. The International Monetary Fund, which is generally the referee in such international agreements, imposing the conditions under which the private commercial banks and foreign governments will forgive or postpone debt or lend new money, was removed from the equation except as an occasional statistician. That meant that Mexico's bureaucracy was now on its own in dealing with the Mexican economy.

For no sooner was the seal placed on the second part of the restructuring in August 1985, than it became obvious that it would not solve Mexico's or the banks' problems. Mexican government officials announced that the country would not meet the austerity targets that had been set in the agreement with the IMF for debt repayment, and New York bankers refused to lend Mexico the "new money"— estimates ranged from $2 billion to $5 billion—needed in 1986 to get the economy growing. De la Madrid, moreover, said only three days after the signing that Mexico would "continue pursuing negotiations to obtain better debt payment conditions." To give muscle to those words, Mexico quietly hosted a meeting of ten Latin American debtor countries to consider ways to ease the common problems of the Latin American debtors. In the wings Fidel Castro, as host of his own meeting, said that the U.S. must forgive all payment since the Latin American debtors simply could not pay. The first act of the new president of Peru, Allan García, was to announce that his country would contribute only 10 percent of its export earnings toward debt servicing and repayment.

"Mexico's latest move is all the more significant because Mexico has been viewed by some of its fellow debtors as a pawn of the U.S. Federal Reserve Board; Mexico's role was thought to be to discourage the region's other debtors, such as Peru and Argentina, from pursuing more radical courses such as unilaterally reducing their annual interest payments to the bank," *The Wall Street Journal* reporter S. Karen Withcer wrote from Mexico City.[7] *The Financial Times* said: "The sharp drop in Mexico's oil income and the enforced readjustment of its prices are an uncomfortable reminder that even the most model of the Latin American debtors is experiencing serious difficulties in sustaining economic recovery."

Mexico's reserves had fallen by 23 percent by mid-summer 1984, and it had to abandon the three-tiered exchange system that Mancera, again governor of the Central Bank after being ousted by López Portillo, was trying to maintain. But with Houston predicting that oil prices would continue to drop well under $20, and perhaps as far as $13, the complicated juggling did not keep the peso from skyrocketing in the border free markets and on the futures market in Chicago.

By February 1986, the Mexicans were back in Washington looking for new credits—blaming their situation on the falling price of crude oil. But the confusion was rampant. De la Madrid called for new credits of $10 billion for the year—a staggering increase over the $4 billion he had suggested were needed in November 1985. Then Finance Minister Silva Herzog lowered the bidding to $6 billion, only $2 billion more than the fall 1985 estimates.

Washington's reaction was that it wanted to see signs of economic reform before any new money was forthcoming—austerity in government, rationalization of the hemorrhaging public sector, export promotion measures, etc. A "mini-address" by De la Madrid in late February did anything but reassure foreign lenders or investors; the president talked about repaying the foreign debt "in accordance with the nation's ability to pay." And the Mexican government began to press for "interest relief" from its creditors behind the scenes, hinting that it wanted to cap interest payments at 6%, a figure suggested by other Latin American debtors and advocated by some experts in the U.S.

As the price of oil continued to tumble, well past the $13 figure which pessimists in Houston had been touting for two years, the mathematics of the Mexican debt became even more tortured. What was clear as spring 1986 approached was that there was no consistent strategy, either in Mexico City or in Washington to handle the problem.

For the restructuring of the outstanding debt would not, of course, remove the basic causes of the debt fiasco. "[D]espite the fanfare surrounding its launch, bankers argue that even such a mammoth rescheduling is, on its own, incomplete as an answer to Mexico's $90 billion debt problem. Far more important is the basic test that lies ahead. Will Mexico's fragile economic revival endure in such a way to allow resumed access to normal market borrowing abroad? Without such new borrowing, which is not written into the agreement, the package would surely founder in the medium term."[8] One can understand why, given the magnitude of the debt and the repercussions on the New York banks if it were repudiated, any bandaid solutions were eagerly sought and trumpeted. But the arrangement simply dragged out the process—Mexico continued to depress her economy to make the payments, in order to maintain her reputation as a reliable borrower so as to borrow more money. If there were not enough new capital to restore confidence or to make the new and heavy investment needed for growth, Mexico would be plunged deeper in crisis. For Mexico was in a pressure cooker, with an economy running on a stop-and-go track, producing a fraction of its capacity much of the time, and at an overall rate far behind the increase in population.

Even if claims of a modest 2.5 percent growth in the economy in 1984 proved out[9]—and one can only question the government's figures—it meant that standards of living must continue to fall as per capita income dropped under the weight of population growth. The question became: when would the foreign banks have to take their lumps and write off a major portion of the debt—or, more likely and euphemistically, permit that it be set aside? Only then could Mexico get on with some program of development rather than pouring its resources into debt servicing.

Nor, on the political side, has the new president been able to reestablish internal confidence. A draconian program of government expenditure reduction—government expenditures represent about 40 percent of the gross national product—brought down inflation (if not to the IMF prescription). But unfortunately it also brought the whole economy to its knees. For a time imports were cut drastically and the international balance of payments looked good, especially compared to the other major debtors in Latin America, Brazil and Argentina. But his largely public relations stunt was achieved at the cost of reducing economic activity to something like 60 percent of its 1980 level.

Norman Bailey, a former member of the U.S. National Security Council, has called this program disastrous. "In the so-called 'realistic' scenario, the debtor countries accept a semi-permanent state of depression. The banks, meantime, continue to pay themselves interest while pushing off amortization into the never-never land of the 21st century . . . Even if such a situation could be sustained for several years, the result would be a Latin America with no private sector, no middle class, and a resentment level ready to explode at any time in the face of our national security."[10]

True, there had been a remarkably successful switch to domestic suppliers of some imported merchandise, but that may be largely explained by a reversal of patterns developed during the long period when it was made artificially cheap to use dollar imports, and some of this may in the long run prove as inefficient and self-defeating as the import-substitution program that gave rise to the whole industrial debacle. Since over 90 percent of Mexico's nonfood imports are now intermediate and capital goods, the large-scale cutbacks have crippled economic growth. The year 1983 saw a minus 4.7 percent growth rate, according to official figures—and it may well have been below that. Nor did there seem much likelihood that Mexico entered a new growth cycle in 1984, despite government predictions and a temporary upturn.

What seems certain is that Mexico faces years of declining income for most of its population. Already, what Mexicans call the middle class, but which is in reality the large group of new urbꭎn entrants in a modern economy and new social environment, is taking a beating from falling living standards—and perhaps worse, the deflation of their hopes for improved living standards.

Mexico cannot embark on a massive investment program necessary to continue growth without a source of capital. And that does not seem at hand. Some estimates of capital flight since the first Echeverría devaluation in 1978 run as high as $60 billion.[11] Banco de México estimated in June 1984 that $30.6 billion had flown the country in the previous seven years, more than $4.5 billion in 1983. Another $4 billion reportedly left the country before the July 1985 elections. And there are estimates that $6 billion left the country in 1985.[12] Morgan-Guaranty Trust Co. in New York estimated in April 1986 that Mexico's debt would stand at a manageable $12 billion if the capital flight were subtracted.[13] Without fear of contradiction it can be said that all the capital which could be moved has left Mexico in the past decade. The conventional wisdom (of the optimists) contends that the Mexican private sector is greedy, and when De la Madrid and the PRI regime come to heel and agree to compromise for mutual profit, the funds will flow back. The Interamerican Development Bank's Ortiz Mena, a man of common sense, says: "If we use money from outside to cover the flight of capital and that capital does not accompany capital which comes back, what we are doing is paying with short-term money, substituting [it for] capital which was formed with many years' work. It is savings which we are having to rebuild. This money cannot be paid for. Either we create the conditions through which capital will return, or we pay it off. How? With exports and services. That is to say, a proportion of our future exports are not going to be used for growth."[14]

There is a fundamental ignorance in the U.S. of the depth of the trauma in the whole Mexican business community produced by the nationalization of the private banks. One reason Humpty-Dumpty will not be put back together again is rooted in the role played by the private Mexican banks. As in Europe, they held large equity positions in the major Mexican manufacturing companies. For the most part owned and directed by the wealthy mercantile-industrial families, they not only acted as a conduit for investment funds but also for all initiatives in the industrial sector. The government has sold most of those holdings back to the original owners, or to other buyers, in order to turn back some 80 percent of the private sector which they constituted.

But the status quo ante can not be resurrected, short of denationalizing the banks. And that the PRI cannot do—even though

De la Madrid, his Finance Minister Jesús Silva Herzog (son and namesake of a leading left-wing ideologue), and Central Bank Governor Miguel Mancera all opposed López Portillo's nationalization. In this, as in so many things, De la Madrid and the regime are prisoners of the PRI's revolutionary rhetoric. There has been talk of a new investment apparatus for funneling investment into the private sector which could be set up among the insurance companies and stockbrokers,[15] but that too would require a resurgence of confidence in the future of the private sector—and of Mexico. De la Madrid has, moreover, specifically knocked down this possibility: "A parallel banking system in Mexico is not possible, and I have told this to the private sector with total frankness. . . . this idea of a parallel banking system is just wishful thinking on the part of some, because they would like to have a financial apparatus that is independent of the government."[16]

A prime indicator of the loss of confidence was the remarkable lack of enthusiasm among the members of the private sector in buying back the equity of the companies the government has offered on relatively reasonable terms—they would, of course, be buying back companies which the government confiscated in the first place. Their reluctance was due less to bitterness than to their doubts over the future of the economy and to the erosion many of the companies have undergone under government management. The bureaucratization of the banks, probably the most efficient entity in the Mexican economic scene before nationalization, is appalling. In the short time that they have been in the government's hands they have been turned into the same sort of chaotic and corrupt mess that exists in the rest of the government bureaucracy.

One additional but little noted effect of the nationalization is that it changed the character of the central bank, Banco de México, which had been a powerful independent voice in economic decision-making because its board was dominated by representatives of the private sector. It was also a training center for the *técnicos* who kept the economic policy-making on track in the 1950s and 1960s. But today the Banco de México is just another government puppet with no independence and decreasing power.

The most pressing long-term economic question is where the capital will come from to produce growth. Even those observers who hold relatively optimistic views about the short-term outlook despair when faced with what lies ahead. It is true that historically Mexico has had a phenomenal savings rate. But that savings rate is eroding as the population explosion makes increasing demands on a stagnant economy. Whatever the nature of the governing regime, it will be hard pressed not to mount a more expensive program of social welfare —however primitive—in order to meet the needs of the population. It is estimated, for example, that 800,000 new workers, for whom there were no jobs, came into the labor force in 1984 alone, a million in 1985, 1.2 million in 1986, and so forth. Those figures will rise annually throughout the rest of the century and into the next.

Foreign investment—even with greater confidence in the future of the economy and the private sector—could never have been more than an ancillary source of capital under the best of conditions. International direct capital investment transfers account for only about 10 percent of investment in the nonindustrial world on a worldwide basis. Although it can be argued that foreign investment is essential as the only proved way of transferring technology from the U.S. and other developed countries to the nonindustrialized world, every new investment attempt has caused contention inside the De la Madrid government.

A Mexican government decree in August 1984 setting up new regulations for the pharmaceutical industry set off a new debate over where policy toward foreign investment was going. "The row may also undermine the careful efforts of the 18-month-old government of President De la Madrid to demonstrate its commitment to a mixed economy. . . . Some drug company executives are already comparing the pharmaceutical industry decree with the banks' takeover," David Gardner, a British observer, writes.[17] The original decree obliged the companies to switch from trade mark to generic labeling some four hundred products, and erected a protectionist infrastructure for the manufacture of seventy key pharmachemicals in a bid to raise raw material self-sufficiency from 40 percent to 66 percent by 1988. The companies argued that in a country with no real patent register, such as Mexico, their only assests are their trademarks which generic labeling would confiscate. The compromise which was finally effected after months of bickering partially satisfied the pharmaceutical companies. But it left behind one more in a long list of psychological impediments for foreign investors. Again, in January 1985, the Mexican government—after a long soul-searching process—rejected the bid of IBM, the world leader in computers, to make a major investment in its present facility in El Salto near Guadalajara. The refusal of the Mexican government to accept IBM's insistence on 100 percent ownership (a worldwide formula that the company's enormous lead in the data processing field has permitted in such equally protectionist and xenophobic countries as Japan) was a double blow, for IBM had proposed to export 90 percent of the plant's production of personal computers to other countries in Latin America, one more instance in which the government's supposed new export orientation was put to question. And, again, the government's refusal combined the usual antiforeign sentiment and the protectionist lobbying of other computer manufacturers in Mexico through their Mexican partners. Whatever the reasons, it again gave the lie to Mexico's purported policy of laying out the welcome mat. After months of delay and debate inside and outside the government, the IBM proposal was approved—and, despite government professions to the contrary, very much along the lines IBM had originally proposed. Needless to say, the fracas left a trail of bruised and angered sensibilities.

In August 1985, the Mexican government again rejected a proposal from a U.S. multinational—this time Chrysler Corporation —to build diesel trucks in Mexico in collaboration with a private sector partner. Not only would the $300 million investment have provided employment, but Chrysler planned to export 51,000 trucks a year. The decision was ideologically based. Mexico had already made two agreements for government-owned companies to produce heavy trucks with Ford and General Motors. Chrysler wished to start the new operation in order to fulfill the requirements of a government decree which would terminate their present operations in a 100 percent Chrysler-owned subsidiary. A reversal might be forthcoming, as in the IBM case. But it is another example of how ideology rather than pragmatism—or the economic crisis—continues to dictate decisions by the *neo-científicos*.

It is also crystal clear that the foreign banks, whatever their inclinations, will not be able to lend to Mexico—nor to other developing countries—in the grand manner of the past decade. Their heavy lending to the nonindustrial world has overtaxed their whole capital structure. Lawrence J. Brainard, chief economist of Bankers Trust Co., New York, and one of the leading world experts on the international debt problem, sums it up: "My central conclusion is that a viable strategy to deal with the world debt crisis must begin by addressing the factors which have contributed to the breakdown of disciplines on developed countries' fiscal and trade policies. The path to sustainable world growth, lower interest rates, and rising levels of trade lies in the old-fashioned virtues of conservative fiscal management combined with the reliance on free markets. Market disciplines coupled with fiscal irresponsibility will lead sooner or later to excessive strains on the financial system and a disruption in financial flows both domestically and internationally. In developing countries, such a situation could lead to growing political instability. . . . It is not a coincidence, in my view, that many of the countries that got into trouble pursued policies of heavy state intervention in the economy and discrimination against foreign and private investment. It would seem overly optimistic to believe, however, that radical changes in such policies will be forthcoming any time soon in Latin America. And, for that matter, prospects that the developed countries will start disciplining their economic policies seem equally remote. Thus, progress toward a solution of the present crisis may be long in coming."[18]

Without a 180 degree turn in policy—which it is difficult to see De la Madrid or any PRI president making—Mexican owners of flight capital will not bring their money home. One is reminded, as so often in talking about Mexico, of that old curse of its proximity to the U.S. Unlike many other parts of the underdeveloped world, even in Latin America, where it takes some sophistication to know how to move money abroad, individual Mexicans have the advantage of hospitable and convenient U.S. financial institutions just next door. Speak to any white collar worker in Mexico City—not to say a businessman or professional—and you will find that he has a bank account in Laredo or San Antonio or San Ysidro. The continuing devaluations of the peso plus that arbitrariness of government economic policy have driven all but that most dedicated patriot, or the citizen with no concern for his future, to keep their savings in dollars abroad. And, for Mexican nationals in Mexico to do so is not the problem that it is for Overseas Chinese in Southeast Asia, the Lebanese in Africa, or the East Indians and Lebanese in the Caribbean. As Mexico City businessmen are fond of saying, if the governments of the two countries cannot keep bodies from crossing the borders as illegal migrants, how can they possibly keep money from penetrating the border between Mexico and the largest free currency market in the world?

All this means that investment in Mexico in the future is likely to have only one major source of capital: export earnings. And there are monumental problems in the way. Traditional mineral and raw material exports are subject to radical fluctuations in the world business cycle. But there are a multitude of problems beyond roller-coaster prices for raw materials about which the Mexican statist economists and their friends in the Rockefeller Brothers Fund have complained bitterly for at least four decades and made the heart of their argument against encouraging the private sector and foreign investment. There is, for example, the inexperience of the Mexican business world in marketing industrial exports abroad. There is that problem of Mexico's relatively high-cost industrial plant. But perhaps most important, there are the risks of entering world markets with a program of export-led economic development at a time when a dozen other nations with similar problems and similar attributes (namely, the abundance of low-cost labor) are attempting to do the same thing.

Despite a good deal of loose writing by commentators after the fact who have tended to make the Japanese ten-feet tall, the great export boom in the Far East which began in the 1950s, which has brought such prosperity not only to Japan, but also to Hong Kong, South Korea, Taiwan, Singapore and much of Southeast Asia, was as much "pull" as "push." That is, the incentives for the early development of markets in the U.S., and later in Europe, came from marketing and industrial firms in those recipient countries who sought out Japanese and other Asian manufacturers, often for products that were already in the market place but which for whatever reason could be produced more efficiently (cheaply) in Asia.

One may well ask why in the 1950s and 1960s some little part of that development, however small a fraction, did not go to Mexico, sitting as it does next door to these same American markets? Why, for example, did no U.S. importer begin to develop an infants' wear supplier among the women embroiderers of Oaxaca just as they did in the Philippines? The answer is, at least in part, that the whole atmosphere in Mexico was hostile to the concept of export and foreign markets and partnerships. In part that was because there was the burgeoning, protected Mexican market. But it was also because Mexico was and remains a highly parochial country. Mexican businessmen, as well as the government, have a great deal to learn if they are to become successful suppliers to the U.S. on the massive scale needed to solve the Mexican development problems.

The sorry spectacle of Mexico's decades-long failure to enter the General Agreement on Tariffs and Trade (GATT) makes this point. The López Portillo government negotiated a remarkably favorable entry into the GATT agreements for Mexico, permitting it in some instances to take as long as eight years to make its adjustments on tariffs and quotas. The entry would have opened up all GATT's markets—including the U.S.—to Mexico's products, asking in return an entry into Mexico's highly protected markets. And Mexico was permitted enormous latitude in delaying the competition from foreign exporters, concessions made to no other member on entry.

Yet a combination of Communist, nationalist, and protectionist forces united in attacking the treaty. A storm of invective against the GATT negotiations filled the media. And it was an issue that neither López Portillo—nor De la Madrid—from the all-powerful presidential throne, was willing to bull through. By the spring of 1984, Mexico tried to negotiate a bilateral economic treaty with the U.S. which would grant her the benefits of GATT in the American market without having to join the world organization. American authorities, in a fit of absent-minded compassion for the Mexican economic crisis, were going along with the effort. But Mexican authorities, even in their dedicated blame of all economic and political problems on U.S. intransigence, had not adequately surveyed the congressional field in the U.S. When De la Madrid made a state visit to see Reagan in Washington in May 1984, his staff expected to carry the treaty back to Mexico as a trophy. They were apparently unaware that in an election year, with Reagan probably facing a protectionist Democratic candidate, the U.S. president would not be likely to take on the brouhaha that such concessions to Mexico would evoke from the Congress. Reagan might have been able to "sell" the idea of concessions to Mexico against the powerful protectionists in Congress—from Florida's tomato growers to Pennsylvania's steelmakers—under the guise of admitting Mexico to the international family of nations of GATT, and an overall appeal to free trade and a fair deal for Mexico as a major U.S. market. But to try to do so on a bilateral basis promised to bring out every protectionist interest in Washington, with the resultant discordant publicity and political animosity.

A facesaving administrative trade agreement was signed by Mexico and the U.S. in April 1985, but negotiators deadlocked until August 30, when a settlement was partially reached on Mexican subsidies to dollar exports. But the new agreement, even without further hitches, promises neither to block growing U.S. protectionism toward some Mexican products nor to change Mexico's barriers to more bilateral trade. By October 1985, there were leaks from Los Pínos indicating that the De la Madrid administration had changed its mind again and would begin the long preparations to enter GATT. Finally, in early 1986, De la Madrid turned back to the GATT option and promised to negotiate entry—ten years, at least, after all pragmatic economic arguments had dictated it. But the process is expected to take at least until 1987 at the earliest—another example of the Mexican administration's procrastination, until too late, in reaching logical decisions on finance and trade.

Mexico, thus, is left with one big hope for earning the kind of foreign exchange it will need to get its economy back on the growth track: oil. Petroleum now provides some 60 percent of Mexico's export earnings, as well as being a major ingredient of domestic economic development. It is an important reason why some observers believe Mexico has the potential to do better than some of her debtor brethren. Brazil must import virtually all her energy. But leaving aside the political sickness that oil resources apparently constitute for any underdeveloped country, whether it be Venezuela, Iran, or Indonesia—and which Mexico has to some extent already experienced —the purely economic prospects are not without severe limitations.

There are, indeed, major oil reserves still untapped, and Mexico may be potentially another Saudi Arabia as some oil experts have predicted. No one can be quite sure, for there has been a great deal of political tampering with the estimates since the oil-debt crisis developed in 1981. (For the first time in a decade, PEMEX authorities scaled back slightly their estimates of proved reserves at the end of 1984).

There are, however, several dampening considerations. Mexico's oil monopoly PEMEX (Petroleos Mexicanos) is one of the most inefficient oil producers in the world; one Houston source estimates that its 250,000 employees produce what no more than 15,000 would in Texas. The inefficiency is only surpassed by the corruption. Since its inception in 1938, the state-owned oil company has become a world unto itself, a monster which was already developing when Cárdenas nationalized the foreign-owned companies. From the early days of the *Porfiriato*, the government had encouraged the kind of bitter rivalry among the investors and the various oil companies that would give the government a controlling hand in the development of oil. Trade unions, which date to the earliest commercial exploitation of petroleum in Mexico and whose existence was formally guaranteed by the 1917 constitution, were seen by the government as a means of putting pressure on the foreign corporations. But after the nationalization, Cárdenas was unable, even with his prestige and popularity, to bring the unions directly under government control. The semi-independent government monopoly PEMEX was the result. And for some fifty years, until De la Madrid launched a press campaign in 1983 using government exposure of the enormous corruption of the union and the leadership of the company as a weapon, they constituted a separate empire of untold riches, bribery, theft, and political power.

"The [Soviet] Politburo is innocent compared to us," an American scholar quotes a Mexico City local oil union leader as saying.[19] For example, PEMEX unions have been acting as middlemen contractors, taking a cut from all subsidiary contracts for the oil monopoly. These profits have totaled millions of dollars, and much of it has been exported from Mexico to U.S. and other foreign bank accounts. The world of PEMEX unions and corruption has become a satrapy within the Mexican state, almost immune even to the power of the presidency.

Although the new president announced a formal end to the contractual arrangements between the unions and PEMEX suppliers in early 1984, the jury is still out on the question of whether De la Madrid will in fact bring the PEMEX unions under control. Having jailed (but not yet brought to trial) the head of the company under

López Portillo, Jorge Díaz Serrano, who however corrupt is viewed abroad as a brilliant administrator and knowledgeable oil operator, the question is not only whether De la Madrid can break the mould of corruption that is fifty years old but whether he can do so without further degrading PEMEX's efficiency. And many Mexican cynics believe that Díaz Serrano is really in jail because of the political threat to De la Madrid. In any case, at this writing—the winter of of 1985 –1986—no possibility of a solution to the whole question of Díaz Serrano and PEMEX corruption is in sight.

In oil, as in so many other things, Mexico is at the mercy of international movements. There is general agreement that whatever the developments in the Middle East, the outlook for the next decade is for a relatively stable real price in petroleum with few if any new price bonanzas for Mexico. Short term, the price seems likely to fall back to pre-1975 levels. Furthermore, just to keep producing at present levels, Mexico will have to reinvest large amounts of capital into the infrastructure of production. In mid-1984 the industry was running at about 2 million barrels a day with about a third of that going to local consumption. The government austerity program curbing inflation has cut back so heavily on investment, even in public-owned companies like PEMEX, that it is unlikely that present levels of production can be maintained without new investment in the ports, oil pipelines, railroads, refineries, and other parts of the infrastructure.[20] Even during the bonanza days of 1980 when Mexico was pumping and shipping all the oil she could at the highest prices, there were logjams in the supply system. And although the Mexicans argued in 1983 and 1984 they have "closed in" some 15 percent of their production in order to help OPEC meet the worldwide effort to hold down production and keep prices up, there is some question whether this was not simply a face-saving device by embarrassed PEMEX and government officials to protect the confidence in their greatest cash-cow.[21]

As other oil-producing countries have found, petroleum, itself, is not the kind of labor intensive employer that Mexico needs to meet the problem of an enormously expanding labor force. Nor does the past in Mexico hold much hope that even if large oil earnings were available, the primitive Mexican political system could transfer them where needed in the social and economic sectors.

The effort of De la Madrid, in pursuit of his image as a moderate wielding a broom, to wage a cleanup at PEMEX was only one in a series of political initiatives. None of them has had appreciable success. De la Madrid got off to a bad start in his 1982 election campaign by adopting the slogan "*Nacionalismo Revolucionario*" to describe his program, a phrase he has continued to use even though it has elicited strong criticism from the private sector.[22] Could the PRI candidate have been unaware that the term "revolutionary nationalism" was invented long ago by the International Communist movement, and that, whatever De la Madrid meant by it, it has a specific meaning in the Mexican context for the Communists and the left wing of the PRI?

The term "revolutionary nationalism" appeared first when V.I. Lenin used it as the theme of the Second Congress of the Communist International in Moscow July 17–August 6, 1920. From its inception in Moscow it has described the Marxist-Leninist strategy and tactics by which the Russians hoped to turn anti-imperialist confrontations in the nonindustrial world into the international proletarian revolution. Eudocio Ravines, once a Comintern agent in South America, explains that the communist strategy is to capitalize on the sentiment in former colonial countries ascribing all their problems to colonialism.[23] Since the decolonization by the Western powers in the 1950s and the fading of nineteenth century imperialism, the term often has been used—in many instances innocently—as part of the rhetoric of the "nonaligned countries" to establish their political position as equidistant between capitalism and Communism. In Mexico, the phrase was used lavishly by Vicente Lombardo Toledano, the charismatic leader of the government-sponsored CTM trade union federation during the 1930s and 1940s. Toledano was pushed out by the PRI leadership for his total devotion to the Moscow line, particularly as expressed through the World Federation of Trade Unions (WFTU). The anomaly of De la Madrid having adopted the slogan as his own in 1980 has, therefore, a double irony.

Nor has De la Madrid's other major political ploy, his campaign for "moral rejuvenation" announced during his presidential campaign, been any great success. A series of dramatic exposures of corruption in high PRI circles has dogged the administration from its inception. With what could only be the support of the president's household, Los Pínos, a press campaign was launched against the former police chief of Mexico City, Arturo Durazo. Durazo was a shady character who had also been a classmate (El Negro) and "protector" of both Echeverría and López Portillo in their grade school days in Mexico City.[24] José González, a man purporting to be a member of Durazo's *camarilla*, a self-confessed hired killer, sold 1.8 million copies of a book entitled *Lo Negro del Negro (The Black Deeds of the Black One)*. It detailed a story of corruption, violence, and immorality seldom equaled in the annals of large city police forces. Whether it was all true or not—and few Mexicans found any reason not to believe it

—the country witnessed the spectacle of a revelation that its capital city had been in the hands of gangster leadership and that its former president was a confidant of the chief offender. Mexicans generally believed that the book could not have been published and distributed —it was hawked on the streets in Mexico City traffic—without the approval of the De la Madrid administration.

After a few weeks, the De la Madrid government put out a call through Interpol for Durazo's arrest, although a disaffected wife in Montreal reported that everyone knew that El Negro could be found in Paris. The whole affair suddenly disappeared from the newspapers when, according to one account, López Portillo, during a short and surreptitious visit back to Mexico—his first since leaving the presidency—told De la Madrid that there was no way Durazo could be indicted without besmirching the former presidency, which would constitute virtual regicide, and ruin not only López Portillo but the whole Mexican system.

Whatever the reason, by late spring 1984 Durazo was reported in Havana, Cuba, dying of cancer and other complications, and the story virtually disappeared from the controlled press after the government confiscated Durazo's huge palatial dwelling (called the Parthenon because of its grandeur) and another at Cihautenango. But in June 1984, Durazo was arrested by American authorities at the airport in San Juan, P.R., when he transited the airport there enroute from the Caribbean, apparently en route to Europe. He was held by U.S. authorities in Los Angeles, awaiting extradition to Mexico. The question, of course, is whether Mexican authorities really want him, whether an airing of the accusations against him would benefit a regime not yet ready to undertake the massive housecleaning that his trial would force on it. Although the U.S. government's move for extradition lost the first round ignominiously in the courts in California, U.S. Attorney General Edwin Meese assured the Mexican press during an August 1985 visit to Mexico City that the extradition was going forward. On April 1, 1986, after extended court procedures and negotiations, Durazo was turned over to Mexican authorities in San Diego. It remains to be seen how or whether he will be brought to trial/justice in Mexico.

Meanwhile, the Mexican police establishment is a shambles. Robbery and assault against private homes—often with heavy weapons —had become almost commonplace by the summer of 1984. And it was widely believed that former members of the Mexico City police whom De la Madrid had purged in his "moral rejuvenation" campaign were directly involved. And corruption continued inside the police force with little sign that anything had changed in the tradition of

Mexican government—except that with more economic distress they had become more acute. There were even accounts during the 1985 earthquake aftermath that the police themselves participated in the looting of damaged apartments.

De la Madrid's *renovación moral* has become a farce, over-whelmed by the magnitude of its task and the refusal of the regime to make the sharp, political break with the past that is required. It was the earthquakes in September 1985, although limited to a rela-tively small area in the oldest parts of Mexico City, that were De la Madrid's most difficult test—and one that found him terribly want-ing. There were extenuating circumstances, perhaps. The tremors— a second followed within less than 24 hours of the first—were of enor-mous magnitude. It was the kind of natural disaster that would have taxed any regime anywhere in the world. The Mexican military had a plan for such emergencies, the DN-III. But De la Madrid refused to permit a declaration of emergency and an army takeover of the evacuation of the destroyed buildings—apparently because he feared the military would not restore civilian control. The military then, in a fit of pique, stood guard around the destroyed areas with their arms, literally in most cases, folded.

Almost immediately after the first earthquake an incredible per-formance between the Mexican government and foreign countries, began—especially with the U.S. Energetic U.S. Ambassador John Gavin who toured the destroyed areas told the American press that there could not be less than 10,000 deaths—Mexican government of-ficials have subsequently acknowledged that the death toll reached at least 20,000, and most observers on the ground believe there were closer to 30,000. Not only the Mexican Foreign Secretary Sepul-veda but the *gringo*-hating Ambassador to France, Jorge Casteneda, castigated Gavin to the press for his "inopportune" statements and went on denying the extent of the crisis. An equally ridiculous ex-change took place in Washington: Secretary of State George Shultz, apparently attentive to the State Department's experts, repeatedly said that the Americans were waiting on Mexico to request aid for the earthquake's victims. Under the best of circumstances, the Mexicans would have found it difficult to ask for help from the gringos. And it was the not the best of circumstances. Sepulveda repeatedly told foreign governments that help was not needed—King Juan Carlos of Spain within hours after the news arrived in Madrid offered help but was told that Mexico could attend to its needs by itself.

But as it became clear that lives were being lost in the ruins, that most of the buildings that had fallen were government-built and be-cause of corruption had been improperly constructed, and that police and government officials were not only negligent but venal beyond belief—e.g., taking money from relatives to remove bodies from the buildings—the city's residents' took control themselves. Volunteers began to dig out bodies on their own. Despite government interference—earthmoving equipment that had been flown in from abroad was held up at the airport by functionaries—foreign volunteers came in to help.

And the newspapers exploded, defying Mexico's traditional unwritten rules of censorship. *El Norte* of Monterrey said: "The attitudes of some functionaries of our government are disgraceful; the offers of our neighboring nations to extend the hand in generosity and goodneighborliness is without limit. An inexplicable pride, which demonstrates an inferiority complex, exists among some of our officials who are psychologically sick. How else can you explain how important officials can keep on saying that Mexico 'has not asked for aid'?" Raquel Díaz de Leon, a reporter writing in Excelsior, said: "The police and the army, ill-fated elements, some too clever by half and some stupid, have been the major obstacles to putting into effect the aid operations of the rescue groups, sometimes permanently halting, in stupid and arbitrary forms, generous foreigners who want to help out . . . My God, why do we have to pay in pain and shame before the world for these imbecile managers of an obtuse and corrupt elite. And . . . the rescue elements from other countries are at the command of these people!" Enrique Massa, a former Jesuit writing in the leftwing *Processo*, said, "The priorities of this country are not men, health, life, school, financial security, and humanity, the dignity of Mexicans. The money that has fled cannot be used for that. And what follows: Since [President] Miguel Aleman until today, rape, sack, corruption, concentrated and illicit wealth, luxury, mansions, debauchery, frivolity, obstentatiousness, white elephants, inefficient expenditures, voyages, contraband, the sacking of safes and the sacking of voting urns, the hundreds of thousands of millions lost which the country needs . . . This is the moment when the government must show us its true intentions."

But even the physical presence of the President was lacking. He did not appear on television until after the second earthquake, and then in his wooden, cold, slightly ridiculous manner. Immediately, there were bad jokes about the number of different leather jackets he had donned when he visited the earthquake ruins. One of his closest advisers, the regent of Mexico City, Ramon Aguirre, repeatedly demonstrated his incompetence—even though rumor had it that De la Madrid would like to have him as his successor in the presidency.

Placido Domingo, the Spanish baritone who had grown up in Mexico and was among the ruins personally directing rescue operation for members of his family, captured the growing impatience and hatred of the city and its victims: "In this dramatic moment, difficult for our country has suffered the tragic consequences of the earthquake, leaders and officials who have robbed with impunity, ought be ashamed and ought to come [back] to help overcome these problems . . . what is handicaping us is the lack of adequate rescue equipment and I have asked the North American First Lady Nancy Reagan, when I chatted with her briefly, to help us. As if this country had not been robbed enough, now we have to confront the crisis of the 19th of September [the date of the first earthquake]. I ask all these thieving people, in a gesture of humanity, if they have that capability, to bring back to the country the millions they have stolen and that now are so necessary."

The earthquake outbursts were unprecedented. They inaugurated, at least temporarily, a new era for the Mexican press, and perhaps for free speech in the country. But the revelations of the earthquake continued: Eight, perhaps as many as 20, bodies of tortured victims were found the basement of the Procuraduria General de Justicia del Distrito Federal. For the first time ever, Mexicans began to talk publicly—and in the press—about what everyone had known had always gone on: the torture of criminal and political prisoners, and often their disappearance. The bodies were foreigners, Colombians, apparently narcotics traffickers who the police had tried to shake down. The Colombian Embassy asked for explanations publicly. Furthermore, a respected criminal lawyer was found shot to death in his car but buried in debris in an attempt to disguise the murder. The whole episode was compounded when the Procurator of the Federal District, until then a young unknown woman, Victoria Adato de Ibarra, denied that there had been torture. She was shortly shifted into a ministry, with accusations on all sides that she was equally unqualified for that job as she had been for the prosecutor's role.

The government moved, finally, to clean up the debris. It ordered attempts at rescue stopped, but had to back off when the volunteer search and rescue units demanded to continue their work with the possibility that more lives of people buried in the debris might be saved. The government sought to move people off camps on the northern outskirts of the cities—more than a 100,000 were without shelter. But the quake victims played a game of hide-and-seek with authorities over the next weeks and months, fearing that if they left the site of the ruins, they would be forced to move long distances away from their work sites with only inadequate transit or lose their claims to destroyed homes.

They were right. The government, using the rationalization that it was necessary to do something about the slums in the area, nationalized some 710 buildings. They were to be replaced by low-cost, government housing. (It had been widely publicized that the government-subsidized low income housing was the scene of the worst loss of life during the tremors as whole floors collapsed because of faulty engineering and construction.) Most of these buildings were said to be dwellings that for years had been rented under Mexico City's rigid rent controls. The owners had been unable or unwilling to make repairs because of the low rents and they had fallen into disrepair. But it immediately became obvious that many of the buildings nationalized did not fall into this category, that in fact some new buildings were being taken over, including at least one new office building belonging to German owners. It was not clear whether the whole effort had been incompetence, corruption, or venality—or the usual PRI combination. But there were negotiations and the order was amended.

Out of the earthquakes and their aftermath—even though the area affected was only a small section of the world's largest city—came a new attitude toward De la Madrid. Members of the educated and upper classes simply dismissed him as incompetent—the most common gesture at the mention of his name was a wave of the hand. Among the mass of poor Mexico City workers, there was growing resentment—Mrs. De la Madrid was driven away from a site of one ruin by local residents throwing rocks. The Administration which had inherited the PRI's reputation for incompetence, corruption, and often venality, now had a new aspect—indecisiveness. And that might be the most serious of its failing for it fired speculation that something was changing in the regime. By early 1986 there was speculation that De la Madrid, still nominally the all-powerful president, might not be able to name his own successor when he left office in 1988.

As the situation continued to deteriorate even further, the head of the powerful oilworkers union warned the president semipublicly in January 1986 that PEMEX was crumbling under the assault of lower world oil prices and Mexican government policy. He warned the president that if PEMEX collapsed, so would the regime and the presidency. A few days later, De la Madrid was to hear the octogenarian, Fidel Velaquez, head of the CTM, the government trade union federation, warn, again publicly in the president's presence, that the country had lost its way. These two organizations, pillars of the PRI regime, now seemed to be drifting into opposition to De la Madrid. That was an ominous portent for the regime.

In the end it is these political problems rather than any economic decisions that will likely determine the nature of the coming crisis of the regime in Mexico. The economic chaos may, indeed, have overshadowed the more profound political crisis of the regime, but it is not as fundamental. De la Madrid and the PRI regime are in trouble, not only because he has inherited a system that is limping, but because he himself appears to be too typically a product of the growing pseudo-technocracy of the regime that had come a cropper in economic development. The *neo-científicos*, though armed with their computer models, simply do not have the answers. Nor have they had the courage to look for new political formulations for the multitude of problems they have inherited from the regime's long period of stable infertility.

Chapter 4: **A Destabilizing Ambiente**

The crisis of the Mexico Model at home comes at a moment when, for the first time since World War I, Mexico is increasingly embroiled in politics beyond her borders.

Mexico, from the consolidation of the PRI regime until the Echeverría administration, had been largely isolated from the affairs of the outside world, including those in the Western Hemisphere. A Chinese Wall had been erected between her international image and her policies at home.

To the world, the PRI preached the glories of the Mexican Revolution, expressed sympathy for radical causes wherever they might be, and decried intervention by other powers, particularly the U.S., in Latin America. It entailed taking stands in the United Nations which were pro-Soviet and at the Organization of the American States (OAS) where Mexico was the lone holdout in the Hemisphere against attempts by the U.S. in the 1960s and the 1970s to isolate Cuba, a Soviet ally.

But at home, the regime cultivated an image of conservatism — even though its statist policies moved the country steadily leftward toward the kind of planning and *dirigisme* in which the Soviets excel. The oligarchic regime favored a small number of families and a political elite, despite rhetoric to the contrary. The regime was also often brutally authoritarian in dealing with any dissidence, on the Left as well as on the Right. A turning point in Mexican history, and the most celebrated incident, was the so-called Massacre of Tlatelolco in 1968 during the administration of President Gustavo Díaz Ordaz. Ironically, on August 13, 1521, Cuauhtemoc, the last of the Aztec emperors, was defeated and his followers slaughtered by the Spaniard Hernán Cortés in the same area, which today is called La Plaza de las Tres Culturas (Plaza of the Three Cultures — Indian, Spanish, Mexican).[1]

"The key to understanding Mexico's tensions in 1968 is to recognize the extent to which it had changed. The marginal population had been growing at an average rate of 19% per year since the mid-1960s, a rate faster than the infrastructure of services could satisfy (elementary schools, for example, grew at a rate of 2.9% in average during that [Díaz Ordaz] sexenio). Agricultural production had grown at an average of 0.96% from 1964 to 1970, while the population grew 3.4%. The high rates of growth of the economy and the government's promotion of industry had attracted an inflow of foreign investment ($1 billion from 1964 to 1970) and had complemented the consolidation of large indigenous commercial and industrial groups. Both the foreign concerns and the local industrial and commercial groups had begun to displace small- and medium-size industrialists and shopowners who could not compete with more efficient and economically powerful entities. . . .

"Mexico was thoroughly transformed, and this was not yet reflected in political participation. What aggravated certain nuclei of the middle classes—as well as intellectuals and students—was the excessive authoritarianism of the government. This impeded public expression and freedom of the press for a population that was rapidly acquiring not only a high standard of living but also the education and the values commonly found in more developed societies, where political expression of such groups was not only common, but key to the main currents of social change. . . .

"Even if the student demonstrations that took place in 1968 had not occurred, the model of Stabilizing Development would have had to be modified or replaced by something else. Politically, the authoritarian policies of the Díaz Ordaz administration and previous governments alienated important sectors of the population, particularly the middle classes, to the point where political institutions had begun to lose their credibility and legitimacy as representative institutions. It became evident through the explosion and later repression of the student movement in 1968, that the political system faced a dilemma of its own creation: It had organized and coalesced new social forces, but it had denied them access to institutions and representation."[2]

With Echeverría as Minister of Gobernación, the government brought in army units to put down demonstrations by radical students at UNAM, organized by the Communist party of Mexico and the fellow-traveling union of university workers. The agitation over a three-month period finally ended in a riot involving students and military units on the eve of the 1968 International Summer Olympics in Mexico City. With the whole world ready to focus on the games, the government moved with determination. As so often in Mexico, statistics on the rioting are not reliable. The government claimed that only fifty seven students were killed; the student leaders countered with 300 students, men, women, and children. Videotapes recorded by North American news agencies show women and children at the confrontation, much as they might be in any public gathering in Mexico City at almost any time of day or night. Therefore the higher casualty figures could well be the more accurate. There were a series of incidents after the initial encounter; and a final amnesty for participants was not declared until López Portillo released the last of the students from prison ten years later, in late 1978.

Many Mexicans regard the episode—because it involved the formerly elitist institution, where so many PRI leaders (and their sons and daughters) had been trained, the principal cultural institution of the Republic—as a turning point in contemporary politics. But there have been equally bloody incidents elsewhere, all but ignored by the U.S. and the world press. They include a battle between *campesinos*—mostly Indians—and PEMEX's security forces in Tabasco state in the fall of 1982 when PEMEX took over land from the local population. Left-wing priests took up the cudgels for the Indians and led them against the PEMEX forces. Little has ever been published about this episode, though by all accounts it was bloody and the casualties ranged in the hundreds.

Today, however, there is a sense that events have moved beyond this kind of single, isolated incident—whether it be in Mexico City or in the countryside—which gets momentary attention and then rests in a footnote in the history of the PRI regime. For it will be increasingly difficult for Mexico to simply appease both sides in the international arena with rhetoric while using authoritarian means to maintain order at home. In the past these domestic eruptions have been largely beyond the purview of the outside world. Mexico's parochialism has been matched by the neglect with which the world press and foreign powers have treated its problems. But no longer.

For in the future, Mexico City will find it hard simply to ignore, among other things, the Cuban role as surrogate of the Soviet Union in the Western Hemisphere. Mexican officials argue privately that the apparent modus vivendi between Mexico City and Havana has bought the PRI immunity from Cuban attempts to target it for subversion as it has most of the governments of the region through its aid and direction of guerrilla groups.

For Cuba and the Soviet Union, Mexico's shipments of oil to Cuba—including swaps for Soviet oil which went to Israel through Romania—have helped scale down Moscow's enormous bill for world Communism's Caribbean appendage. And Mexico City has provided a haven for left-wing political exiles from all over the continent, allowing Cuba, through its mammoth embassy in Mexico City, to maintain contact, organize propaganda, and plot the overthrow of anti-Communist and pro-U.S. regimes in the region. The propaganda, of course, presents the Castro-PRI modus vivendi as based on a sympathetic and idealistic relationship.

Interestingly, in the 1950s, Fidel Castro found haven as a political exile in Mexico with his friend, the Argentine revolutionary, Che Guevara—Castro from Batista's Cuba and Guevara from Guatemala after the fall of the pro-Moscow government of President Jacobo Arbenz in 1954. Both were already firmly in the Moscow camp— Guevara had been a member of Arbenz' secret police. Castro was released from a Mexican jail through the intercession of former President Cárdenas after his revolutionary activities against the Batista government had been discovered by Mexican police. The Mexican Left provided additional help and he was able to renew training and set sail from Mexico.[3] The evidence that Castro and his closest collaborators were recruited by the Soviet KGB long before Castro moved into power in Havana, (much of which activity took place in Mexico) is recounted convincingly by Castro's former guerrilla comrades, like Juan Vives.[4] And it was Mexico which alone refused to break relations with Cuba after a resolution of the OAS condemned Cuba for its attempts to overthrow other governments.

But that issue receded somewhat when Castro's efforts at subversion ended temporarily with the capture and death of Guevara in Bolivia in October 1967 and the failure of his guerrilla movement. By the 1970s, Cuba had developed a new and more sophisticated role: Havana was to be the catspaw for Moscow in Latin America and in the non-alligned movement of Third World states where Cubans were more acceptable than Russians.

The new Cuban role was conceptualized and defined in 1965 after a bitter confrontation between the Soviet KGB and Cuba's own DGI (Directorate of Government Intelligence), its secret police.[5] The argument that went on over a period of six months resulted in a compromise between Havanna and Moscow. Cuban intelligence and secret services were split into two organizations. One was the old DGI, tasked by the Soviet KGB, just like the other satellite secret services, to perform missions for the Russians where Soviet penetration might be more difficult. At the same time, a high level Committee for the Americas was created, a section of Cuban intelligence with direct ties through Castro to Moscow, which would exploit non-Communist left-wing and democratic proclivities in the Western Hemisphere—including the U.S.[6]—for Communist ends.

The new organization was dedicated to the destruction of anti-Communist forces allied with the U.S. throughout the hemisphere.

The Committee for the Americas has worked out an increasingly effective strategy and tactics for uniting dissident leftist groups— even those which have historically been opposed to Moscow domination, like the Latin American Trotskyist splinters—into effective armed revolutionary insurrectionists. The bait appears to be more the prospect of power—these men have spent a political lifetime outside the power structure in their countries—than a dedication to Marxist-Leninism.

The case of Havana, itself, dramatizes how power came to Castro in Cuba (and to Maurice Bishop in Grenada and to Lt. Col. Desire D. Bouterse in Suriname) through his cooperation with pro-Soviet forces in Latin America and the world. It is this history of success in the pursuit of power, more than any other factor, which motivates the guerrilla leadership in El Salvador and Guatemala in the face of opposition of the U.S., traditionally the dominant force in the area. As the crisis deepens in Central America, Cuba's role in unifying and arming the leftist guerrillas (with Moscow's help) in Nicaragua, El Salvador, Guatemala, and Honduras, has become a central concern of Washington policymakers. But it is one for which Washington has no remedy—at least thus far. As the problem of Latin American subversion and guerrilla warfare intensifies in the coming decade, Mexico City, the hemisphere's non-Communist center for subversion and espionage, will become increasingly important to the U.S.[7]

De la Madrid has continued Mexico's policy since the 1960s of trying to maintain a balance with the Cubans. In this respect, Mexican maneuvers at the UN are often only rhetorical flourishes which have little concrete meaning except as they aid the propaganda campaign of the Soviet bloc against Washington. An example occurred in August 1983 when the U.S. used all its persuasion to thwart a United Nations motion to condemn Washington as a colonialist power in Puerto Rico. Porfírio Muñoz Ledo, the former Mexican ambassador to the United Nations (his colleagues call him *Don Perfidio* because of his irascibility and shifting loyalties) refused his government's instructions to vote against the resolution and Mexico abstained. He later told other Latin American diplomats that he would not "bow to *gringo* pressure." The incident takes on added significance as Muñoz Ledo has been a serious candidate for the presidency and could be again.

But at times, these rhetorical excesses in the United Nations and elsewhere do have important concrete implications for the U.S. Cuba's Communist regime backs the terrorist wing of the Puerto Rican *independista* movement. A major terrorist figure in that movement, Willy Morales, was captured in Mexico in 1983, after his escape from a New York hospital following an incident where a bomb he was making blew up in his face. He was captured while plotting a bombing of the annual U.S.-Mexican congressional members meeting in Puebla. The U.S. has asked for his extradition, but the disposition of the case remains something of a mystery at this writing.

Mexican efforts to pacify the Cubans are expensive in more than ordinary dollars and cents. Only weeks before he was sworn in as president of Mexico, De la Madrid went with then President López Portillo to Havana which greeted them with extensive and warm public ceremonies and private conferences. Many in Washington are prepared to rationalize such irritants to the U.S. as part of the complicated foreign policy dance in a complex world where Soviet power (as expressed in Latin America through Castro's Cuba) is an important consideration for all countries. They argue that Mexico's overtures to Cuba are only part of a game of mutual blackmail. Mexico, afraid of Cuban subversive techniques, buys off Havana at relatively little cost to itself—and the U.S.[8]

The "bottom line" may well be whether the Cuban Communists are, in reality, being bought off. In October 1983, two Cuban diplomats were arrested and later left the country after having been involved in delivering explosives to anti-Communist Cuban exiles posing as leftists who had entrapped them in a sting operation on the eve of the state visit to Havana of Minister of Finance Jesús Silva Herzog and Minister of Trade Hector Hernández, both considered "moderates" in the De la Madrid administration. But the incident did not hold up the visit nor deter the Mexicans from extending the Cuban Communists a $55 million credit, only a few weeks after U.S. creditors, through the intercession of the Federal Reserve Bank, had arranged a rescheduling of Mexico's $90 billion external debt, more than 40 percent of it owed the U.S. banks.

Cuban activities in Mexico are so elaborate and of such magnitude that it is doubtful Mexican authorities have a full knowledge of them. Mexico City is, for example, a convenient transit point for other Latin Americans who are taken to Havana for indoctrination or for the more serious pursuits of espionage and terrorist activities. And in late 1983, the Cubans gave it some fancy window dressing by setting up extremely cheap tourist fares from Mexico City to Havana at a time when middle-class Mexicans found they could no longer travel abroad because of the economic crisis. There is little reason not to believe that the Cuban DGI agents operating in Mexico are "tasked" by the Soviet KGB just as when in the U.S., at the United Nations, and elsewhere. For in both North and South America, the Cubans can penetrate circles which are closed to the Russian Communists.

Nor is the problem of Cuba's involvement in Central America an academic one that Mexican diplomats can handle at arm's length in the OAS and the UN. Mexico's interest and involvement in Central America goes back to the Spanish colonial period—and indeed its huge and relatively untapped southern state of Chiapas came into Mexican hands only after independence from Spain in 1823 when Guatemala seceded from the ill-fated and short-lived Mexican Empire of José Iturbide. The history of Chiapas is as much an irritant to relations between Mexico and its southern neighbor, Guatemala, as the history of Texas and the Southwest is to Mexico and the U.S. There have been sporadic attempts at rebellion in the state against the Mexican central authorities, and a *Chiapas Independiente* clandestine radio broadcasts from time to time, from Managua or Havana. The state of Chiapas, like the area south of the border in Guatemala, is heavily Indian, descended from the great Mayan civilization of southern Mexico and Central American which rivaled the Aztecs of high plateau where Mexico City lies today. This heritage reinforces the local antagonism to the central government. The area is backward and isolated and has long been neglected by the federal government.

A new dimension has been added to the traditional animosity by the continuing guerrilla war in Guatemala, where three groups of guerrillas are precariously united through Cuban efforts. The war— the terror and counterterror all too familiar in recent decades in Latin America, Asia, and Africa—has sent tens of thousands of the local Guatemalan population scampering across the Mexico-Guatemala border for refuge since 1981. The Guatemalan army maintains, with considerable evidence, that the refugee camps in southern Mexico have been used as sanctuaries and recruiting pools for the guerrillas who cross into Guatemala. The border—a 1,500-mile jungled terrain that stretches from the Pacific to the Caribbean—is virtually indefensible from either side. For centuries, dating from the Captain-Generalcy of Guatemala and the Viceroyalty of New Spain (Mexico), trafficking has been a major enterprise on the border. The local populations, moreover, on both sides of the line have more in common with one another than with their own countrymen; and both areas have been treated as low-priority regions for development funds and talent by the central governments. Add to this the explosive ingredient of oil, located on both sides of the border, and you see why the area has become as potentially dangerous to Mexico as it has long been to the regime in Guatemala.

Were all this not enough, a new political ingredient has been injected by naive but activist Catholic churchmen, some of whom are prepared to make common cause with the Marxists. The bishop, Manuel Ruiz, at San Cristóbal de las Casas, the traditional center of Chiapas, is a member of the left wing of the Mexican church, a believer in the so-called liberation theology which preaches that the here-and-now is the chief concern of the Church.

"Liberation theology developed from the people [of Latin America]," said Philip Scharper, editor of Orbis Books at Maryknoll, a major publisher of the works of liberation theologians. (The American Maryknoll fathers and sisters have been among the most active in promoting liberationist concepts in Latin America.) "It is not academic and it's not theology of the theologians but it did grow out of the work of trained theologians. It grew out of the fact that Third World theologians had trained in Europe and then returned to Latin America and looked around and said, how can we use theology we learned in Europe in the old mode? They saw the dehumanizing poverty that affected the continent. They asked themselves how can we take the good news of Christ to people who have been marginalized?" [9]

One of the most influential of these theologians is Father Gustavo Gutiérrez, a Peruvian priest who studied psychology at the Catholic University in Louvain. Gutiérrez' 1973 book, *A Theology of Liberation* (Orbis Books), provided the movement with its name and many of its basic ideas. Gutiérrez has written that "the poor man is someone who questions the ruling social order." He asserts that "the poverty of the poor is not an appeal for generous action, but the demand for the construction of a different social order."

One of the main features of liberation theology, according to Philip Scharper, is an emphasis on "sinful structures, and sinful societies that live in defiance of what God intended for His children." Scharper said that liberationist group reflection in peasant villages employs biblical themes to help the people grasp their political and economic realities. "When these people read the Magnificat," Scharper said, "and Mary bursts into joy and says God will pull down the mighty, they know who the mighty are." He also said that group reflection on, for example, Christ's statement that He is "the living water" can lead the village to become more aware of the pollution of their drinking water.

"Liberation theology uses Christian concepts like conversion or change of heart in a drastically new way," explained Father Virgilio Elizondo, who heads the Mexican-American Cultural Center in San Antonio (Texas) and who works closely with the activist and pro-liberationist Bishop Patricio Flores of San Antonio. "To respond to God's call, is to become a new person and live in the world in a different way and change the structures of society."

Another liberation theologian defines repentance as "the power to disaffiliate our identity from the faults and oppressive power systems of fallen reality." In her sympathetic book, *Liberation Theology: Human Hope Confronts Christian History and American Power*, theologian Rosemary Radford Ruether gives a startling view of liberation theology's interpretation of Christ's Resurrection. "Liberation for the oppressed," she wrote, "thus is experienced as a veritable resurrection of the self. Liberation is a violent exorcism of the demons of self-hatred and self-destruction which have possessed them and the resurrection of autonomy and self-esteem, as well as the discovery of a new power and possibility of community with our brothers and sisters in suffering. Anger and pride, two qualities viewed negatively in traditional Christian spirituality, are the vital *virtues* in the salvation of the oppressed community."

Bishop Ruiz in San Cristóbal de las Casas has gathered around him a group of radical churchmen and laity who minister to the 45,000 Guatemalan refugees, as estimated by the UN High Commission for Refugees. They are housed in camps and fed through gifts, largely from American Catholic and non-Catholic donors—who have been kept, as has the UN agency itself, from overseeing the dispersal of the aid in the area.

Guatemalan authorities have charged that the refugee camps give, in fact, logistics support to the guerrillas, and that wounded guerrillas have been treated in a local Mexican hospital in the border area which is headed by a surgeon prominent in the Mexican Communist party. Calls for dispersing the refugees from the area have in the past met with stiff resistance from these church-affiliated groups who see the refugees as an injured party with the right to return to their villages in Guatemala—whatever their politics. It is also clear that the more radical members of the aid operation consider the refugees capable of waging a continuing campaign inside Guatemala against the government in Guatemala City.

Although no evidence has been made public, there is a widespread belief in intelligence quarters in Guatemala and Mexico City that Cuban and perhaps East German[10] agents have operated with the guerrillas in the area on a continuing basis. Cuba is a short distance away and the Yucatán peninsula has a long and rich history of contacts with Havana, especially in times of political trouble. The Cuban consulate in nearby Merida (which caused controversy when Echeverría permitted Havana to open it) is large and has radio communications equipment far beyond the needs of a local consulate. One piece of circumstantial evidence pointing to a sophisticated international Communist infrastructure operating in the area is that the occasional border clashes between Guatemalan government forces and the guerrillas are broadcast over Havana radio within hours, with details unavailable to anyone not on the spot.

In May 1984, the Mexican government announced a plan to move the refugees to the state of Campeche in Yucatán on the Gulf of Mexico after forces from the Guatemalan side of the border raided some of the camps with casualties to both refugees and Mexican civilians in the area.[11] The Guatemalan government denied the charges. But it is clear that they stemmed from anti-Communist forces inside Guatemala, and it is equally clear that the Mexican military, with antiquated equipment, poor communications, and small forces, would not relish an encounter with the better-equipped, better-trained, and better-armed Guatemalan army. The whole setting has the familiar ring of a Cambodia or a southern Lebanon to those who have watched the Communists exploit a refugee-border situation to build a guerrilla infrastructure. The Communists today have the opportunity and the facilities to do that on the Mexico-Guatemala border, and unless Mexico City carries out its plan to remove the refugees from the border area and break off their contact with the guerrillas, the area will pose a problem as difficult of solution as Cambodia and Lebanon have been for their anti-Communist neighbors, Thailand and Israel.

Nor has it escaped the notice of some military authorities that this threat lies in the region of Mexico's precious oil resources. One Mexican general, now retired from one of the highest posts in the military structure, worries that Mexico is today totally vulnerable to air attack on its oil fields, that its "entire oil establishment could be wiped out in fifteen or twenty minutes by aircraft coming from Guatemala." It is clear that Mexico's interests lie in a stable and friendly Guatemala on its southern border, probably the only way that difficult terrain could be defended. Yet the policies of both the Echeverría and the López Portillo governments led to a shaky relationship with Guatemala, including at times a breakdown in diplomatic relations. Whatever the protestations of Mexican diplomats who purport to see only an indigenous revolutionary impulse there, a Guatemala in the hands of a regime such as the Sandinistas in Nicaragua would constitute an external threat of enormous dimensions to Mexico and one which it is hard to envisage its armed forces handling.

There has been some improvement in bilateral relations with Guatemala since De la Madrid took office and they may improve more with the new Christian Socialist government installed in early 1986 in Guatemala.[12] But in the long run, effective resistance to Communist aggression in the Central American region will depend on the multilateral relations in the region. The Communists have been extremely agile in exploiting the old feuds among the Central American states.

Only cooperation by the non-Communists on a regional basis—with U.S. assistance—is likely to allay the threat in the long run. The careful game of blackmail and counterblackmail which has gone on for twenty years between Mexico City and Havana would certainly enter a new phase if Guatemala were to fall to the Communists and become allied with Havana. That, in turn, depends to a considerable extent on the outcome of the civil war in El Salvador. Whether one calls it "the domino theory" or not, the reality is that it is inconceivable that Guatemala would not have an infinitely more difficult time controlling its insurgency were it to face a pro-Havana regime on its southern border. The Salvadoran struggle, in turn, is allied to events in neighboring Nicaragua from which the insurgency against the present regime was launched—and which still plays an important part in fostering the Salvadoran guerrillas in every respect.

The Nicaraguan Sandinistas, from the outset of their accession to power in Managua, have stated plainly that one of the aims of their revolution is to spread revolutionary regimes to the other Central American states, including Guatemala, and the contest in El Salvador is very much a part of that strategy.[13] They have, in fact, picked up where the League Against Imperialism, a Soviet Comintern operation, left off in the 1920s when it operated from Mexico City to subvert the Nicaraguan regime of that time.[14] It was thwarted when the U.S. intervened with the Marines, an eight-year occupation that ended in pacification and stabilization but unhappily with the installation of the Somoza family dictatorship.

Whatever the outcome of the struggle in Central America between the Communists and their allies and the U.S. and its friends, the situation is extremely troublesome for the PRI, given its own growing crisis. Mexico City is likely to become more and more dependent on Washington's largess, which would have to come out of the pockets of the U.S. taxpayer. And this at a time when the cost of America's security vis-à-vis Central America is likely to grow. The Kissinger Commission on Central America asked for expenditures of $24 billion for economic aid alone in Central America during the period 1984–1990, a totally arbitrary figure but probably as realistic as any other estimate of what it would take to get those long stagnant societies moving.[15]

But economic cost is only one of the factors produced by the complicated Central American crisis. That situation is coming to a boil just as Mexico's relationship with the U.S.—which has, for the most part, been on "hold" during the past fifty years—is again at a crucial juncture. Relations with the U.S. have been the central thread, and one might say almost the only constituent, of Mexican foreign policy since the defeat of the French attempt to establish a European empire in Mexico in the middle of the nineteenth century. This goes back to the military clashes of the nineteenth century but is also manifest in the overwhelming presence of the U.S. everywhere in Mexico— from the ridiculous antics of the tourists to the sublime influence of missionaries, intellectuals, and businessmen.

And it sometimes unites Mexicans of the extreme Right and Left in their chauvinistic antagonism. An example, full of ironies, in the present political scene is the continuing campaign by the Communists and the extreme Left of the PRI against an American fundamentalist missionary group called the Summer Linguistics Institute. This organization, in the exercise of its belief in the sanctity of the literal word of God as found in the Christian scriptures, has tried for the past fifty years to spread the Christian Bible's teachings to illiterates in Latin America through instruction in local languages, including the Indian dialects. In many instances, they have had to analyze and codify languages which have never been written, leading them to remote parts of the continent, including southern Mexico and Guatemala, where they have worked with the local Mayan family of tongues. Their work among the Indians was one of the first uses made of modern scientific anthropological techniques and they were originally welcomed to Mexico by President Lázaro Cárdenas, the patron saint of the Left who can have done no wrong. That connection has proved the only defense the missionaries have had—in addition to their hard and selfless work—against a totally baseless campaign in the Mexican press which claims that they are agents of U.S. imperialism, the CIA, etc. But the campaign against them has united the Left with the more xenophobic Catholic elements, some of whom have become allies through "Christian Marxism" (liberation theology).

The fear of any U.S. presence dominates the political discussion and cultural life of the country. It has justified many of the actions and policies of the present regime. One can explain this Mexican paranoia with that old cliché: "Just because I am paranoid doesn't mean that I am not persecuted." Mexico and Mexicans have a long list of grievances against the U.S., sometimes skillfully paraded.

A visit to the Museum of the Interventions in suburban Mexico City is an experience for an American interested in this aspect of Mexican social history. The museum displays the evidence of foreign incursions into Mexico in this lovely former nunnery and former site of a battle in the U.S.-Mexican War of 1847. The presentations are geared to current Communist-line politics. The tipoff of the party line is the more tolerant attitude taken toward the French-sponsored Mexican empire of Maximilian as opposed to treatment of incursions by the U.S. which never attempted annexation of the heartland of the country. A Mexican historian can present the American acquisition of Texas and the U.S. Southwest as an example of nineteenth-century imperialism. But in the process he must ignore the fact that Spanish claims to the whole of this vast territory were just that, European claims in dispute among the major powers. Important, too, was the Mexican family fight over decentralization and federalism that was an important part of the Texas issue. A Tejano (a Texan of Mexican origin), Lorenzo de Zavala, wrote the first Texas constitution. He has been a proponent of Mexican federalism but despaired of it ever becoming a part of Mexico's constitutional structure and opted for Texas independence.

At the same time a Mexican intellectual, perhaps because he knows little about U.S. history and institutions—often far less than about those of Europe—is strangely oblivious of the very real differences between the two societies. Thus even an intelligent and educated Mexican nationalist can, for a brief moment, look at Texas and California (as well as New Mexico, Arizona, Nevada, Utah, and parts of Colorado) today and *see them in their present state* as losses to Mexico. The argument that their development is an integral part of the difference between the U.S. and Mexico, that there might have been little if any development had they remained a part of Mexico, is lost somewhere in a chauvinist miasma of self-pity and a search for a scapegoat.

For a Mexican nationalist who lives at the furthermost reaches of this shuttered world—and make no mistake, few Mexicans, however sophisticated and out of sympathy with the current regime, escape a blind nationalism based on opposition to U.S. domination—the situation today is intolerable. Mexico's fashionable leftist intellectual establishment believes—because of the tragic nineteenth-century legacy between the two countries—that Mexico's overwhelming concern is how not to be subsumed by the U.S. And many of Mexico's elite, it is no exaggeration to say, can rationalize their own failings in the belief that the U.S. is the country's only political problem. Porfírio Díaz put it as well as anyone when he allegedly said, after a meeting with President William Howard Taft: "Poor Mexico, so far from God and so close to the United States."

Today the anti-Americans and their fellow-travelers inside the PRI find themselves—in their own terms—more in the hands of the *gringos* than ever before, more in danger of being drawn completely into that maw of "the Colossus of the North." Nor does it take much imagination to see the current situation in that light. Mexico owes the U.S. banks vast sums. While it is unlikely that it will ever pay the debt servicing, much less the enormous capital repayment, it must maintain its credit in New York if Mexico is to have access to the savings of even its *own* citizens which have flown abroad (mostly to the U.S.), not to mention foreign capital for development.

Mexico is now dependent on U.S-subsidized food imports to feed her growing millions. The U.S. Commodity Credit Corporation has sold Mexico more than $2 billion worth of food on extended guaranteed credit since 1980. Mexico depends on Houston to set the oil price for her "black gold" which was, alas, supposed to have been the answer to all her problems—particularly in dealing with the *gringos*. Mexico must also look to the U.S. to absorb a significant part of the surplus population that threatens to choke it. And Mexico's more astute economists are saying that the only hope of climbing out of the hole of poverty is to develop exports for the largest market in the world—next door in the U.S. However distasteful, the fact remains that obligations to the U.S., and, ostensibly, the ability of Washington to dictate the terms of the relationship, have grown enormously.

In every aspect, it seems that the Americanization of daily life in Mexico continues apace—the fast-food restaurants, the introduction of American consumer goods, the infrastructure of modern life which resembles more and more that of the U.S. It has been true for years that Mexico in many ways is more "American" than Western Europe: commercial standards and forms, for example, are more imitative of the U.S. than any American trading partner except Japan. And, final insult, today English or an American business school diploma appears to be the ticket for advancement—even in the PRI, supposedly the most Mexican of Mexican institutions. It is yet another abomination to these nationalists. That they, themselves, are often in part the product of American universities, that they draw deeply for their vulgar Marxism on American critics of U.S. life and policy, is only one of the anomalies of the situation. All this has driven the fashionable leftist políticos in Mexico into near hysteria.

Out of this chauvinistic fury comes the bitter anti-Americanism and even the pro-Soviet and pro-Communist positions that dominate Mexican intellectual life. When Octavio Paz—generally recognized as Mexico's greatest living poet and dean of its literary figures—told a television audience in the spring of 1984 that, while he still considered American imperialism a threat to Mexico, it paled in comparison to the threat of Soviet totalitarianism to the whole Western world, he was ignored by the establishment Mexican press. The two-part series presented by Televisa, the private Mexican television network, was fascinating as an insight into the thinking of a major Mexican intellectual as also into the conflicts within that community. And though Paz no longer reflects the Marxist views of his youth, he still carries many of the dichotomies of the Mexican intellectual's approach to his own and the world's problems. His analysis of "revolution," for example, which negates much of the conventional interpretation of the Mexican Revolution, nevertheless does not preclude his allegiance to what he calls the goals of that revolution.

The program was virtually blacked out in the Mexican press, and for some time Paz, himself, was a social outcaste from the left-wing Mexican intelligentsia. For reasons that still remain somewhat obscure,[16] the De la Madrid administration chose to pay homage to the old man and in mid-summer 1984 a national gala was sponsored for him. He was eulogized, although some of his colleagues (notably, Carlos Fuentes, the novelist and frequent propagandist for the PRI in the U.S.) hinted at their strong disagreement with his recent views.

One has to cast back to post-World War II France, the late 1940s, to find an example of the ferocity and the superficiality of Mexican anti-Americanism. How foolish it now sounds to remember the French campaign against the introduction of Coca Cola, the threat to France in the 1950s of "Coca-Cola imperialism." For it is clear that France remains as Gallic today as before *l'imperialisme cocacola,* which then was of such crucial concern to French intellectuals. And one has little difficulty in concluding that the Mexican ethos, however difficult it may be to define, will endure the onslaught of Denny's fast food chains and Sears Roebuck stores in the new, American-style suburban shopping malls that dot Mexico City and other large city's suburban rings.

Whatever the natural tendencies of any society to resent the encroachment of another, particularly with a history as difficult as that of the U.S. and Mexico, there are other more specific factors. The penetration of the educational institutions—particularly the so-called autonomous universities, whose budgets are upward of 90 percent met by state funds—by acknowledged Communists and their fellow-travelers since the mid-1930s, has taken a heavy toll on objective thinking and cut deeply into Mexico's heritage of Western humanism. Not only UNAM but most of the huge Mexican state universities outside the capital have faculties—particularly in economics and political science—which are overwhelmingly and openly Marxist and often of the pro-Soviet stripe. At Puebla, Mexico's fourth largest city, for example, the chief executive of the university is a former secretary-general of the Communist party of Mexico, a Lenin prize winner, has turned the university into a platform for his politics.[17] Communist politics are an acceptable norm in Mexico and there have been significant recruits from the families of the elite, though the base of the party appears to be very thin.

That the Communists have made so little inroads among the ordinary people in Mexico—despite the confusion engendered by the Communists and the PRI leadership by their loose talk of revolution —is something of a miracle. Part of the long history of failure of the Communists in Mexico is their inability to build a nativist structure. Whether that will obtain in the future as the crisis of this regime deepens remains to be seen. The Communist persuasion may, too, be only a passing fad to the spoiled youth of the upper classes, the university faculties, the media, the intellectuals and the artists. But it may, as in Italy and Argentina in the 1960s, prove that some of these upper class young people are, indeed, convinced Communists should their services be required by an organized revolt from the Left against the regime.

This setting and the onset of a metamorphosis of Mexico's relations with the U.S. have produced a pseudo-intellectual response, mainly centered in the Mexican foreign ministry. There, in the hothouse of diplomacy and alienation which seems to afflict the diplomatic corps of all the Western states, a bizarre theory of Mexico's relationship with the U.S. has developed, about which more below. It flowered in the Echeverría administration when the deputy foreign minister's post was held by Jorge Castaneda, a vituperative, vindictive, anti-*gringo* intellectual who fathered a whole generation of acolytes, including the current minister of foreign affairs, Bernardo Sepulveda Amor, and his shadow, the former Mexican minister to the United Nations, Porfirio Muñoz Ledo, an aspirant to the presidency against López Portillo. Sepulveda, before his move into the upper reaches of the foreign ministry, was treasurer of the Fundación Lombado Toledano, an organization devoted to the Soviet version of Marxist-Leninism and Moscow's subversive efforts in Mexico, allied with El Partido Popular Socialista (People's Socialist party), a splinter party that has never in all the post-World War II history of the Communist bloc deviated from Moscow's line.

Sepulveda's predecessor and mentor, Castaneda, evolved a theory of *dependencia*, the dependency of Mexico and the other Latin American states on the U.S. in every aspect—economic, social, and political. The answer, Castaneda and his followers in the Mexican Ministry of Foreign Affairs believed, to the *dependencia* on the U.S. is for Mexico to become the leader of a Latin American block aligned against Washington. Castaneda's president, Echeverría, speaking of the problem on a tour through Latin America in July 1974, said: "Latin America cannot return to bilateralism with the United

States . . . If we realize that our problems have a common origin and that we should make a common effort to resolve them, nationalism is converted into a principle of action, en route to economic liberation." If a Latin American bloc could be formed in opposition to the U.S., it could be used to give Mexico City leverage on Washington, to equalize Mexico's relationship with the growing power of the *gringos.*

There are, however, two inhibiting factors to such a strategy. The first is that Mexico has not only never been a leader of Latin America, but during her long history she has never held any such pretensions, as have so many Latin-American countries, from Argentina to Colombia. Furthermore, Mexico today, as a debtor nation, with a faltering political system, faced with old intra-Latin American hatreds, has no basis on which to build such a strategy. The only possibility Mexico has for such maneuverings is if it would be willing to use the Cuban-Soviet network in the region, a tactic which would undoubtedly be acceptable to the Communist fellow-travelers in the foreign ministry. Efforts of this sort have taken place in the past few years. The most gradiose was the organization by Mexico, during the height of the oil inflation, of both the economic and political aspects of the Conferencia Permanente de Partidos Políticos de America Latina (COPPPAL), the Latin American Conference of Political Parties. COPPPAL was created as an instrument of Mexican foreign policy, a bridge between Mexico and the Socialist International (SI). The SI, through its Latin American Committee, dominated by West Germany's ex-chancellor Willy Brandt and his protégé in Latin America, José Francisco Peña Gómez, a former mayor of Santo Domingo and secretary-general of the socialist party of the Dominican Republic, has swung its net far beyond the social democratic parties and forces in the continent and courted the Castroite parties in the hemisphere, such as the late Maurice Bishop's New Jewel party of Grenada. Brandt has justified this appeal to nondemocratic parties and elements in Latin America, with no real commonality with European Social Democracy, as necessary because of the differences between Europe and Latin America. It amounts to a kind of racism that contends that while democracy is necessary for European socialism, it is not for lesser species in other parts of the world.

COPPPAL, with its thirty-odd member parties, represents Mexico in the SI's Latin American circles. COPPPAL is also a way of soothing the furor created by the West German Social Democratic party's (SPD) Friederich Ebert Foundation in Mexico, which has stirred up an intellectual whirlwind in Mexican industrial circles. The Ebert Foundation had supported conferences in Mexico looking to the creation of a so-called social sector in the Mexican economy, that is, a sector of the economy in which ownership would be neither by the government nor by the private sector but ostensibly by the workers. That agitation so infuriated the Mexican private sector that, coupled with Mexico's traditional refusal to join international political organizations in pursuit of the thesis that the Mexican revolution was unique, the Mexican government and the PRI formally remained aloof from the SI. But as an important off-stage voice in the Latin American committee of the SI, COPPPAL has supported the most radical—and antidemocratic—elements in the Latin American Left. And it has been used as a platform for anti-American agitation by such old-line Communists as Tomás Borge, a member of the Sandinista junta in Managua and a vice president of COPPPAL.

A columnist in *El Día*, the voice of the left wing of the PRI, summing up the 1982 meeting of COPPPAL in la Paz, Bolivia, suggested the potential of what has until now been a largely rhetorical and innocuous organization: "The COPPPAL is a sensitive antenna for the concerns which animate the struggle of the people of Latin America, which after the weighty experience of the Malvinas [the British-Argentine war over the Falkland Islands], and before the pressures of the international financial system, alone can recover the road which indicates Latin American nationalism and advance toward the victory in the fight for unity and the liberation of our peoples."[18] In other words, viewed from Washington, COPPPAL is an organization which could unite Latin America against the U.S. Still, when a group of Latin American nations chose to meet to talk over their international debt problems in June 1984, largely at Mexico's behest, the COPPPAL forum was not used, apparently because it was considered too controversial by some of the participants.

Perhaps Mexico's most effective diplomatic effort in the past decade has been in the Contadora Group—Mexico, Colombia, Panama, and Venezuela. The organization, taking its name from the first meeting of its foreign ministers at the luxury resort on an island off Panama in January 1983, has as its aim the settlement of the problems of Central America which have led to civil war in El Salvador and fighting between U.S.-backed guerrillas and the Sandinistas in Nicaragua. The Contadora Group has sought to find a peaceful solution through extended negotiations covering all issues in the Central America region. The Mexicans and the Venezuelans, meanwhile, have used their leverage gained from the sale of petroleum to the Central American and Caribbean states at discount and on credit to help them through the post-OPEC oil crisis. The Mexicans, as defenders of the Sandinistas—and in a joint declaration with the French in 1981, in which Mexico City and Paris declared the Communist forces in El

Salvador "a legitimate political force"—and other pro-Communists in the area have often found themselves in disagreement with the other members of the group. Mexico has insisted that the destabilization in Central America stems from age-old conditions of economic and social poverty which were only manipulated by outsiders. Mexico City also holds that the eruptions of the Left in Central America are not important, that the revolutionary sparks could be neutralized if generous economic aid were provided. Fair elections, moreover, are not necessary if "ideological pluralism" in the region is condoned, i.e., the acceptance of leftist dictatorships.[19]

The Reagan administration has treated the whole effort coolly but formally welcomed the Contadora Group as a mediator in the dispute. But by mid-summer 1984, the Reagan administration was welcoming what seemed a turn in the attitude of the Mexican government, which sent Foreign Minister Bernard Sepulveda Amor to the inauguration of President Napoleón Duarte in San Salvador—despite the fact that Mexico does not have diplomatic relations with the U.S-supported government and permits rebel operations to function openly in Mexico City.

Washington aside, many Mexicans, in and out of government and despite the official propaganda line, are worried about the growing internationalization of the crisis in Central America.[20] For Mexico has not only supported the Sandinista regime in Nicaragua with statements in international forums, but one retired Mexican high army officer insists that arms and oil have been shipped from Mexico to help support the Nicaraguan Communists against the U.S-backed contras who seek their overthrow. According to Mexican opposition politicians, there have also been some five hundred *internationalistas* (the Sandinista term for foreign Communist experts and policy advisers) in Managua aiding the regime—including Mexican military paid for by the Mexican taxpayer.

In the hands of Foreign Minister Bernado Sepulveda Amor, a representative of the extreme Left of the PRI and the bitter anti-*gringo* feeling that permeates the Mexican foreign ministry, and Washington and Mexico City's positions on Central America have continued to widen. After Sandinista junta Chairman Daniel Ortega returned from a "laying on of hands" ceremony in Moscow in the spring of 1985, following the farce of the Nicaraguan elections and his elevation to the presidency, he announced that Managua would no longer import petroleum products from Mexico. Earlier Ramón Beteta, head of the Mexican oil monopoly PEMEX, had suspended shipments to Managua in conjunction with Venezuela. Both had accumulated substantial debts under the San José Accord which had shortly after the oil crisis extended joint credits to the Central American and Caribbean countries hard-hit by the OPEC price increases. And the economic crisis in Mexico, pressure on oil production, and most of all, Beteta's rationalization program for PEMEX pricing, seemed to dictate a tougher policy toward the Central American debtors at a time when domestic Mexican price for petroleum prices was being raised sharply. Ortega announced that Nicaragua could no longer abide by the San José conditions—80 percent commercial payments and 20 percent extended credits—and would look for oil suppliers elsewhere, presumably from the Soviet Union which has long supplied Cuba.

When the Reagan administration instituted commercial sanctions against the Sandinista regime in retaliation for Managua's new move toward Moscow, Mexican UN Ambassador Porfírio Muñoz Ledo denounced the U.S. action. And after some weeks of confused statements, Sepulveda announced that Mexican oil shipments were continuing to the Sandinistas on the same basis as before. As U.S. pressure—exerted through the American-supported anti-Sandinista contra guerrillas—increased against the Managua regime, Sepulveda attempted to organize counterpressure. Secretary of State George P. Shultz rejected Mexico's insistent pleas that the U.S. resume direct bilateral talks with the Managua regime which had been sponsored by Mexico in the resort city of Manzanillo.[21]

Sepulveda had upped the ante a few weeks earlier by staging a new meeting in Cartagena, Colombia, in late August 1985 where the Contadora powers—headed by Mexico and including Venezuela, Colombia, and Panama—were to meet with a new grouping, the so-called Contadora "support group," consisting of Argentina, Brazil, Peru, and Uruguay. All four had recently elected left-of-center governments with strong sympathies for the Sandinistas and united in their cry of non-interference by the U.S. in Latin affairs. Furthermore, Sepulveda was proposing that these governments together with the Contadora powers organize a multinational military force to keep the peace in Central America by sealing off Nicaragua's borders, starting with its southern border with Costa Rica. The contras and their allies in the U.S. and Central America saw this as a deliberate Mexican attempt to help the Sandinistas who, despite their growing military support from Cuba and the rest of the Communist bloc, were facing a growing internal resistance on top of the heightened contra campaign, which threatened to escalate to a "two-front" war—from the Costa Rican border, in the south and the Honduran border in the north.

"Unfortunately," Sepulveda said in an embittered statement replying to "leaks" in Washington that Mexico was moving away from support of the Salvadoran Communist guerrillas, "confrontations and battles between countries and between national factions persist in the region. We have still not succeeded in dislodging the interference of countries outside the zone."[22] This latter was interpreted as a reference to the U.S.—although had it not been Sepulveda, it might easily have been a reference to Cuba as the chief supplies of weapons and training to the Communist guerrillas in the region. How far Mexican policy was simply an attempt to distance itself from the U.S. in the Contadora Group and how far Mexican leadership really believed that the conflict in Central America was a replay of the Mexican Revolution—a favorite theme of Mexican critiques of the U.S.—was not clear and may never be.

Mexico played a nefarious role toward the end of 1984 in attempting to persuade the Central American states to accept a draft of a Contadora treaty which would have disarmed the region's anti-Communist groups but set up no enforceable standard by which the Cuban, Soviet, and other Communist bloc aid to the Sandinistas would be monitored and halted. On the eve of the October foreign ministers meeting between the European community and the Central American states in San José, Costa Rica, the Mexicans presented a draft of the treaty to the Sandinistas who immediately signed it and called on the Americans to sign a protocol acknowledging it and agreeing to abide by it. The draft did not accede to demands by either the U.S. or the other Central American powers for adequate guarantees against a growing Sandinista military presence in the region.

Nor was the bilateral process of negotiations between the Sandinista regime and the U.S. more encouraging. The Mexicans, who insisted against U.S. wishes in becoming the permanent hosts for the talks, had set up a parallel meeting during the U.S.-Nicaraguan talks taking place in the same hotel among Mexico, the Sandinistas, and the Cubans—one more example of Mexico's perception of its role as intermediator between the U.S. and Communist forces in Latin America. Again in the summer of 1985, Mexico attempted—with the help of Venezuela—to set up a *zona sanitario* (a neutral area) inside Costa Rica along the Nicaraguan border. The move was presented as an effort to keep the civil war between the Sandinistas and the contras from spilling over into Costa Rica. Opponents of the maneuver saw it as an attempt to keep opposition to the Sandinistas from mobilizing Nicaraguans along the Costa Rican border as they had previously done on the Honduran border region in the north.

Mexico has also joined a number of economic organizations in the area which include Communist Cuba, and which have helped Cuba to break out of the isolation imposed largely through American initiative in the 1960s. One is the Caribbean Multinational Shipping Company (NAMUCAR), ostensibly a commercial undertaking but one which some Central American anti-Communists believe has been used for shipping weapons secretly to guerrilla groups fighting established governments in El Salvador and Guatemala. When Mexico proposed, along with Venezuela, to create a Latin American Economic Organization (SELA), Castro enthusiastically endorsed it and participated in a ministerial meeting in August 1975 in Panama. Again at the initiative of Mexico, Cuba was brought into an international sugar organization representing Latin America.

None of these organizations is likely to mean much in terms of solutions to the problems of the region. But they provide a propaganda network, one more avenue of access, in which Cuban (and therefore Soviet) propagandists and subversives can operate. And it is highly unlikely that they will take their lead from the Mexican "moderates" who want to use them for Mexican-U.S. bilateral problems.

What appears to be happening, in sum, is that Mexican egos, so long accustomed to playing the role of Latin America's leading economic role model, but paradoxically, so long isolated from much of the rest of the hemisphere, will continue to be blind to the growing peril in the region. Nor will the PRI regime recognize that the crisis, though ostensibly brought on by economic problems, is being politically exploited by Cuban penetration backed by the Soviets.

Chapter 5: **What Kind of Explosion?**

Where people gather—often in Mexico, occasionally in the U.S.—to discuss the crisis of the Mexico Model, there are two classic scenarios divining where the current crisis in that country is leading:

One group of analysts (the optimists) holds that Mexico is, indeed, in the midst of the greatest crisis in its history. But the PRI, with its special mystique, will see the country through the current difficulties as it has so many times in the past. This line of thought admits that the PRI is a bundle of hypocritical contradictions, caught between its professed revolutionary character and its very real unadorned opportunism, that it is not ideological in any real sense, and that it is incurably corrupt. But for these very reasons, the PRI will continue to "co-opt" any viable opposition on the Right or on the Left. It is precisely its character, the argument continues, that permits the PRI to swim through Mexican history, swinging right or left as the currents take it, enveloping opposition with its pragmatism and opportunism.

Another group of analysts (the pessimists), pointing to the growing and long-term problems of Mexican society led by the demographic explosion, see the PRI and all it stands for as an anachronism, an ossified political structure. It is a catastrophe only waiting to happen, a fossil ready to be toppled by a truly revolutionary conspiracy which will replace it with a government either of the Right or of the Left—or both.[1]

To predict the exact scenario of a breakdown of Mexican society would be foolhardy. Only determinists who see preordained certainty in their logic of history make this sort of prediction. But all logical signs point to an increasingly difficult situation in Mexico, where population pressure, the failure of the economic system, and the political incompetence of the leadership are producing an entirely new political environment. One must examine the possibilities of developments in terms of conventional political labels and attitudes that in a period of great crisis and flux would probably prove to be inadequate. Nevertheless, an examination limited to right-wing and left-wing opposition to the regime appears to be only one way to sort out possibilities as the crisis deepens.

Paradoxically, solutions to the present situation are not likely to come from the innate conservatism of the Mexican people expressed through existing conservative political organizations. Mexican conservatives and moderates are overwhelmed by the all but total dominance by left-wing thinkers and fellow-travelers of the Mexican intellectual world and the government's revolutionary rhetoric that comes out of that domination and which acts as a deterrent if not a brake on policy formulation.

At its outset, the De la Madrid administration had only one ideologue with a sufficient grasp of the Mexican political processes to maneuver in the Byzantine world of the upper reaches of the PRI for a new approach to the problems of the regime. He was Jesús Reyes Heroles, the minister of education, the leader of the Left within the PRI. Reyes typically commanded a prominent *camarilla* (band of comrades in politics) in the federal government based on close ties to Tuxpan, his birthplace in the state Veracruz where he once briefly served as mayor. Reyes's ideological base was formed in the Escuela Nacional Preparatoria, the premier school leading to the national university (UNAM), which is dominated by left-wing thinkers and activists, and later in his studies as a distinguished student in UNAM's law faculty. He has occupied positions in government since his emergence from UNAM in 1944, although he served as an assistant to a presidential secretary as early as his first year in law school in 1939.

Unlike most politicians in the highly personalized Mexican political world, Reyes pursued a career under different sponsors. The conservative President Miguel Alemán in 1946 appointed him as secretary to the newly organized ministry of national resources under an old professor from the Preparatoria, and he brought many of his friends from there into the government. His six years as head of PEMEX, no doubt laid the foundations for the patronage that set up his *camarilla*. Reyes epitomized the new bureaucrat-politician who has come to dominate the PRI, since he occupied elective or party posts only briefly (as elected deputy from Veracruz and in 1972 chairman of the Executive Committee of the PRI under Echeverría). But as minister of Gobernación under López Portillo and then, until his death in the spring of 1985, from his post as minister of education, he led a brilliant fight for left-wing policies within the De la Madrid administration in bitter infighting—ironically often opposed to an old student and protégé, minister of finance Jesús Silva Herzog, who has assumed leadership of the moderates within the De la Madrid administration and who hopes, himself, to be the next president. Reyes had only one chink in his political armor: His father was a Spaniard, and the Mexican constitution not only requires birth in the country, as does the U.S. constitution, but also Mexico-born parents. But this, in a sense, threw Reyes back on his Spanish background, and tied him to the group of left-wing politicians intellectually descended from the Spanish Republican emigration. After his death De la Madrid "replaced" him with a colorless and mediocre friend—another example of the narrowing circle of the government and the power of the presidency. It was the end, many felt, of any new and effective effort to revamp the PRI—either from right or left.

PRI moderates, like Minister Silva Herzog, are politically castrated because they find it necessary to spout the rhetoric of the Revolution while pursuing policies which run diametrically counter to its slogans. To believe that this will succeed in the long run, is to believe that ideas have no meaning and that there is no price to pay for rhetoric in the modern political process, whether in Mexico or elsewhere. In the end, the conservatives and moderates of the PRI are going to find that they have destroyed their own base for building any program, that they are at the mercy of the agenda of the Left. The erosion has already bitten deep; it accounts for the leftward movement of Mexico's governments though they have been largely in the hands of moderates or even conservatives.

The whole question of bank nationalization is a typical example of the process. Until as recently as 1980, the proposal to nationalize banks had been advanced only by the Communists and the extreme Left in the PRI. When López Portillo suddenly decreed it on Sept. 1, 1982, it was not only against the advice of the right-wing PRI *políticos* but also against the advice of the overwhelming majority of the establishment's *técnicos*. As a result, men like Silva Herzog, who opposed bank nationalization and foresaw the annihilation of confidence it would bring on, now have to try to salvage something from the ashes. It will not be easy. There has never been any question of denationalizing the banks even though De la Madrid opposed it himself and took office only a few months after it had been decreed and, indeed, before it had been institutionalized with an administrative organization for the banks and a constitutional amendment.

Other fundamental ideological issues, totems of the Left, are also festering inside the PRI establishment. One of the most important is education. The politicization of the universities by the Left—led by the Communists—and the unprecedented growth of their student bodies in the last twenty-five years have virtually destroyed them as viable educational institutions. The Communists early on targeted the faculties of economics and political science and they now dominate most of the disciplines in the principal state-supported universities, often supported by the extremely radical university employee unions. More recently they have gone after schools of business administration and have organized boycotts of textbooks by U.S. authors or those to do with American business models. Several of them have changed their designation to schools of public administration and are using East bloc texts.

In the vacuum for quality higher education that has developed, a group of alternative educational institutions has grown up, many of them in the last decade, largely organized by anti-Communists, often with a Catholic ethos, and with the help of the private sector. In many instances, they educate not only the children of the PRI's opposition, but the sons and daughters of the PRI leadership. The reason is simple: if one wants a decent university education in Mexico today he must attend a private non-Marxist facility. Reyes Heroles—and the whole Left in and out of the PRI—has of course made Catholic private schools a major ideological target for government "reform."

The battle over the schools has already begun. The first target appears to be the normal schools. Since they require government certification, they have been under pressure to reduce enrollment. Some private schools have moved to change their registration from federal to state governments, which are more sympathetic, to escape pressure from Mexico City. But in the end, the relatively small number of students enrolled in the private schools probably means that private education could be a token of freedom without in any way affecting the Marxist orientation of the bulk of Mexico's educational apparatus. At any rate, for the moment, the PRI has not succeeded in "nationalizing" the private universities.

But just as nationalization of the banks was effected, though unlikely only months before it happened, the political system in Mexico —with its unlimited executive powers—could focus on the schools in a new fit of perversity. Education is certainly a high priority for the Left; having infiltrated the influential faculties in the major state universities, the Communists and their friends fear the intellectual opposition that is being formulated in the private universities. At a moment of crisis, "nationalization" of the private schools could be the next Christian cast to the lions by the opportunistic PRI to keep the circus going.

All this is to emphasize once again that despite the innately conservative nature of the majority of the PRI, their opportunism and lack of ideological commitment make them putty in the hands of a better-organized left wing in the party, buttressed by the bogus "revolutionary" cant. The vacuity of PRI rhetoric is nowhere better demonstrated than in the slogan chosen for the celebration of the fiftieth anniversary of the "revolution" in 1984, "La Revolución es México!" (The Revolution is Mexico!).

Unfortunately, it is also difficult to maintain that the political opposition on the Right outside the PRI will arbitrate the future. Mexican moderates and conservatives are extremely fragmented and weak. The Partido Acción Nacional (PAN), the largest of the conservative opposition groups, is backed by some elements of the business community and of the Church. But the business community—especially that centered in Monterrey which has been the mainstay of PAN and which as late as during the Echeverría administration could bring enormous pressure to bear on the central government—has been castrated by the economic crisis. As one Monterrey industrialist put it to the author, referring to the series of economic decisions leading to the present international debt crisis, "Make no mistake about it: it was a great party and the private sector was right there at the head of the line." He referred, of course, to the massive borrowing by both private and public sectors on the same false assumptions which preceded the 1982 financial collapse.

The Monterrey group, before the financial disaster overtook it, included the largest single private corporate entity in Latin America; but the ALFA group of companies is no longer likely to play a decisive political role. The nationalization of the banks, the flight of capital, the demoralization of the business leaders—because of their defeat at the hands of the bureaucrats or their willingness to compromise their liberty and power—and the nature of the economic crisis which does not permit easy or quick solutions, have all eaten into the business community's ability to affect the political situation.

The PAN also suffers from the divisions within the Catholic church which has seen even some of its hierarchy seduced by Marxist concepts of social justice—government intervention, division of property, and radical concepts of religious commitment to a Marxist program for the poor. The origins of this movement in Mexico go back to the 1920s when church leaders during the worst of the anticlerical agitation of that period decided that the Mexican church must have a modern social program. The Church set up the Mexican Social Secretariat (SSM) to oversee social action programs. From its inception, the SSM took up the cudgels against economic liberalism—identified since early in the nineteenth century with the anticlericalism of the liberals' creed on the Continent in Europe, particularly France and Italy—although, in its denunciation of classical capitalism, the SSM brooked no acceptance of Communism.

But with the growing difficulties of the Mexico Model, criticism of the economic system escalated in church councils. As early as 1950, an SSM leader, Father Pedro Velázquez, argued that capitalism was " . . . saturated with injustice . . . desirous of producing prosperity for a single class, creator of the greatest hatreds that humanity experiences today, the bearer of responsibility for the present chaos which confronts the world."[2]

Out of this background and with the threat that Castro's Communism posed for Mexico, the Mexican Catholic hierarchy and lay leaders in the 1960s feverishly sought new social solutions, consonant with the Catholic faith, to the growing problems of the country. The encounter between students and the government at Tlatelolco in 1968 had the same dramatic impact on church sociologists as on the Mexican political structure. One SSM leader, Father Alejandro Morelli, argued that the failure of the Mexico Model and other developmental schemes in Latin America was the result of a conspiracy by the wealthy nations and the national oligarchies to maintain the status quo. Morelli sought to interpret Christian scripture as primarily an experience of liberation and he was joined by Father Manuel Velázquez, another SSM official, who called for participation in revolutionary action to bring about change. In this way they were following in the footsteps of European and Latin American theologians who had accepted Marxist analysis of social problems— and, in some instances, Marxist solutions as well.[3]

But it was the former bishop of Cuernavaca, Sergio Mendez Arceo, who retired in 1983 reportedly under Vatican pressure but at the age of seventy-five, who dramatized the radical changes that the left wing of the church in Mexico proposed to make in traditional doctrine and to represent those beliefs abroad. "Don Sergio" has been an outspoken advocate of a Marxist-Christian alliance, a frequent visitor to Managua and Havana, and even to the East bloc. "The Red Bishop" in April 1971, in Santiago de Chile with the blessings of the Allende government, was a founding member of an organization among Latin priests that later came to be known as "Christians for Socialism." Earlier in 1968, at a meeting of the Conference of Latin American bishops (CELAM) at Medellín, Colombia, this group and other like-minded members of the Latin hierarchy were able to put through resolutions on social problems that were interpreted as an endorsement of liberation theology and for collaboration with the Marxists. These endorsements were reversed in 1979 at a Latin American Eucharistic Congress in Puebla, perhaps Mexico's most Catholic city, under the direct influence of Pope John Paul II who was present.

Bishop Mendez Arceo has had relatively little influence with the Mexican hierarchy, who have repeatedly repudiated his statements.

But he has, over the years, given protection and aid to a group of scholars, lay and priests, who have worked closely with Marxist political factions, and to like-minded clergy in Mexico and Central America. Father Ivan Illich, a Jesuit who has since left the priesthood, conducted a center under Mendez Arceo's "protection" to train clergy for work on social issues in Latin America. Many of the individuals and organizations in Central America who today foster the program of the liberationists trace their intellectual origins and their organizational methodology to this center.

Some of these social activists have moved out of the Church and into radical politics. José Alvarez Icaza, a lay leader of the Mexican delegation to Vatican II, for example, today is a leader of the ultraleft Partido de los Trabajadores Mexicanos (PTM), formerly a member of the five-party PSUM alliance led by the Communists, but which entered its own candidates with considerable success in the 1985 parliamentary elections.

Bishops Ruiz García of San Cristóbal de las Casas, Chiapas, and Arturo Lona Reyes of Tehuantepec, are two leading members of the minority in the Mexican church who hold to liberation theology briefs. Lona claimed, in an informal interview with this author in 1984, that all ten bishops in the south (out of the ninety-odd total bishops in the Mexican episcopate) see such activities as land reform as one of their principal pastoral missions. The bishop claimed that he and Ruiz and the other "progressive" clergy were the victims of a campaign of vilification and calumny. He said he believed that such programs as land reform were crucial to any program for social justice in the country. But he also acknowledged that there were technical problems involved that suggested that they would not, ultimately, solve those problems; e.g., that even were all the land in Mexico divided on an equitable basis, the problem of food production would remain. And the bishop conceded that there were deep moral concerns—corruption, for example—that had impeded any progress and which received less emphasis in his preoccupation with revolutionary forms.

The region is, of course, the most volatile in the country with its large indigenous population, its poverty, and its proximity to the violence in Central America. Both Ruiz and Lona have been extremely active in pastoral work among the Guatemalan refugees in the border areas,[4] and they have bitterly attacked the Guatemalan government—particularly its former pentecostal Christian leadership, which they stigmatize as religiosity without social conscience.[5]

The Mexican Cardinal Primate Ernesto Corripio Ahumada has fought back by denouncing the Guatemalan military for its excesses, but at the same time condemning the Nicaraguan Sandinista regime as inspired by Cuban Marxism. The conflict over the flirtation of some left-wing priests with Marxist-Leninist confrontational tactics if not actually with Communist guerrillas has split the Mexican church into at least two camps. Nor has the denunciation of the Marxists and their collaborators within the Church by Pope John Paul II during his visit to Mexico and Central America in 1982 been enough to quiet the activists who have allied themselves with the Communists in that struggle in Nicaragua. The presence of a number of Nicaraguan priests—who have refused to accede to the Vatican's orders to withdraw from active politics or leave the Church—in the Sandinista regime has further widened the fissure.

On the other hand, a number of priests in northern Mexico with close affiliations to PAN have attacked the government for its refusal to honor fair elections, in effect those where the PAN was the probable victor in local contests and the Mexico City hierarchy has pushed all Mexicans to participate in the electoral process. A new group in the Mexican church called "neoconservative" has made a determined effort to stem the liberationist tide with an informed, coolly analytical response to the liberation theology dictums.[6] Its most effective spokesman is Bishop Javier Lozano Barragan of Mexico City, a serious student of Marxism and a protégé of Alfonso Cardinal López Trujillo of Medellín, Colombia, the current head of CELAM and one of the pope's most trusted and effective surrogates in fighting the liberationists in the Western Hemisphere.

José Angel Conchello, a former chairman of PAN, acknowledges that this ideological split inside the Church has caused problems and that some Panistas have flirted with the liberation theology movement, but argues that it is now in the past. That seems optimistic at best, since liberation theology has an enormous appeal in a country with such desperate economic problems as well as to a party like PAN, whose ideology tends to be vague as its growing support becomes more and more simply accumulated from an anti-PRI electorate.

Furthermore, the left-wing "networks" in the Church are far more developed than those of the moderates or the conservatives. These elements in the Mexican church—as throughout Latin America —get enormous intellectual reinforcement through the intervention of radical European clergy (particularly French and Spanish Jesuit and Dominican missionaries serving in Central America) and some U.S. Catholic missionary societies, who serve largely as propagandists for the new version of the Faith. There is also considerable funding from abroad, not the least from American church sources.[7]

In addition to their problem with their Catholic alliances, the Panistas have a problem of image. By and large, their leadership belongs to the same elite as that of the PRI. Right or wrong, much of the country feels that PAN is an ineffective opposition tolerated by the regime to give credibility to its claims to democracy. And Panistas do tend to reflect elitist governing concepts not that different from that of their PRI colleagues. No new PAN leadership is likely to emerge, at least before the onset of large-scale violence.

But perhaps the ultimate question for the PAN, as for any democratic opposition group in Mexico, is how it can hope to wrest power peaceably from the PRI. Pledged to the process of the ballot box, how can the PAN hope to take over from a PRI, many of whose leaders announce publicly that they intend to hang on to power by whatever means necessary. Nor is it realistic for the opposition to hope for a split in the PRI—at least not until too late to allow a transfer of power to a new ideological group. Again, paradoxically, the right wing of the PRI, despite its ideological sympathies and familial ties to the PAN and the private sector, is more fervent—at least publicly—than the left wing in its advocacy of strong arm methods to hang onto power. That is logical since the success of the PAN would diminish the leverage of the right wing inside the PRI.

But there are other ways to power than through the ballot. And in Mexico, as in other Latin American societies, the potential for a *caudillo*, a charismatic figure, particularly a military figure, during a crisis of the regime is never to be ruled out. The tradition of military rule is deeply imbedded in a history that goes back to the *reconquista* in fourteenth- and fifteenth-century Spain, when small groups of feudal Christian *guerrilleros* under charismatic leaders reconquered the Iberian peninsula from the Moslem Moors. Some historians have posited that the Spanish conquest of Latin America was, in a sense, a continuation of this phenomenon. And because of almost four hundred years of Latin American experience with military dictatorships— including Mexico's—the role of the army is a frequent subject for speculation in consideration of the present crisis.

But one must immediately point out that the Mexican army is far less dynamic than its counterparts in other Latin American states. The Mexican army has seldom been, as in other Latin American states, the guardian of the *status quo* or the continuity of the republic. The Mexican military who were an important part of the PRI's revolutionary family in the 1920s and 1930s were, after all, not a professional officer corps but rather the product of two decades of civil war that had thrust dozens of local political leaders into command positions. "Generals" were local *caciques* who could pay, command, and keep together a few hundred, or at best, a few thousand men, often *campesinos* who had joined the fray in the general breakdown of society because they had no jobs nor livelihood. That has given the Mexican military a tradition of populism if not radicalism, a nonprofessional background which the institutionalization of the past fifty years has not wiped out, especially as the role of the military (and its funds) declined precipitously.

Mexico's military, through a complicated decentralization of command at the center and through thirty six military zones around the country, would find it hard to assume leadership even in a crisis. In addition to the fractured command structure, with a separate army and navy commander-in-chief, there are three heavily armed battalions of the presidential guard which report directly to a chief of presidential staff in Los Piños. Loyalties in the military, even more than in civilian life, are based on personalities. The phasing out of the military as a component in the revolutionary family since the late 1930s has been so thorough that officers have played a minimal political role for decades—even to the extent of not dictating its own policies in armaments and recruitment. The Mexican military establishment has become a lackey of the PRI with its first loyalty to party largess. Nor has it been able to maintain itself as an effective force. As one of its former commanders said in a private conversation, the Mexican army "is not an army but 120,000 men deployed around the country without adequate training, equipment, or leadership."

Mexico does not, in consequence, share the military tradition of Argentina, Chile, or Brazil, or even of Colombia or Venezuela, countries where a breakdown in the political order in the 1950s led to a takeover by soldier-politicians. Mexican soldiers did not fight in World War II and have been insulated from smaller conflicts since. Nor does Mexico remember a recent military dictatorship such as has dominated Venezuela and Colombia as late as the post-World War II period, regimes which, however discredited in the end, were popular when they came to power at the failure of a civilian political process. A military dictatorship or directorate such as took over in Chile in 1973 after the defeat and death of Salvador Allende, the Marxist president, is difficult to hypothesize in Mexico. There simply are not enough qualified officers to lead it. One can only postulate that at a certain level of general disorder in the country, the Mexican military might step in with conservative civilian advisers to try to control a chaotic situation.

That is not to deny, however, that there has been a renaissance of sorts among the Mexican military. Beginning in López Portillo's administration, the PRI began to increase drastically the budget of the military. And it was generally believed that the armed forces would almost double to 220,000 over a five-year period. This decision was made by López Portillo at the urging of an extremely able and effective minister of national defense, Gen. Felix Galvan López. (Galvan had earlier served as military attaché at the Mexican Embassy in Washington, an almost traditional route upward for Mexican military men who have strong PRI connections. He has since retired to his ranch in northern Mexico, under something of a cloud.)

Why López Portillo decided to put this new emphasis on the military is less than clear, given the strong suspicions with which the civilian PRI officials have regarded the Mexican army in the past fifty years. The explanation may lie in the contradictions which beset López Portillo's view of Mexico and his own personal problems which certainly contributed toward the collapse of his policies. One report, for example, is that during a visit to the Guatemalan border early in his administration, he was flown by helicopter along the jungle frontier. He returned to Mexico City convinced that there was no defense of the border, and that, as with so many other issues, Mexico should make the best of a bad situation by refusing to acknowledge that the problem existed. But in the process of this rationalization, he apparently was persuaded that something had to be done to secure as best possible Mexico's oil fields which lie close by the border and the violence in Central America.

In pursuit of that policy, in 1981, the combined army and air force budget was increased 54 percent over 1980, bringing it to 1.6 percent of the gross domestic product. But even more revolutionary, for the first time in living memory, López Portillo bought major U.S. military equipment—12 F-5 jet fighter planes. The choice was between the American aircraft, the French Mirage, and Israeli aircraft. Whether or not the decision was dictated by the practicality of having their engines maintained and serviced out of Texan airports, the Mexicans implicitly gave up—at least temporarily—the long-held concept that the U.S. was the only potential enemy and therefore could not be a source of military hardware. But the modern fighter aircraft are only the tip of the billions of dollars which would be needed if the Mexican military is to be modernized to even minimum standards.

It appears likely, moreover, that the austerity program which has overtaken the country will force major cutbacks in any kind of military expansion and modernization for some time. De la Madrid, however, not only exempted the military from the enormous cutbacks in real income of state employees in 1983, he gave the military a 100 percent salary increase, partially compensating for the massive devaluations of 1981–1982.

The nature of the modernization gives some indication of just how far the Mexican army has to go to become a modern fighting force: for example, exchanging horse cavalry for modern maneuver brigades using Mexican-built personnel carriers. A construction program was begun to build modern installations for the regional zone commands, perhaps so as to make use of them in maintaining public order. Of more political significance is the effort to upgrade the inferior military colleges and academies, most of which are at the U.S. high school level or below. (An exception is the Military Hospital in Mexico City which, along with its teaching staff, is considered one of the best medical institutions in the country.) A new equivalent of the U.S. War College, the Colegio de Defensa, has been set up where officers are taught, in addition to strategic and military subjects, economics, politics and "social action"—interestingly enough, in some cases, by civilian instructors who are not members of the revolutionary family.

The Mexican military are so removed, not only from the high echelons of the PRI, but also from civilian society, that there is little to indicate their political views. Conventional wisdom holds that their senior officers have been neutralized, bought off by the PRI—there are approximately five times as many generals as in the U.S. army —and kept isolated from civilian political life. The completely volunteer force—both officers and men—tends to come from the poorer rural strata of Mexican society, and thus, it is assumed, is generally conservative. But precisely for this reason, the men share a certain populist feeling. Recruiting is undertaken at the local level, and new soldiers may serve in their home areas; although, as with the civilian bureaucracy, a growing number of the military officers are recruited from the lower middle class in the valley of Mexico around the capital. One Mexican educator, with contact among younger officers, argues that a left-wing populist movement among the younger officers, much like that which took place in the Peruvian army in the late 1960s and 1970s, is not to be ruled out. In the case of the Peruvian army, large numbers were converted to a pro-Moscow position, if not out-and-out Communism, which led to massive purchases of Soviet equipment and the entry of large numbers of KGB-military trainers into the country.

Some foreigners with contacts among Mexican officers report a vehement feeling in the military that they do not want to be tarred with the same brush as the police who, particularly in the corrupt-ridden sexenium of López Portillo, came into such total disrepute. And that could lead to a growing perception by the senior military that they must protect the Mexican people against a corrupt civilian bureaucracy. The record is also clear that, despite enormous pressure during Echeverría's administration, the high command has avoided any official fraternization and collaboration with the Cuban Communist military beyond the norms of protocol.

The question of the relationship between the Mexican and the U.S. military will be crucial in the coming decade. The traditional concept of the U.S. as the historical enemy of Mexico and of the Mexican military—their heroes are almost exclusively those who have distinguished themselves in combat with the U.S., like the youthful cadets who committed suicide during the Battle of Chapultepec in the Mexican War—has long prevented relations between the two countries' armed forces from being much more than formal and correct. However, occasionally there are Mexican officers in U.S. military schools, and at times the Mexican military tour U.S. facilities. But when, in the spring of 1984, forty senior Mexican military—brigadier-generals and up—planned a visit to Washington and to various military installations around the country, it caused a political fracas in Mexico. And that although the tour was initiated by the Mexicans and had the okay of Los Piños. The trip was canceled, but then resumed after the commander of the prestigious Colegio de Defensa, who apparently had opposed it, was transferred.

Mexico did not participate in the massive U.S. military assistance programs to Latin American armies in the 1960s and the 1970s. U.S. military attachés in Mexico have only the most superficial and formal contact with Mexican commanders in the field. Most of the intercourse between the two countries' armed forces has taken place through the Mexican military attaché's office in Washington, whose officer is often tapped to become an important figure. Ironically, the Mexican military who are critical of the policies of the government today look to the U.S. and the American military for support.

A conservative military takeover—were it to come—would be greatly dependent on Washington for support, not only in terms of logistics for its military machine but to set up a functioning civilian apparatus to govern the country. The U.S. record in Vietnam and elsewhere does not evoke much optimism in this respect. Any Mexican military government, furthermore, would not only face all the present problems but, if conservative or even moderate, would run up against the significant opposition of the Left.

If, then, the overthrow of the present regime—or a significant modification of it through some evolutionary process—from the Right does not seem to be in the cards, what do we find on the Left of the political spectrum (always bearing in mind that these terms may not be relevant in the cataclysm that could overtake the regime)?

Any analysis of a possible overthrow by, or radical lurch to, the Left in Mexico must first of all deal with the strange dichotomy that has always characterized left-wing politics in the country. It results from the profound attachment to the thesis of the nineteenth-century intellectuals—in Mexico as in most of Latin America and Spain —which held progress as synonymous with the European liberal agenda. First and foremost on that agenda was a break from what was perceived as domination by the Catholic church which had so influenced Latin American civilization. And given the deep religiosity of the ordinary Mexican—the effective welding by the early Spanish missionaries of Catholic concepts with the traditional beliefs of the Indians—a gulf was created between the elite's fashionable European anticlericalism overlaid with its infatuation with the Left, and the mass of the people, religious and conservative.

Although Zapata has become the quintessential revolutionary for many latter-day leftists in Mexico, Zapata and his followers were fervent Catholics. "Despite its conservative bent, the Church kept the loyalty of Emiliano Zapata, and his peasant armies, spokesmen for the rebel agrarian wing . . . The Virgin of Guadalupe, anathema to the *come santo*, saint-baiting, rebels in rival camps, adorned their banners. . . .To their dismay, Carrancista politicians discovered that priests, the hated *curas*, had staunch allies in the villages of Oaxaca, whose inhabitants welcomed no attacks on the churches."[8] One could argue that there is nothing so unique in that; that in all countries political theory is relegated to the educated elite and the mass follows in the wake. But it may be a question of degree; and the caste differences, so strong in the Mexico of the past and still so apparent in contemporary society, have made this cleavage even wider. Communism and socialism, essentially European doctrines, from the early decades of this century have appealed almost exclusively to the upper stratum of Mexican society. And, in fact, the history of the Marxist movements in Mexico has been intimately connected with foreigners, particularly with Americans.

As with Russia, the originators of socialist and Communist theories never thought that Mexico was ripe for their philosophies. To the contrary, in Mexico as in the rest of the nonindustrialized world, the early Marxists saw imperialist domination as a step toward progress. Friedrich Engels, writing to his friend Karl Marx on Feb. 14, 1858, referred thus to the U.S. war against Mexico: "In America we have witnessed the conquest of Mexico, and we are happy about it. For a country which until now has been busy exclusively with its own affairs, perpetually torn by civil war and impeded in every development, a country whose highest prospect was to come under the industrial vassalage of England—for such a country to be dragged into historical activity by force is indeed a step forward. It is in the interests of its own development that henceforth Mexico should be placed under the tutelage of the United States."[9]

American Communists in the 1920s, who dominated radical politics in Mexico, acted as though they took their cues from this evaluation of the Mexican War of 1847. The Mexican Communist party was, in fact, founded by a group of American, European, and Asian Communists working in the U.S. radical movement under the direction of the Third International and the Comintern headquartered in Moscow.

Funds and orders for the organization of the Mexican party were given by Moscow to Carl E. Johnson (party name "Scott"), an American radical from Boston of Lett descent and a member of the Cheka, the Soviet secret police. Johnson was part of a special committee, which included Sen Katayama, a Japanese Christian Socialist converted to Communism who acted as Comintern agent around the world and was one of the founders of the Communist party in the U.S., and Louis C. Fraina (Lewis Corey), one of the principal figures in the split of the American socialist movement which resulted in the founding of the Communist party, and M.N. Roy, a famous Indian revolutionary who became a Communist in the U.S.

The first efforts of the committee went astray because Fraina allegedly squandered funds allocated for the operation in Mexico and was "tried" before the party in a process that was to become famous in the 1930s under Stalin. Roy, who was to become one of the most famous agents of the Comintern, escaping to Mexico from his conspirational activities in the U.S. involving plots against the British in India, founded the Communist party in Mexico at a congress from Aug. 4 to Sept. 15, 1919, with members of Mexican socialist groups whom he had rallied with a newspaper he edited called *El Socialist.* Roy believed that Mexico, if destabilized by a leftist conspiracy, could help deflect U.S. aid to Britain during World War I and thus enable Indian revolutionaries to succeed in his native India. John Reed, who had sent Roy a picture of Lenin for the dais at the congress, told Roy, when they both arrived for the Second Congress of the Comintern in Moscow in July 1920, that the Mexican party was the first organized outside the Soviet Union, and that he, Roy, had stolen a march on Reed, who had hoped to organize an American Communist party first. Roy financed the Mexican socialists with funds given him by L.K. Marten, who was in Mexico as a representative of the Bolshevik government in Moscow (which was still not formally recognized by the Mexican government).[10]

The dominance over the Mexican Communists of the U.S. Communists, as the vehicle of the Comintern, was blatant in a "Letter from the Executive of the Communist International to the Communist Party of Mexico."[11] C.E. Ruthenberg, an American, writes in the foreword: "Under ordinary circumstances a communication to a party in another country, dealing with the problems of that country, would not be of sufficient interest for publication [in the U.S.], but this is not true of the document contained in the following pages." The interest of the American party in the Comintern document becomes clear from its penultimate paragraph: "The Russian Revolution is the heroic prelude to the World Revolution. The victory of the working class in the most important countries of Europe assures the victory of the proletariat in all countries. But the destruction of the last stronghold of capitalist imperialism, the overthrow of the North American bourgeoisie, is the task of the workers and peasants of all the American countries."

In 1924, Mexico established diplomatic relations with the Soviet Union—the first country in the Americas to do so. A brilliant ambassador, Alexandra Kollontai, presided over an extremely popular Soviet establishment in the late 1920s. The social whirl that surrounded the Russian embassy in those days had a great deal to do with laying the foundations for the infatuation of the Mexican elite—particularly the artistic elite—with the Soviet Union and with their acceptance of Communism as a legitimate political doctrine that persists to this day.

But it was trips by American Communist leaders in 1924 and 1925 to Mexico that led to the formation of the Pan-American (later All-American) Anti-Imperialist League in 1925, one of the chief conduits for Communist party activities in Mexico and throughout the hemisphere. The organization had an American branch, but its Central American secretariat was set up in Mexico City where it published the Spanish-language monthly, *El Libertador*, edited initially by B. D. Wolfe, an American Comintern operative, who later became famous as the ex-Communist biographer of Lenin, Trotsky, and Stalin.[12] The organization claimed to have national sectors in eleven countries as well as individual members. In Puerto Rico and other areas, the Anti-Imperialist League, as it was commonly known, prepared for the emergence of indigenous Communist parties by organizing Marxist study groups and linking radicals of like-minded persuasion. The organization played a role in supporting the resistance movement of Gen. Augusto C. Sandino against the U.S. Marine occupation of Nicaragua, building on an early important episode in which Porfírio Díaz rescued an anti-American Nicaraguan leader by dispatching a Mexican gunboat.

But, " . . . Sandino refused to be used by forces extraneous to his cause. Thus, although for a time in the late 1920s he received rhetorical (and some small material) support from both the U.S. and the Mexican Communist parties, he steadfastly refused to follow Moscow's dictates and even denied that a social revolution was necessary in Nicaragua. This eventually led him to sever personal relations with Farabundo Martí, a Salvadoran Communist who for a time served as the Comintern's envoy to the Sandinista forces."[13]

The U.S. wing of the Anti-Imperialist League never amounted to more than a letterhead organization, one of many such groups in the Communist movement. Its Mexican operations were partially hampered by the suspicion and caution of President Plutarcho Elias Calles, who set a pattern for Mexican foreign policy (until the 1970s) wherein Mexico, while hospitable to all political refugees on the Left, officially kept its distance from revolutionary activity in the rest of the hemisphere.[14]

In 1933, the Anti-Imperialist League gave way to another organization, the American League against War and Fascism, whose activities were directed toward the coming storm in Europe rather than Latin American affairs. Meanwhile, by 1929, the Mexican Communist party (PCM), under Soviet direction, had initiated a radical program for revolution and confrontation with the Mexican government despite the Mexicans' pride in their own revolutionary credentials.

In a bitter complaint against the tutelage of the party by Moscow, José Revueltas, a dissident Mexican Communist, wrote in 1962: "[The Mexican Communist party] considered it sufficient at that time [1929] to be the Mexican section that was recognized by the Communist international in order to regard itself automatically as the conscience of the Mexican working class. The result was, in any case, that during its first period of life, until 1929, instead of playing the part of the socialist worker's conscience and thereby becoming the vanguard of the proletariat, it merely carried out the function of being the vanguard of bourgeois democracy, and thus became a radical agrarian party of the petty bourgeoisie."[15]

Revueltas' complaints about the twisting of the party line and its destructive effect on the movement in Mexico are not that different from similar complaints of Communist dissidents all over the world, complaints that the policies of the national parties have been bent to the needs of Soviet foreign policy. When the amateurs in the movement launched their offensive at Moscow's insistence, the government cracked down on the tiny party and its leaders were deported to the penal colony of Las Islas Marías.

The Mexican government refused to believe Moscow's disclaimers of responsibility for the actions of the Mexican party and, in 1930, Mexico broke relations with such abruptness that for more than a decade the Soviets demanded an apology before reestablishing relations. Despite the leftish sentiments of the Lazaro Cárdenas administration in the 1930s, Cárdenas continued to refuse to make that gesture. This attitude was reinforced by the influence of Leon Trotsky and his anti-Stalin dissidents within the world Communist movement and the Mexican Left. In 1936 *Pravda* announced an all-out war against Trotsky and his sympathizers within the international Communist movement. Trotsky chose Mexico for his exile—probably because of its proximity to the United States, his principal concern after the Soviet Union, as well as his difficulty in finding refuge in any other country. In Mexico, Trotsky was befriended by many of the artists and notables of the Left and protected by Cárdenas.

But in May 1940, a group of Mexican Communists (led by the muralist David Alfaro Siqueiros) attempted to assassinate Trotsky in his house in Coayacán near Mexico City—at least the second attempt after the successful murders of his son and many of his leading collaborators in Europe. When they failed, Moscow organized another elaborate effort to penetrate the Trotsky household using members of the Trotskyist movement in the U.S. The former leader of the Red army was killed on Aug. 20, 1940, in his home by a trusted visitor using a mountain climber's ice pick; an assassin who was the son of a famous Stalinist woman leader in Republican Spain.

Prior to this, and partially as a result of the first attempt by Josef Stalin to assassinate him, J.B. Mathews, chief investigator of the U.S. House of Representatives Special (Dies) Committee on Unamerican Activities, invited Trotsky to come to Austin, Tex., "for the purpose of testifying before it. . . . The Committee desires to have a complete record on the history of Stalinism and invites you to answer questions. . . .Your name has been mentioned frequently by such witnesses as [Earl] Browder and [William Z.] Foster. This Committee will accord you opportunity to answer their charges." Trotsky enthusiastically accepted the invitation "as a political duty," but the assassination intervened.

In a lengthy article laying out the basis for the first attack on him in Mexico, printed posthumously in the American Trotskyist organ, Trotsky maintained that the attack was organized by the Soviet secret police, the GPU, and was a direct outcome of the struggle for control of the Mexican party as well as the international persecution of him and his followers by Josef Stalin, by then the all-powerful Russian dictator.[16] Trotsky quotes at length from the *Voz de México*, the Mexican Stalinist newspaper, which publicized his dealings with the Dies Committee. Trotsky writes: "It is not at all a question whether the so-called 'principles' of the Communist party are good or bad. It is a question of the activities in which the Communist party engages and the real relations between the Central Committee of the Communist party and the GPU. The GPU is not merely the secret police of the USSR, but something far more important. The GPU is the instrument of the totalitarian rule of the Stalinist clique over the USSR and the Comintern. One of the most important and unremitting tasks of the GPU is the physical destruction of the most resolute and dangerous opponents of Stalin's dictatorship. Within the USSR this destruction is semi-camouflaged by legal formalities. Outside of the USSR it is carried out through plots, attempts, and murders from ambush." Trotsky then goes on to document the longstanding relationship between the Comintern and the Mexican Communist party and its fellow-travelers in the country.

Unfortunately, Trotsky's murder precluded the presentation of this and other evidence before the U.S. congressional committee.[17] It was not until the creation of the international alliance against Hitler that Mexico in 1942 again established relations with the Soviets. And not having broken off relations during the Cold War period after 1948, as many other Latin American governments did, Mexico has maintained the longest uninterrupted contact with Moscow of any country in the area.

Today, the Soviet Embassy in Mexico City is one of the busiest in the world and has the largest contingent of KGB secret police outside the Soviet bloc. There is a consensus in the Western intelligence community concerning the reason for such a massive Soviet security presence. Eighty percent to 90 percent of the Soviet establishment in Mexico City—a large part of whose members are non-Spanish-speaking—devote their energies to problems connected with Mexico's neighbor, the United States. Almost no autobiographical material of former Communists in the U.S. or testimony of Soviet defectors is without its references to the clandestine going and coming of Russian agents to the U.S. through Mexico. Russian communications facilities in Mexico City are considered second only to those in Havana in the hemisphere and may in some ways be superior to them. They are used to spy on the U.S. and to aid Russians to steal American high technology.

In post-World War II Mexico City became the jump-off point for Latin American Communists, Soviet agents, their sympathizers, and others who could not get through the American security screen in their travels to and from Europe. At the height of American vigilance against Soviet operations in the U.S. in the 1950s, a Dutch airlines flight which flew passengers Mexico City-Montreal-Amsterdam to avoid U.S. immigration was jokingly called "The Red Express" in commercial airline circles because it carried such large numbers of Latin American Communists and Soviet agents. When the Rosenberg nuclear espionage case broke in the U.S., nineteen American scientists fled to the Soviet Union—through Mexico. President John Kennedy's assassin, Lee Harvey Oswald, was involved with Soviet agents before he defected to Russia through the Soviet embassy in Mexico City. In 1960, two young employees of what had previously been the secret U.S. National Security Agency defected to the Soviet Union with key information on the U.S. "spy-in-the-sky" satellites, and they escaped from U.S. authorities through Mexico.

More contemporaneously, the constant and often successful Soviet penetration of the electronic industrial secrets of Silicon Valley in California are run out of Mexico City. A former "hit man" for the Communists, Maurice Malkin, in his book, gives a raw picture of this international scene of intrigue and moral squalor in Mexico, as well as intimate details of how these operations are carried out.[18] Evidence mounts that this route is used more often than any other clandestine conduit for Russian agents and information to enter and to leave the United States.

The Soviet facilities in Mexico City—with the help of the huge Cuban embassy—are also the center for much of Russia's activity in the whole Latin American region. The Aeroflot route which spreads out from Mexico City throughout Latin America facilitates Soviet movements, carrying both legitimate Soviet diplomats and clandestine agents, and offering concessional passage to Latin American academicians, scientists, tourists and businessmen who visit Moscow. The Soviet Union, which uses its fishing fleet for espionage and communications operations all over the world, has cooperation agreements with Mexican fishing interests. Today Soviet-built Cuban "fishing" trawlers with communications gear often stand off the coast of Panama and Nicaragua, monitoring U.S. communications and backing up clandestine arms shipments and communications for the Communist forces in El Salvador and guerrillas in other Central American countries.

A cultural treaty signed in 1968 set up a mixed commission to expand the above-ground cultural and propaganda operations of the Soviet embassy in Mexico, which are enormous. Soviet officials often visit Mexico; up and coming "young" Russian Communist leaders like Geidar Alief, a protégé of former KGB Chief Alexei Andropov, and a confidant of the new party chief, Mikhail Gorbachev, visited Mexico in April 1982. Every East bloc anniversary—the forty-fifth anniversary of the Bolshevik Revolution, the thirty-third anniversary of the German Democratic Socialist Republic, etc.—is celebrated by an enormous hoopla in Mexico City, complete with access to the government-owned television where Communist artists and producers abound.

Mexico is also the prime distribution point for dozens of Soviet journals and periodicals and hundreds of books published in Spanish and Portuguese by Moscow for Latin America. A steady stream of cultural exchanges keeps Mexican intellectuals and students moving back and forth to Moscow. Mexico City, far more than Havana, is the headquarters of Communist dissident movements throughout the hemisphere. The Salvadoran Communist guerrillas, for example, have kept their external political and propaganda headquarters in Mexico City. Large numbers of Chilean Communist exiles from the Allende period and exiles of the Montonero movement in Argentina (including some of the *desaparecidos*, the disappeared, purported victims of Argentine suppression) reside in the Mexican capital.

But the Soviet and Latin Communist presence and the pro-soviet proclivities of the Mexican intellectuals have not translated into voting strength for the Mexican Communist party in part, perhaps, because of its relatively brief history as a legal party. It was only in 1979 in the López Portillo administration, as part of his "political" reform, that the Communist party was again legalized. Whatever the reasons, the Communists remain a minor electoral force despite the overwhelming Marxist character of the intellectual community and the obvious impact Marxism and Soviet propaganda have in education and the media.

Today the Mexican Communist party (PCM) is part of a new popular front party, El Partido Socialista Unificado Mexicana (PSUM), formed in 1981. The new party aimed at broadening the support of the Moscow line beyond the PCM faithful to include left-wing elements disaffected from the PRI. There was also a suspicion in nongovernmental circles that a deal had been struck between the government and the Communists from which both hoped to profit. PRI leadership wished to avoid what had overtaken the older Communist parties in Cuba, Nicaragua, and El Salvador which had been, like the Mexican Communists, part of the political establishment of those countries through much of the post-World War II period. Even in Somoza's Nicaragua, the Communist party functioned. Its origins include the emigration to that country in the late 1930s—at the instigation of the elder Somoza who wanted their skills and abilities—of Spanish Republican refugees, many of them Marxists. The Communists functioned semipublicly in Nicaragua and were reluctant to join the anti-Somoza guerrilla campaign until it was well on its way to power. Several of the members of the present Sandinista junta pro-

Moscow government in Managua trace their family and intellectual origins to these "establishment" Communists.

Ultraleft forces associated with Fidel Castro's Communism more than with Moscow's traditional representatives in these countries have made an "end-run" around the old-line Communists, lining up help from Castro for a unification of all the forces on the left, sometimes including groups which had their origins in anti-Moscow left-wing activity including Maoist pro-Chinese movements of the 1950s. The "Popular Front" tactic, of course, is not new to Communist politics, especially in Europe in the 1930s where Moscow used the threat of fascism to forge temporary alliances with democratic and left-of-center parties.

But in Latin America, these more recent attempts at leftist unity have in these special cases not been initiated in the old-line Communist circles who often were accepted members of the status quo as in Mexico. One strong motivation for the new popular front is the "lessons" drawn by the Marxist-Leninists of the area from the overthrow of the Allende government in Chile in 1973. How not to repeat "the Chile model" has been a watchword in the Communist movement in Mexico, as also elsewhere in Latin America, and most particularly in southern Europe.

Taking a lead from Fidel Castro's orchestration of leftist unity movements in Central America, the Mexican Communists apparently hoped to emulate the process; that is, unify the various political groups, make a strong bid for power, and then envelop the older Communist organizations—with Moscow's blessing. One curious aspect: the Mexican government made public that it had agreed to permit the Communists to organize the PSUM with the provision that the PCM had the right to withdraw from the PSUM and reconstitute itself independently should it so choose.

The first goal does not appear to have been achieved. In the election for president in 1981, the PSUM with its 112,000 members garnered only 3.6 percent of the vote. That did not, however, deter the PSUM and the Soviets from organizing a "cultural blitz" in August 1983 around a party congress, attended by six hundred delegates and forty "fraternal delegates" from Communist parties around the world, led by Aleksey M. Skolnikov, Soviet ambassador to Nicaragua and a leading Soviet Latin American expert.

During 1983 when the De la Madrid administration was permitting relatively fair municipal elections, the opposition to the government took a strong swing to the Right, but not to the PSUM, except in some remote areas of the south. And that trend continued in the 1985 congressional, gubernatorial, and municipal elections—although new radical, populist parties on the Left have picked up some of the old PSUM-cum-PCM support. These shifts appear to confirm the historical tradition that the people of Mexico, while given at times to radicalism and violence, are immune to the electoral appeal of orthodox Communism, even when coated with popular front slogans. But that has not precluded the Communists from spending money and organizing electoral activity in strategic border regions in the north where, in fact, there was no possibility of winning mayoralty elections. In the fall of 1981, for example, the Communists were spending relatively large sums of money in local elections in the state of Coahuila, just across the border from Texas, with the obvious intent of winning friends locally. Since they had no chance of electoral success, it appeared to be an effort to build on the existing Communist infrastructure along the U.S. border for purposes other than electoral.[19]

It appears likely that Moscow long ago decided that the primary function of the Mexican party was to cradle the Soviet espionage and propaganda apparatus that operates from Mexico City against the U.S. The attempt to gain power for itself in that country, given the difficulties, would have to take a lower priority in the interests of the socialist fatherland. Long-time observers of Communist activity in Mexico hypothesize also that Moscow must always restrain the Mexican party and its more adventurist cadres from trying to exploit "revolutionary" opportunities in Mexico. Intelligence sources speculate that important elements in the Soviet Union weigh any possible success in their bid for power, or the creation of difficulties for the Mexican regime—and the U.S.—against the relative impunity with which the Russian espionage and propaganda can now operate from Mexico against the U.S.

But it is also clear that the Soviets have been tempted from time to time to exploit "targets of opportunity," even including violence. In 1971, Mexico expelled five KGB Soviet secret police officers masquerading as Soviet diplomats, when they were implicated in the Revolutionary Action Movement (MAR).[20] MAR, organized by a Mexican KGB agent, Fabricio Gómez Souza, was made up of cadre of "students" trained through fellowships to the Patrice Lumumba University in Moscow. But Mexican authorities arrested the "students" when they reentered the country, and they confessed to having had training in North Korea in sabotage, terrorism, robbery, and guerrilla tactics. The Mexicans believed that the Soviets had used the North Koreans as a surrogate in order not to become implicated themselves. Apparently the whole affair was an outgrowth of the 1968 student agitations at UNAM, in which Mexican Communists participated and which at least some Moscow planners must have seen as a new era with possibilities for developing a new revolutionary movement. That is why it cannot be said with certainty that the Russians, in the crisis of the whole society anticipated in arguments here, would forgo the temptation to fish in troubled waters—even with the enormous stake they have in maintaining the status quo.

If the Communists do make a power grab in Mexico it will come through a Fidelista putsch—some kind of alliance between the Cuban network which undoubtedly has been laid down in the country (backed by the Soviets) and a radical populism springing from an economic and political breakdown. There is some evidence that such an effort was in progress in the 1960s. A series of bombings, radical union activities, kidnappings, and minor guerrilla skirmishes indicated that at least some elements of the Mexican Left thought the time had come for a major effort in what the Marxist-Leninists characterize as "a revolutionary situation."

And, in fact, one guerrilla faction led by a charismatic schoolteacher, Lucio Cabanas, operated in the mountains of the west-central state of guerrero (Acapulco) until the mid-1970s. Cabanas and three companions organized the Party of the Poor with its Peasants' Brigade Against Injustice which fought for almost fifteen years against the Mexican police and army forces. It took a major deployment of the Mexican army, operating against a few hundred guerrillas, to bring the insurgency under control. And, at least as left-wing mythology has it, it was then defeated only because of a betrayal by Havana, which had initially given Cabanas some support as had some radical Chicanos in the U.S. Southwest. The insurgency, however, was never more than an isolated local political movement, even though it did excite the nominal support of some radical Mexico City intellectuals and student groups.[21] Perhaps the local guerrilla movement's most lasting effect was the influence it had on López Portillo to whom the poor military showing against Cabanas was evidence of the need to beef up Mexican military.

Mexico, with its crazy-quilt of volcanic mountains that cuts the country up into a patchwork of isolated areas, is ideal terrain for the kind of guerrilla warfare that has erupted all over Latin America in the post-World War II period, backed by the Communists but based on local conditions. It is not even necessary to hypothesize any Soviet belief in the ultimate success of such operations to see how in a certain situation Moscow would be tempted simply to stir the pot of Mexican discontent for the repercussions on the United States.

The discontent may show in the coming months in the trade union sector where Mexico's organized industrial workers, in the past a privileged class, are being asked, along with the new middle class, to bear the brunt of the austerity program. The government dominates the bulk of these trade unionists through its alliance with the CTM, led by old Fidel Velázquez who ousted the charismatic Moscow-line leader, Lombardo Toledano, some thirty years ago. Velázquez' arrival to the leadership of the CTM was the consolidation of the alliance, in fact the control by the PRI, and the regime of its hold on the trade union organizations. They have been one of the pillars of the regime. That is why all Mexico was startled in early January 1986 when Velázquez took the occasion of the annual Congress of the CTM to fire off a blast in De la Madrid's presence, warning him that "the country had lost its way." A photograph of the two attending the Congress on the front page of Mexico's leading newspaper, *Excelsior*, showed them glaring into the camera, ostentatiously ignoring one another as they sat side by side. It is no secret in Mexican political circles that the old trade unionist opposed De la Madrid's selection as the candidate of the PRI in 1980. And although he has reiterated several times over the past few years that he would not permit the economic problems that the country is suffering to initiate a break with the PRI and the De la Madrid administration, it is obvious that rocky times are ahead as his own constituency demands a more forceful policy toward the government's anti-inflationary program.

Velázquez can continue to maintain some of the vast social welfare system of the CTM with resources other than those which come directly from workers' union dues.

The CTM unions now own 180 companies valued at 200 billion pesos (more than $1 billion). According to Velázquez, there are sufficient funds in the union to continue buying companies, "but we are not going to buy those that might be a burden."

But the question that many in Mexico ask is: what happens to Velázquez' organization when the octogenarian dies? Will it remain in the hands of the moderates in the PRI like himself, or will the splendid organization fall into the hands of more populist leadership? The history of the CTM is, like most Mexican institutions, highly personalized. Velázquez' personal intercession has often been the deciding factor in settling intraunion and employer disputes. The question of succession has been asked often in recent years, by members of the Left as well as of the Right, with whom Velázquez has learned to deal. Arnaldo Hoy, writing in a popular Mexican magazine of the Left, says: "Fidel Velázquez has succeeded in harmonizing and maintaining a diversity of personal interests and constituencies. It is unlikely that any of the major CTM leaders now on the scene, either among

those of equal age or among the younger leaders who have been indicated as future leaders, will adequately replace him. The severe internal factionalism which broke out following the death of Jesús Yurn [a
close associate of Fidel Velázquez and long-time leader of the Federal
District Workers Federation, FTDF] and the schism which ruptured
the FTDF and resulted in the creation of a rival federation competing
for the same union constituency may well forebode a similar outcome
following Velázquez' death . . . the challenge posed by the leadership
transition may also coincide with a broader crisis in the control structure of the 'officialist' labor movement, offering new opportunities for
more mobilized, autonomous labor actions."[22]

While the transition to a successor may be orderly, it also is possible that, in a period of great economic strife, a more radical leadership will take-over. Certainly trade unions, even in the nonindustrial
world, have always been prime targets for Communist and Soviet
strategy, offering the possibility that in a crisis where the PRI lost
its control over these organizations, they might become transformed
from organizations of control by the ruling party to agitation instru-
ments against the status quo.[23]

For the moment, Soviet strategies and tactics in Mexico are
somewhat obscure. Speculation in Soviet literature on Mexico and its
politics is, even in volume, very sparse. "Relations with the U.S.S.R.
and other members of the socialist community during the détente
period of the 70s came to occupy an important place in the foreign
policy of Mexico, which was guided by economic as well as political
aims," says a recent summary of developments in Mexico prepared
under the auspices of the Institute for Latin American Studies, one of
the regional propaganda and research organizations of the Soviets.[24]
The book is a scholarly evaluation of Mexican developments in the
1960s and 1970s. It would appear to be a handbook for Soviet readers
interested in a broad, panoramic view of Mexican developments and
is largely based on Mexican sources. Curiously, it barely alludes to
the economic crisis of 1981–1982—a seemingly attractive target for
the stereotypic denunciations of the international banks, capitalism,
imperialism, etc., endemic to Soviet publications. The authors tread
lightly over many difficult—from the Soviet point of view—areas
in Mexican economic and political development, perhaps because of
the initiation of a new presidential administration in Mexico and
precisely because of the economic crisis. It is, however, again typical
of the very careful approach of Soviet propagandists and scholars to
Mexico—much more deferential and ambiguous than to other Latin
American states.

Since the 1960s, the Soviets have been circumspect in their dealings with the Mexican government. The old warhorse of the Mexican

Communist movement, Valentine Campa, in an informal interview with the author in early 1984 complained somewhat caustically of the failure of the international Communist movement to "appreciate" the situation in Mexico, apparently indicating that the Mexican Communist party has paid a price for Moscow's even-handed relations with the Mexican government. And one senses a certain restraint by Soviet propagandists when they deal with the Mexican scene. But it is not clear why Mexico is given a low priority in the open Soviet press. What does seem certain is that the Communist movement of Mexico put the highest priority, particularly in the post-World War II period, on providing the cradle for Soviet espionage against the U.S. and American interests in Latin American generally.

It is not hard to hypothesize a constant battle inside the Soviet intelligence and foreign policy bureaucracy in which the enormous importance of Mexico as a base for operations against the U.S. is weighed against the potentials of a more adventurous policy in which the weaknesses of the Mexican regime would be exploited—not so much to push the Communist movement in Mexico, as to create problems for the U.S.

That is much easier to do today than it was a generation ago and not only because of the chaotic conditions. Until the middle of the López Portillo administration, when the political and economic climate worsened dramatically, Mexican and U.S. intelligence and police operations had a close working relationship. American officials were constantly told by their associates in the Mexican government to disregard the rhetoric which was employed in the international forums against the U.S. On specific matters, such as on drugs, foreign agents, the exchange of information on Cuba and the Soviet Union there was cooperation at the working levels, which dated back to the eve of World War II when Cardenas and Roosevelt made strides to bury the memories of the 1920s and the 1930s. After the war, American intelligence was instrumental in organizing the Mexican Dirección Federal de Seguridad (DFS).

Old hands in American intelligence claim part credit for rooting out and destroying enemies of the Mexican regime in moments of crisis. U.S. intelligence officials in Mexico had direct access to the president's office, often initiating projects that in other countries might have waited on formal diplomatic channels. But that relationship has passed into history.

The worldwide disinformation campaign fired up during the 1970s to discredit the U.S. Central Intelligence Agency (CIA) had its counterpart in Mexico. The most popular columnist in Mexico, Manuel Buendia, with intimate ties to Fidel Castro, made a specialty of "exposing" CIA "plots" in Mexico in his column in the newspaper *Excelsior*, until his assassination by unknown assailants in early 1984.[25] Buendia had excellent sources inside the Mexican government and was said to be a frequent visitor to De la Madrid after his ascension to the presidency. De la Madrid ordered a state funeral for Buendia after his murder, which was seen by some as a warning to the president himself, and called it an attack on freedom of the press.

Cooperation between the U.S. and Mexico is now formal and limited. When Secretary of State George Schultz visited De la Madrid in 1982 and made an attempt to bring up the subject of expanding Soviet KGB activity he was abruptly told that the Mexicans did not need U.S. assistance in that area.

There is no one single reason for the breakdown in the old relationship. In part, it was one of the casualties of the López Portillo presidency, which came to office dedicated to improving relationships with the U.S. (and one could say the same of its counterpart, the Carter administration). There was also the long battle over the price of Mexican natural gas and the boorishness with which Energy Secretary James Schlesinger handled the issue. One of the principal causes of the breakdown was the failure of the domestic development schemes of López Portillo, which persuaded him to turn to foreign policy issues where anti-Americanism is a rule of thumb in Mexico.

But, the most significant single incident was the arrest and capture of Miguel Nassar, then head of the DFS office in Los Angeles, in April 1974. Gossip in international intelligence circles has it that the arrest of the Mexican official on charges of running a car theft ring in Mexico and drug trafficking was a "set-up". One of the U.S. officials intimately involved in the episode does not deny that Nassar may well have had a hand in illegal activities of this sort. Later events have shown the extent of the participation of Mexican security officials in such trafficking. But he insists that, in this instance, the affair was deliberately arranged to break the U.S.-Mexico operational connection. It is also rumored that the arrest may have been related to the continuing and incessant feuding between the U.S. Bureau of Federal Investigation (which operates out of the Mexico City Embassy though barred in other parts of the world) and the Central Intelligence Agency. In any case, it seems to mark the nadir in the relationship between the two countries' security forces.

The *modus vivendi* between Communist Cuba and the Mexicans is, of course, an important element in evaluating the potential of the Left in any future destabilization. Mexico serves as a friend and supplier of petroleum to the Cubans and the Soviets inside the respectable Latin American family of nations. The Mexicans have been invaluable allies of the Cuban protégés, the Sandinistas, in their struggle in the face of growing discontent at home, American pressure and the growing fears of their Central American neighbors. In the diplomatic world, the Mexicans are the chief spokesmen for the Sandinistas; and until he was withdrawn in the late summer of 1985, the Mexican ambassador in Managua was known as "the tenth comandante" in the Sandinista junta of nine men.

In assessing what Moscow's current attitude is toward Mexico, it is possible that the Soviets were also gulled by the relative stability of the Mexico Model. They also could have believed what many Mexicans believe—that the U.S. would never permit Mexico to move into the Communist camp and that Soviet resources expended to that end would be wasted. And then, as mentioned, there could be the bureaucratic disagreement between the value of Mexico for Moscow's "housekeeping arrangements" in Mexico, her ability to use it as a listening post and sanctuary for intelligence operations in the U.S. Still, it is hard to believe that if Mexico begins to show signs of destabilization, that Moscow would miss the opportunity to try to create even greater problems there for the U.S., understanding (as it must as the chief American adversary) how deeply events in Mexico could affect U.S. security interests.

But, after all the conjecture, the future of Mexico may not be limited to the options of classic right-wing and left-wing take overs if a breakdown in the Mexican *status quo* should take place. What may well be in the cards is a repetition of earlier historical patterns in Mexico. Mexican society, for all its weaknesses and failures, has proved through the centuries to have inner resources, great flexibility, and built-in attributes that keep it operating against enormous odds. These include close family relationships that provide economic and social security in a society that has few government welfare services, and a feudal hierarchy in the villages and city *barrios* that keeps order and provides an indigenous social organization, however archaic and undemocratic, to the modern eye. The tradition of *aguantar*—to bear suffering and affliction—which is so much a part of the Indian heritage of the poor in Mexico, also permits the society to ride out bad economic and political periods that might destroy a more rigid and sophisticated culture.

And, finally, one can see the present crisis as the third in a chain. The two great convulsions in Mexican history, after the Spanish conquest, were in the early nineteenth century when Mexico finally broke with Spain, and again early in this century when the stage for the present regime was set. Both of these eruptions constituted a breakdown in the established order, a devolution into chaos, a falling away from stability—a process of erosion rather than revolution. And looking at the present Mexico scene, one could predict a replay of history rather than the launching of a conspiracy that would overthrow the government and establish a new and revolutionary regime. Indeed, one can already make a case that the PRI is losing power gradually, that its control over the daily affairs of the country is disintegrating, and that even should the PRI turn to repression, as it has in the past, it may not be enough to save the present system. The PRI rule may simply deteriorate until law and order finally breaks down, and the vast numbers, the vast distances, and the regional antagonisms of Mexico will combine to bring on a new period of disorder. That would repeat the history of the break with Spain and the breakdown after 1910. And it may be a far more likely development than the neat scenarios for revolution and new regimes that obsess the minds of so many participants and observers.

From the standpoint of U.S. interests, such a breakdown in Mexico could produce results as bad—or almost as difficult to resolve —as if a Castroite regime were to come to power in Mexico. Because chaos in Mexico would breed problems for the U.S. in such volume and of such variety that they are hard to calculate, much less remedy.

Part II:
The United States of America

Chapter 6: **Mexico as a Problem for U.S. Foreign Policy**

The 2,000-mile border that separates the United States and Mexico is the only land barrier between the industrial world and the nonindustrial world, the so-called Third World. One could argue, of course, that the line that separates the countries of Western Europe from the East bloc Communist satellites is also such a division. But there is a difference: culturally Central Europe includes both Germanies, just as it includes Hungary and Czechoslovakia and Austria. And were the Iron Curtain between the Communist and the non-Communist world to disappear tomorrow, the Europeans would take up where they let off in 1939—with the memory of the past forty years' distinction between East and West only one more complication in Europe's myriad political past.

The U.S.-Mexican border, on the other hand, is not only a frontier between two relatively new nations in the New World, but as the Mexican poet and historian Octavio Paz says, the U.S. and Mexico represent two important and different cultural entities carried over from the Old World to the New. As Paz points out, in many ways Spain and England represented the extremes of the European society, and their differences and long conflict were basic to the establishment of the modern age. Those differences in the European cultures are as distinct as the dissimilarities between the nomadic Indian tribes which the English settlers found in North America and the elaborate Aztec empire which the Spaniards enveloped along with its peoples in the new society they built in Mexico. The clashes that have taken place between the U.S. and Mexico represent not only the expanding power of the *gringos*, but the clash of those fundamental cultural values between two branches of European civilization. Again, as Paz says, if you could visualize a Mexico tomorrow, shorn of its underdevelopment and a major world power, its distinctiveness from the U.S. would be greater, not smaller.[1]

The differences between the North Americans and the Mexicans, then, are not just those of economic development and the prosperity that it has produced in the U.S. They are endemic to the basic approach to many of life's fundamental problems.

"Of course, it goes without saying that any generalization about the collective character of either America incurs a logical risk, but there is no other alternative than to take the risk if we would understand," says the philosopher Patrick Romanell.[2] "This is no denial of the responsibility to search for the most adequate interpretation of the national character of any people, nor is it a denial that the national characteristics themselves are subject to historical change and thus in continual need of empirical reinterpretation." Romanell then goes on to say that there is a crucial difference between the two cultures in North America: "Whereas Anglo-American culture is essentially European, Hispano-American culture is only partially European, having as it does Indian (and to a lesser degree, Negro) cultural components." And Romanell reminds us of what the Mexican historian and philosopher José Vasconcelos said: "Whenever two civilizations meet, one or the other becomes predominant, but they both undergo change; they both lose certain traits and win others. What happened to the Spaniard during the Arab invasion, happened to the Indian during the Spanish invasion."[3]

Romanell says that all this leads to a basic difference between Mexican and U.S. societal foundations. "[T]he dominant preoccupation on which Hispano-American culture rests is the *tragic* sense of life and, in contrast, that on which Anglo-American culture rests is the *epic* sense of life . . . The theme common to the tragic and epic forms of literature is a dramatic situation involving the inevitability of moral conflict arising out of the pursuit of some goal by a personality or a group. As to their difference in content and context, briefly stated, it is: while the epic soul struggles endlessly to conquer obstacles external to himself, the tragic soul has the difficult job of conquering himself. . . . Whereas North American thought has been largely motivated by an interest in the problems of knowledge, Latin American thought has been inspired essentially by problems of conduct. . . . Finally, to sum up, the secret imaginative background of the philosophizing characteristic of America is, on the one hand, the tragic sense of life rooted in Latin American existentialism and, on the other, the epic sense of life rooted in Anglo-American pragmatism."

Paz, more poet than philosopher or historian, has captured these differences perhaps more poetically than logically. "The North Americans are credulous and we are believers; they love fairy tales and detective stories and we love myths and legends. The Mexican tells lies because he delights in fantasy, or because he is desperate, or because he wants to rise above the sordid facts of his life; the

North American does not tell lies, but he substitutes social truth for real truth, which is always disagreeable. We get drunk in order to confess; they get drunk in order to forget. They are optimists and we are nihilists—except that our nihilism is not intellectual but instinctive, and therefore irrefutable. We are suspicious and they are trusting. We are sorrowful and are sarcastic and they are happy and full of jokes. North Americans want to understand and we want to contemplate. They are activists and we are quietists; we enjoy our wounds and they enjoy their inventions. They believe in hygiene, health, work and contentment, but perhaps they have never experienced true joy, which is an intoxication, a whirlwind. In the hubbub of a fiesta night our voices explode into brilliant lights, and life and death mingle together, while their vitality becomes a fixed smile that denies old age and death but that changes life to motionless stone."[4]

In addition to the very real disparities between the two cultures, Prof. Philip Wayne Powell has laid out in detail the origins of the enormous body of prejudice in the Anglo-Saxon and Germanic world against the Spaniards, all their works, and their intellectual offspring in Latin America, which dictates American attitudes toward Mexico and the Mexicans. Powell argues, too, that the Ibero-Americans have been victimized right up to modern times, by this false evaluation of the Spanish world.

"Spain was the first summit power of modern times, preeminent in Europe and presiding over an empire that dwarfed those of Rome and Genghis Khan," Powell writes. " . . . With tasks and goals of such magnitude, Spain inevitably depleted herself in blood and treasure and went into decline in Europe, where her long sway finally receded before France and England, successors at the summit. But the centuries of Spanish imperial power created a host of enemies who, mixing fear and envy, and the intense hatreds of religious conflict made Spain and Spaniards the first to feel the impact of the printing press as a propaganda weapon. Spanish power was the target of devastating attacks, which launched a Western fashion of denigrating Spain, Spaniards, and most of their works—propaganda which became entrenched as History. The story of the Black Legend, which purports a unique Spanish depravity . . . and knowledge of the growth and perennial fruiting of the 'large spreading tree of hate' is essential to an understanding of the vast Hispanic world. . . . "[5]

The Mexicans have had to wrestle with this problem of their real and perceived dissimilarity with the U.S., fitfully if serially, throughout their history. It has not, of course, always been the problem they would have us—and themselves—believe. For it often provided and continues to provide a rationale for their failures to deal with their problems effectively. Ironically, if you speak to other Latin Americans, they will tell you—at least those who want a democratic society modeled on the only successful contemporary models, those of the U.S., Western Europe, and Japan—that they see Mexico's geographic position and concomitant exposure to the United States as a great advantage in developing the kind of economy and society they would like to have in their own countries. In the considerable animosity which exists throughout Latin America toward Mexico, one element is precisely this jealousy over what other Latin Americans perceive, rightly, as the special beneficial relationship Mexico enjoys with the U.S. because of the intertwining of history and geographical proximity.

The vast market that the U.S. has provided for Mexican products in the past and the supply of modern manufactures at cheap prices just next door have been important ingredients in making Mexico one of the economic leaders of Latin America. The imitation of many U.S. institutions, from credit cards to philanthropic foundations, has made Mexico a more modern society. And despite the clichéd aspersions made in Mexico City cocktail party circles by American expatriates as well as Mexicans on North American puritanism, materialism, decadence, and so on, Mexico has been heavily influenced throughout her history by U.S. concepts of individual and collective political morality.

It is interesting that Paz, once a Marxist and still a forthright defender of the concept of the Mexican Revolution, has returned to a defense of what once would have been called the *petit bourgeois* democratic ideals of Francisco I. Madero, the nineteenth-century leader in the overthrow of the Díaz dictatorship, and to the 19th century Mexican liberals. Madero, who was sent to school at Berkeley by his wealthy father, looked to the U.S. for his political idealism. Benito Juárez, the sainted Mexican president who fought the imposition of French rule in Mexico during the American Civil War, also owed much of his intellectual heritage to U.S. thought and institutions, reinforced during an eighteen-month exile in New Orleans to escape political persecution from the *caudillo* regime of Santa Anna.[6]

The U.S., as the senior partner in this relationship, has been able for a good part of its history if not to ignore Mexico, at least to give it a very low priority in its foreign policy concerns, particularly since the early 1930s. Behind this amnesia toward our important southern neighbor is the strange ghost of guilt and ignorance that dominates U.S. attitudes, built on the hubris of the nineteenth century relationship between the two countries. The Mexican War of 1846–1848, followed so swiftly by the great and tragic civil conflict inside the United

States, is almost forgotten in U.S. history. Yet the war was as important as any event in American history. It was a vastly successful war—not only as a smashing military triumph but in setting the stage for the later development of the U.S. It ended the long, drawn-out border disputes of the American West, and incorporated vast new territories that would focus U.S. policy on the Pacific.

"The United States at mid-century was a nation still in search of itself and the war would become an exercise in self-identity," writes historian Robert W. Johannsen, in a recent book on how the war was perceived in the U.S. at the time.[7] "It was a major crisis faced by the American people during a period of dramatic social and economic change. Older values of patriotism and civil virtue seemed threatened by newer concerns for commercial, industrial, and material advancement. Furthermore, the romanticism that had molded the American imagination during the earlier nineteenth century seemed to be on the wane; a golden age of heroism and chivalry (to paraphrase one of the period's spokesmen) was giving way before a brazen age of commerce. . . . For a time and for some people, the war with Mexico offered reassurance by lending new meaning to patriotism, providing a new arena for heroism, and reasserting anew the popular assumption of America's romantic era."

The distinguished historian and Librarian of Congress, Daniel J. Boorstin, characterizes it thus: "It was an offensive war. Undertaken as a political decision by people ignorant of the military problems, the Mexican War resembled most of our later military enterprises. The same exigencies of federal representative government which had drawn us into conflict also prevented us from considering calmly the implications of our entry, from weighing the cost of war or the benefits of victory. The very fact that the war was limited to one small part of this hemisphere, that it was conducted without allies, and that it was relatively unconfused by world issues, makes it a particularly vivid illustration of our domestic shortcomings."[8]

Otis A. Singletary, in his slim but useful volume on the war argues that its obscurity is in part attributable to the fact that it was not the kind of "total war" that came in this century nor a "total victory," since it was terminated by negotiations rather than a dictated peace. "Still another reason for our apparent indifference to the Mexican War lies rooted in the guilt that we as a nation have come to feel about it. The undeniable fact that it was an offensive war so completely stripped it of moral pretensions that no politician of that era ever succeeded in elevating it to the lofty level of a 'crusade.' The additional fact that we paid Mexico $15 million after it was all over —'conscience money,' some called it—seemed to confirm the ugliest charges of those who had denounced the war as a cynical, calculated despoiling of the Mexican state, a greedy land-grab from a neighbor too weak to defend herself. The land hunger was there, to be sure, for expansionism was a dynamic force in America in the 1840s; but there were causes other than greed as there were consequences other than gain."[9]

Singletary argues effectively that while the U.S. annexation of Texas was the immediate cause of the war, there were many others, for the acquisition of Texas was only a part of the American movement west. Furthermore, the brutality and atrocities committed by the Mexican government, including actions against her own citizens, were a cause of intense feeling against Mexico among all Americans as well as the Texans. The political instability in Mexico, due to her unresolved breakaway from Spain, is another explanation for the failure of twenty years of diplomatic negotiations with the Americans over Texas.

And there were massive miscalculations on the Mexican side. The false pride of the Mexicans, sure that their European-style army was superior to the Americans, who at the outbreak of the war had a total force of fewer than 7,000 men, one-third of them foreign-born.[10] At the very moment the war broke out, congress was debating whether West Point should be continued to train professional officers. Mexican leaders were equally sure that the U.S. would not have the stamina for the war, divided as the country was over issues like tariffs and slavery (that is, the possibility that any new territories acquired in the southwest would add to the slave states influence). Furthermore, the Mexicans counted on the fear the French and British had of American growth and power for their intervention against the U.S. if it tried to annex Texas.

But the signing of the Treaty of Guadalupe Hidalgo on Feb. 2, 1848, after sixteen months of fighting in which the Americans distinguished themselves (despite occasional outrages by undisciplined volunteers) left no doubt about the victor. The treaty ceded the Mexican provinces of California and New Mexico to the U.S. and confirmed the U.S.-Mexico border along the Rio Grande in exchange for a payment of $15 million plus the assumption of $3.2 million in debts owed U.S. citizens by Mexico. And, as any Mexican is never slow to remind any American at any given time, it denuded Mexico of almost half the territory to which she laid claim.

The war did more: it established a new relationship between the powerful and growing United States and the economically backward and unstable Mexico. "The Mexican War played an important part in the breakdown of American parochialism," writes Johannsen.[11] "It marked America's first intimate exposure to a life and culture that differed significantly from anything in the American experience. The war was a 'window' through which Americans could see a strange and exotic land of alien manners, customs, and attitudes. America, some were convinced, would never be the same again."

Nor would it be the last encounter in the nineteenth century between Americans and Mexicans. The incidents of further U.S. intervention on the eve of World War I—the petty Veracruz episode of 1914 (which involved the unsuccessful diplomatic efforts of López Portillo's grandfather and could account for some of his grandson's visceral reactions to American policies; the more serious Veracruz episode in 1917 (wherein decorations were lavished but not on Douglas MacArthur, Jr.); the farcical pursuit of Pancho Villa by John J. Pershing in 1916 (which almost destroyed the career of the future World War I commander) were comic opera as seen from the American side. But they inflicted further deep psychological wounds on the Mexicans.

Franklin Delano Roosevelt's decision not to use force to halt Cárdenas' expropriation of the foreign oil companies in Mexico in 1938 marked the end of U.S. attempts to guide Mexican policy through the open application of force, whether in the petty concerns of North American business interests or the broader issues of Mexican stability and progress. Nor did Washington do much more than whimper when the Mexican government in the following decades moved on to nationalize U.S.-owned land, transit systems, electrical utilities, and mining companies.

But, paradoxically, while this tolerance seemed to go a long way toward soothing the century of troubled relations with Mexico, it also contributed to the growing concept of Mexican state capitalism—that the solution to the country's economic development problems lay in state intervention through the creation of government-owned business enterprises. Because of this secondary effect, many conservative Mexican democrats hold Washington partly responsible for the consolidation of its antidemocratic, statist regime—another example of how criticism of the U.S. unites both the Left and the Right in Mexico. Whatever America's responsibility, it is clear that each expropriation of mineral rights or land was one step farther away from the principles of market economy upon which some of the nineteenth century liberal politicians in Mexico, including Juárez, had hoped to build as they moved away from traditional Spanish economic mercantilist interventionism.

Nor were these moves, even then, simply manifestations of an all encompassing anti*gringo* sentiment among Mexicans. Today particularly, there are few reliable ways to measure Mexican feelings toward the U.S. The constant anti-American campaign in the Mexican media reflects the extreme left-wing tendencies of the media personnel rather the animosity of the readers, or even of the government which manages the press. It is one of the contradictions of the current situation that those elements in Mexico which so long were the chief repositories of criticism and opposition to the U.S. —the old families with their ties to Spanish culture who feared the encroachment of American democratic institutions, the old wealth which feared the American competition, the Roman Catholic church —are now no longer anti-American but, in fact, America's main defenders in Mexico. Occasionally, one hears a xenophobic nationalist of the old school who says, "we do not want to become Americans," as though anyone assumed that they could or would.[12] These people, who see America as synonymous with the worst aspects of modernism —from sexual license to unbounded materialism—nevertheless look increasingly to the U.S. for help in resolving what many fear is the crisis of the regime and Mexican society. Paradoxically, a curious attitude which is just below the surface—certainly on the Mexican Right but also on the Left—is the almost mystical faith that should things in Mexico turn very bad, somehow, some way, Uncle Sam, will descend on Mexico, wave a magic baton, and make everything right.[13]

Wherever you look in Mexico, you find that kind of ambiguity about the *gringos*. There is admiration of and confidence in and warm feelings for Americans, and at the same time that there is envy, fear, and hate. Most observers, both North American and Mexican, agree that as one works one's way down through Mexican society, from the wealthy to the poor, from the educated to the illiterate, the antagonism toward the U.S. diminishes. And, ironically, the northern areas of the country, which have had the most exposure to the U.S., and often some of the nastiest historical experiences with American incursions and anti-Mexican racial prejudice, are the most favorably disposed.

How is it that the United States has for so long either ignored Mexico or accepted the simplistic view of the Mexico Model and the claims for its success?

All perceptions are ephemeral and difficult of analysis under the best of circumstances. But in this case, perhaps the most fundamental reason is the overriding drive of the Americans to develop their rich and huge country—the movement West, and the whole rapid blossoming of the American society and ethos that absorbed intellectual energies into the 1940s. The American cultural bias to look back to Europe or over the Pacific to the exotic East—underpinned by the Black Legend—is another important factor.

It is probably the media, however, that has been crucial in creating a wholly false image of Mexico since the end of World War II and into the 1980s. One looks in vain to the U.S. daily press and the weekly news magazines for any sustained reporting on Mexico. Few of the major American news media were represented by staff reporters in Mexico City until the 1981–1982 financial crisis and then the earthquakes of 1985. And even now there are only a handful of American newsmen in the Mexican capital. Not only are important political and economic stories not covered, but the most newsworthy stories on crime, adventure, and personality happenings—grist for the mills of the popular press—also go by the boards.

There is, for example, the famous case of the kidnapping in the fall of 1982 of the young grandaughter of Francisco Madero, the martyred president of revolutionary Mexico, and niece of the candidate of the principal opposition party, PAN, in the 1980 presidential elections. It had all the elements of a marvelous tabloid yarn: A seventeen-year-old heiress to a large fortune, beautiful (all young heiresses are beautiful!), kidnapped by *bandidos*. The Mexican police, with methods that would never win the approval of the American Civil Liberties Union, rounded up suspected leftist sympathizers and with the toughest police tactics (standard for Mexico) were able not only to rescue the young woman, but to bring in several dozen Latin American left-wing exiles who were implicated, including the brother of famed Che Gueverra, the Argentine guerrilla leader and one-time collaborator of Fidel Castro. It is not so clear what happened to the huge ransom, nor, as so often happens in Mexico, to those arrested. But during the weeks when the story was "hot," it was blacked out entirely in the major U.S. press except for a small item in *The New York Times*. This is typical of the attitudes of the American press' ability to simply ignore what goes on below the Rio Grande—most especially when a story is not favorable to left-wing causes.

The extent of the neglect of events south of the border cannot be exaggerated. When De la Madrid, reviewing the annual 1984 May Day parade from a balcony of the Palacio Nacional in Mexico City's famous Zócalo square, was the target of two Molotov cocktails thrown by radical students with suspected Cuban connections, neither *The New York Times* nor *The Washington Post* took note. Nor did they report the ensuing interesting and confusing official explanations, even though the violence occurred on the eve of a much-heralded visit of the Mexican president to Washington. Even the English-language newspapers in El Paso, Texas, did not print the news although it did appear in a semi-official version in newspapers in Juarez, El Paso's Mexican twin just across the border.

More often than not, when news of Mexico does appear, it is late, incorrect, or misinformed. It also reflects the bias of the leading liberal media outlets, especially in the eastern United States, whose belief in the "revolutionary" character of the Mexican regime deters it from the kind of scrutiny that would be applied to Latin American conservative governments, particularly those allied to the United States.

Something we can surely look forward to if Mexico's troubles increase and an even heavier hand is used to put down dissidence, is a sudden turning of the American and international press against the regime.[14] Then those Mexican officials who have long complained about their neglect in the U.S. media will find a more valid cause for their grievances.

One turns, of course, to the academic community for more enlightenment. And there, too, there is great disappointment. The subject of Latin America including Mexico, has not been a chic course of trendy endeavor for U.S. academic specialists—especially in the two-decade heyday of international studies after World War II.

No major figure in the State Department or the foreign policy establishment had been associated with Latin America until the Reagan administration chose outspoken Jeane Jordan Kirkpatrick, a professor at Georgetown University and an authority on Argentina, as its outspoken ambassador to the United Nations. That has been followed by Henry J. Kissinger who gave his panache to the regional studies by heading the Presidential Bipartisan Commission on Central America in 1983.

Kirkpatrick's appointment arose out of her special political talents rather than her Latin American expertise: her virtuoso defense of a Reaganesque position of differentiating between friendly, traditional, authoritarian states and dedicated enemies of the U.S. with pseudo-democratic credentials; her effectiveness as a polemicist; and the fact that she filled the role of a female member of the cabinet. Her appointment, unfortunately, was an indication that the Reagan administration, like most of its predecessors, does not regard the United Nations as a high-priority posting. Her emergence there as a principal foreign policy spokesman, as well as policy contributor, was serendipity. Kissinger's new-found interest in Latin America was evidence of the growing awareness of the mounting crisis in the region.[15] More importantly it was a sign of Kissinger's search to return to the halls of power through a rapprochement with Ronald Reagan, who apparently as a result of his concerns as California governor, has a deep and abiding interest in Latin America and the problem Mexico may one day constitute for the U.S.

All through the post-World War II period, Latin America was considered an American "backyard"; the action was in Western Europe, the Middle East, Southeast Asia, and China-Japan. When President-elect John Kennedy sought to lay out a new Latin American policy even before he took office, he turned to the academic community. It was partially out of that effort that the Alliance for Progress was formulated in his Administration. And it may well be that the program's singular lack of success was attributable to its often theoretical and impractical aspects which came from those academics.[16]

Even the eyeball-to-eyeball showdown of the Cuban Missiles Crisis in 1962, wherein Kennedy traded withdrawal of Soviet weapons for the immunity of the Castro regime from U.S. attack, was short-lived indirect attention to Latin America. Soon, the pressure of events in Southeast Asia and the continuing problem of how to defend a fractious but resurgent Western Europe against Soviet imperialism absorbed all Washington's intellectual energies.

True, Washington has dipped into the academic reservoir from time to time looking for ideas concerning our southern neighbors. And a vast array of tomes tumbles out, including those compilations of the endless rounds of ill-prepared conferences which seem to have become America's second largest industry. But academe is prone to focus its attention on relatively narrow concerns, to retreat into highly arcane research, rather than to face the existential question: how can the U.S. live beside a mushrooming Mexican population which increasingly demonstrates its incapacity to feed and govern itself? Or, in an attempt to curry favor with fellow academics south of the border—rationalized as "coopting the left" or "meeting Mexican scholars halfway"—these conferences turn into stale reprises of past meetings full of Mexican rationalizations. And the epidemic of scientism—the belief that computer printouts and statistical models can substitute for political genius—which dominates the American academy today, often leads to ignoring historical trends, discounting the mystery of dominant personalities, and ignoring just plain common sense applied to our problems in Latin America and as elsewhere, in favor of statistical analysis.

There is, also, an unfortunate if understandable attempt by American academics to maintain intimate relations with their Mexican counterparts even at the risk of adopting some of their prejudices, and worse still, their taboos—what is called "localitis" when it afflicts State Department cadres. Example: An American academic tells you that in order to involve the "moderate Left" in his project he has coauthored a book with a radical Mexican Marxist economist who is dedicated to destroying any concept of a mixed economy in Mexico, much less cooperating with U.S. capitalism. It is pretty hard to see how he could have reached further left for a collaborator. And, in fact, he has coopted no one; he has simply given the Marxist more respectability and a better platform in the U.S. from which to influence Mexican policy, so attentive are the Mexicans to what is trendy in U.S. academic circles.

One can understand—if not excuse—why Mexican academics do not write about corruption, about the influence on modern Mexico of race, color, and caste; why, despite their constant complaints about American domination, there is no major Mexican work on U.S. intellectual influences on Mexico, and on and on. These are all taboo subjects in Mexico. They are subjects of investigation which Mexicans in their authoritarian society would find dangerous to their careers, their livelihoods. A major work on Mexican corruption by Mauricio González de la Garza led to the author's absenting himself from Mexico during the latter part of the López Portillo administration.[17] His book, *La Ultima Llamada*, is an intimate portrait of what happens when a member of the Mexican elite attempts a muckraking piece on the society, even with the collaboration of a member of the ruling family; López Portillo's sister apparently was one of the author's principal sources.[18] But one asks in vain for a commensurate reason why U.S. academics have not pursued many of these subjects, as important as they are to understanding the current crisis in the country.

The domination of Latin American studies in the post-Vietnam era by left-of-center ideologues is notorious, although their vulgar Marxism is often so primitive that one dignifies it by calling it ideology. But it is this pervasive anti-anti-Communism of the American academic community which is more of a deterrent to understanding. "Fostered initially by the Truman administration to mobilize U.S. resources for the reconstruction of Western Europe, anticommunism gained a viselike grip on the public at large," writes Cole Blasier. "The hysterical proportions which it reached were first and foremost due to ignorance. Stalin shut off the Soviet Union from the West; what Americans did not know and did not understand they feared. Soviet capabilities were exaggerated to inhuman proportions. Soviet policies and ideologies also posed a direct challenge or offended vested interests in the United States: property owners, union leaders, the free press, the churches, Jews, and Eastern European immigrants. Anticommunism became a rallying point for diverse interests: it united liberals, conservatives, and reactionaries. The consensus was so broad, the majority so great, that the pressures for conformity approached a kind of social tyranny. . . . The extent of U.S. fear of communism was demonstrated in the extreme hostility of the U.S. responses to the Guatemalan and Cuban revolutions and the Dominican revolt. U.S. policy makers were afraid that the communism allegedly infecting these countries would spread elsewhere in Latin America." [19]

This passage by a respected Sovietologist and Latin American specialist, with its oversimplifications so gross as to defy refutation, is not an atypical example. It obscures, for instance, the real nature of the Soviet tyranny and the American people's proper need to fear it, the origins of the U.S-Soviet post-World War II confrontation, and takes the stereotyped view that any attempt within the U.S. to oppose the expansion of the Soviet bloc, particularly in Latin America, is *ipso facto* morally wrong.

A look at the Latin American bookshelf in any university bookstore will reveal a surfeit of just this sort of literature on problems of the region today. But perhaps even worse is the effort of so many American academics writing on Mexico to curry favor with their colleagues in Mexico—most of whom, again, belong to the conventional Marxist world of the Mexican intellectual, even though these leading "revolutionary" lights tend to "bleed" for the proletariat in Mexico from lifestyles of considerable splendor in Paris, Madrid, Boston, New York, or Washington.

But a new era is beginning for U.S.-Mexico relations, whether or not it is perceived in the academic world or in the news media. It has been brought on by a number of developments, many of them the product of several decades, others the result of new forces during the past few years. The new relationship between Washington and Mexico City arises out of the following:

1. The inordinate growth of communications, even among the poorer areas of the world like Mexico, resulting in the integration of all lands into a "world village." [20]

2. The growing interdependence of the world economy, which finds the U.S. increasingly dependent on the rest of the world—including Mexico—for raw materials and markets.

3. The expanding Mexican population and the need for development, which can only come through integration with the world economy—most importantly with that of the U.S.

4. The shift in U.S. population, both geographically and sociologically, to the Sun Belt, and the growing proportion of the population which is Mexican-American.

5. The spreading turmoil in Latin American—particularly in Central America—which threatens to involve both the U.S. and Mexico.

6. The increasing role of the Soviet Union, as a world power which through its surrogate in Cuba can now project power and influence into the Western Hemisphere.

Perhaps nowhere is the enormity of the worldwide communications revolution that has affected the most remote parts of the world so great as in Mexico. In a rural area in Mexico, one does not know what to make of a young Indian girl boarding the intercity bus in a desolate desert area while wearing Jordache designer jeans. Or, what is one to conclude from the fact that villagers in remote areas watch telecasts of "Dallas"? On a hot spring night, the traditional plaza in Tehuantepec, not exactly a major Mexican regional center, is filled with transistor radios tuned into programs as far away as Havana or San Antonio. Direct dial on most U.S. telephones into virtually any Mexican telephone helps circumvent the pitfalls of mail service on both sides of the border—and the unofficial Mexican political probing of the mails. Half of Monterrey seems to carry a Laredo National Bank checkbook. The menu at Denny's in Mexico City's Zona Rosa is not so different from one of the chain's outlets in San Diego.

And it is in this environment that the old ways of doing things— whether the Mexican attempt to inhibit the free flow of ideas or the American tendency to ignore what happens south of the border, is being modified rapidly. The mosaic of U.S.-Mexican relationships that has been built up in the 75 years since the outbreak of the Revolution in 1910 is enormous. It began with the emigration of perhaps 10 percent of Mexico's population during those troubles (even though some 300,000 were forcibly repatriated in 1930–1932 during the Great Depression). Then, during World War II and afterward, hundreds of thousands of contract laborers were imported to work in the agricultural areas of Texas, California, and Arizona during the manpower shortages. And finally there has been the flood of illegal emigrants, particularly since the 1960s—perhaps as many as 15 million of whom 80 percent are Mexican.

The intricate relationships between these emigrants and Mexico has become a network of communications at an informal level which has brought the two societies together in a way they have never known before. Estimates of the earnings remitted back to Mexico are one index. And although calculations of the sums are open to speculation—especially because of the wide difference between the official rates of exchange and the shadow free markets which operate along the borders—the annual total appears to be somewhere in the neighborhood of $6 billion, second only to Mexico's oil earnings. In many border areas, particularly in the northwest of Mexico, the "dollarization" of the economy is a given that most economists accept

—that is, the use of the dollar as the medium of exchange rather than the peso, a trend that is likely to increase as confidence in the Mexican currency erodes.

The argument is often made among Mexicanologists that the border areas of northern Mexico and the southwest of the U.S. form a new region wherein the local population finds more in common with its neighbors across the border than with its fellow countrymen. It is a romantic concept that many, on both sides of the border, particularly in the business community in the border areas themselves, would like to believe. The argument certainly can be made for the northern states of Mexico, whose cultural background and historic antagonism to Mexico City have been principal factors in Mexican politics, rooted in the Spanish colonial period. But to include the U.S. border areas in this region is more romantic than factual.[21]

For while the border areas of the U.S. that abut on Mexico are among the poorest in the country, living standards are still higher than in the northern regions of Mexico, even though they are some of the richest in that country. For example, take the question of housing: One estimate is that in the late 1970s there were 150,000 houses on the U.S. side of the border that were substandard. But, because they were even worse across the border in Mexico, emigrants into the U.S.—mostly illegal—were quite ready to occupy this housing. Mexico City officials like to hand out statistics indicating the poverty and suffering in the mushrooming border Mexico cities.[22] That is undoubtedly true. But it is also true that in cases such as infant mortality, only Mexico City, Monterrey, Guadalajara, and Puebla—the major and most modern Mexican cities—have conditions as good as or better than those in the border cities. The complexity of this border relationship has been infinitely complicated by the onset of the financial crisis of 1981, the subsequent need to reevaluate the whole economic relationship between the U.S. and Mexico, and the failure of the assumption that oil revenues had changed the traditional dependency of Mexico on the U.S.[23]

Furthermore, the enormous slums of Mexico City are as bad if not worse than any in the border urban area. The huge slum Netzahualcoyotl, which lies just off the main road to the southeast near the international airport contains somewhere between 3 and 4 million people and is growing at the rate of 15,000 persons a month. A Roman Catholic bishop who works closely with the people of the area estimates that at least 250,000 have neither water, electricity, nor waste disposal. Much of the area, while demonstrating the enormous ability of Mexicans to make do against great odds, consists of improvised housing.

Of course, these slum settlements are not a new phenomenon and were reported in brilliant detail in two books by Oscar Lewis over twenty years ago.[24] At the time of their publication, Mexican authorities denied their authenticity and harassed the author. It is a comment on the acceptance of this new kind of urban poverty that Lewis's books are now a commonplace in the literature on modern Mexican life and routinely sold in bookstores in Mexico.

The border towns in Mexico virtually lean up against the frontier for support. Juarez and its environs, across the border from El Paso, is now a city of 4 million people—the fourth largest in the country. Matamoros and Brownsville, Nuevo Laredo and Laredo, El Centro and Mexicali, Tijuana and San Diego, all are border towns with the same kind of symbiotic relationship. The dependence of these Mexican border towns on their U.S. neighbors is unmistakable. Thousands of their residents cross the border daily to work on the American side, and tourist income is of prime importance to the Mexican side of the border.

That dependent relationship was somewhat obscured during the temporary period of the Mexican boom in 1979–1981 when the over-valuation of the Mexican peso against the U.S. dollar made American goods and services incredible bargains for Mexicans, and they flooded across the border as both retail customers and tourists. Laredo, one of the main points on the border for financial transactions and an old emigration funnel into the U.S., which had profited from the boom, by 1984 had 26 percent unemployment, one of the highest in the country. In early 1984, its downtown area looked like a ghost town as a result of the devaluation of the peso which had cut Mexican buying power in U.S. dollars by more than 60 percent from the 1980–82 boom years.

But a far more representative picture of the sort of long-term relationships that have developed in this border area is the dependence of the Mexican border towns on their U.S. sister cities to handle mutual problems. Many of these problems, if the American side were not concerned and did not have the funds, would not be attacked. Some examples: Brownsville wanted to relocate railroad sidings and crossings in order to lessen congestion and increase safety in its activities as a port for northern Mexico. The U.S. is contributing $24 million to the project, which specifically permits the Mexicans to use it on their side of the river. The financial outlay is necessary if Brownsville is to continue to function as the major sea port for the Mexican industrial complex of Monterrey; Mexico has not had the money or the ingenuity to create a viable port of its own for north-eastern Mexico. El Paso offers its trucks, personnel and spraying equipment to keep the mosquitoes down on both sides of the border because Juarez does not have the money or the expertise—and the mosquitoes don't honor the international frontier. San Diego, to keep its prize beaches clean, is processing 13 to 15 million gallons of Tijuana sewage daily on an "emergency" basis that has lasted for over two decades. The remainder of Tijuana's 20 million gallons of waste a day is poured untreated into the ocean south of the city or north into the Tijuana River and its U.S. tributaries and poses a serious health hazard for San Diego. Early in 1984 the Federal Office of Management and Budget in Washington turned down a request for a $710 million in federal funds to build a treatment plant on the U.S. side of the border. But a near crisis, when Tijuana sewage pipes burst in late 1983, emptying another 3 to 5 million gallons of raw sewage across the border, finally got Washington's attention. Sooner or later the federal government will have to pick up the $1.8 million a year that San Diego residents are paying for the Tijuana problem. In Laredo, local boosters have spent their money and influence to attract multinational plant locations to Nuevo Laredo across the river, for the local banking operations depend heavily on Mexican business.

But because of the complicated psychological and political barriers between the two countries, these arrangements are generally informal, amorphous, and unpublicized at the national level. Mexican local governments have little autonomy to make arrangements, and Mexico City sees formal agreements with the *gringos* as more evidence of the distrusted *Norteños* (Northern Mexicans) being sucked into the maw of American influence. And there is the fear on the American side that U.S. assistance could be flowing into a bottomless pit, since the opportunities and living conditions in the Mexican border areas act as a magnet on the huge poverty-stricken population in the rest of the country.

Chapter 7: **Mexicans for Export**

Just as the population explosion is at the root of so many domestic Mexican problems today, so it is an underlying cause of the new relationship that has developed between the U.S. and Mexico.

Mexico in 1985 had some 80 million people. One can only appreciate the enormity of these figures by seeing the rate at which the population has exploded over the last few decades, indeed, the last few years. At the beginning of the troubles in 1910, Mexico had only 15 million people (the U.S. had 92 million). Between the end of World War II and 1970, the Mexican population, largely as a result of a declining infant mortality rate, had doubled to 53 million. And by the early 1990s, it will have doubled again.

There is a general consensus among observers that her former population growth rates—which were as high as 3.3 percent a year only a decade ago—have declined as urban patterns cut into traditional rural customs and fertility dropped. There is, however, room for debate here. Mexican statistics are highly suspect, and the experience in other parts of the world has been that urbanization initially has the opposite effect on fertility; that is, families moving in from rural areas initially tend to grow even more rapidly because no matter how urban slum conditions appear to Westerners, they are usually an improvement in terms of nutrition and hygiene over the previous conditions in the rural dwellings. In any case, consensus has it that Mexico's population will grow at well over 2 percent annually into the next century.

The old traffic metaphor is very apt: will the brakes applied to a speeding automobile, however effective, halt it before it hits the wall? By the year 2000, Mexico will have at least 100 million people, perhaps as many as 112 million—and by some calculations, as many as 132 million people. One Mexican authority estimates that if population should rise above 126 million in the year 2000, Mexico will move by the mid-twenty-first century to a total population of 500 to 600 million.[1] Today more than half of Mexico's population is under fifteen years of age. The population explosion and the inadequacies of economic development mean that poverty is universal in the country.

Mexican per capita income, a not very adequate way to judge the quality of life but a measure of relative wealth, was only $1,640 in 1979. That means that the total national economic product divided by the number of inhabitants was about one-tenth of the same figure for Americans, or one-half of that for Venezuelans. And because of the disparity of income within the country, the situation was even worse than the per capita figures indicate. Some 20 percent of the population with higher incomes accounted for more than 57 percent of total national household income in the 1970s. In 1980, 11.7 percent of all Mexicans lived without water in their homes, 46 percent had no sewage disposal, 58.4 percent had no baths, and about a third of the families lived in a single room.

Furthermore, the distribution of the Mexican population complicates any attempt to improve their livelihood and standards of living. Only 15 percent of Mexicans live on the coastal plains where there is an abundance of water, readily available energy, and a large part of the arable land. More than 60 percent of the population is crowded on the high central plateau around Mexico City where an infrastructure is difficult to provide. But despite the squalid slum conditions, urbanization continues as the masses migrate into these cities looking for jobs and food.[2] By 1980, 66 percent of all Mexicans were living in urban areas. Mexico City, where some 20 percent of the total population now lives, has been growing at the rate of 30 percent annually during the last ten years. It has grown from 8.9 million in 1970 to 16.4 million in 1980 to more than 18 million in 1985 and, unless some radical changes in present trends take place, there will be a megalopolis of 40 million people living in the Valley of Mexico by the turn of the century.

The effect of all this is visible to the naked eye of the most casual observer, even though it is possible for a tourist to escape the spectacle of the wretched makeshift slums that encompass much of Mexico City. More and more people are living on the streets, even in the fashionable areas. "Marias," the Indian or meztizo women who come down from the mountains to sell handicrafts or lottery tickets with three or four small children in tow, huddle in downtown doorways at night, are an increasingly common sight. The quality of the air, a grave problem aggravated by the absence of oxygen at the 8,000-foot altitude, has reached abominable conditions with almost 2 million cars—more than half of the total in Mexico—concentrated in the area with no emission controls. Overcrowded buses roll down the streets belching huge clouds of black smoke and debris from barely burned diesel oil. So bad did the situation become because of a temperature inversion in January 1986, that medical officials feared an epidemic of pulmonary failure.

Virtually no new rental apartments have been built in the last decade due to lack of incentives for private investors. Tens of thousands were without any kind of housing even before the earthquakes of 1985 destroyed the homes of a hundred thousand people. Rents have skyrocketed. Mexico City planning Director Javier Caraveo Aguero in 1984 said that there is no solution to the housing shortage. "Let's say that the 800,000 housing units now needed could be built in 50 years. By that time the population would have grown and housing needs would have again increased, so there would still remain a shortage. . . . Each one of us in Mexico City has less than two square meters of green space, and according to some international organizations, there should be a minimum of 10 square meters for each inhabitant."[3]

Following the earthquake in September 1985, the government announced it would expropriate 7,000 privately owned buildings in downtown Mexico City over a total of 625 acres in order to build 180,000 housing units for the estimated 200,000 people who have been put out on the street by the catastrophe. "The term expropriation scares a lot of people, but it must be remembered that in Mexico the right of property is not absolute," comes the blunt reminder from the PRI's Senate leader Antonio Riva Palacio López. The rationalization for the expropriation was that many of the buildings destroyed by the earthquake were under Mexico City's rigid rent control regulations. Their owners had made no repairs for years and many of them were decrepit. The government, it was argued by the authorities, would take over the ruins, clear them, and replace them with modern low-cost housing. Leaving aside the argument that the greatest loss of life in the earthquake had been in badly built and improperly designed government housing, the whole affair was exposed as the usual government swindle. It turned out that many of the properties had never been under rent control, some were new and in good condition, and some were not affected by the earthquake. After a howl went up in the private sector reflected in some newspapers, the government backed off, amended the expropriation order. The final result trails off into the kind of unrecorded history that overtakes so many government actions in Mexico.

It is clear that even if this ambitious project were accomplished —owners promised to seek injunctions to delay if not prevent the government from acquiring the land—it would only exacerbate the already impossible housing situation created by the government's bungling intervention.

The water supply is also in jeopardy. An addition of only 10 percent in the late 1970s required a supply of electric power equivalent
of that needed to light and power Mexico's second city, Guadalajara.
And because Mexico City lies in a valley on the plateau, waste has
to be pumped up over the mountains for disposal. The only major future source of water is the Tecolutla River almost three hundred miles
away. Meanwhile, the city continues to pump water from its subsoil—
a once abundant supply for the pre-Columbian city of the Aztecs was
built on islands in a lake on the plateau—which has caused the gradual
sinking of major structures all over the city, in some cases leading to
dramatic tilts. There is a constant need to repair and rebuild the major
historical monuments, like the sixteenth-century cathedral and the
nineteenth-century Palacio de Bellas Artes. When the subject of water
rationing comes up—as it does perennially during the frequent shortages—the idea is immediately abandoned since there is no infrastructure to permit an equitable division of the existing supply.

None of the remedies which have been suggested, plotted, and
partially implemented has even begun to meet the population challenge. Birth control programs have run into the same problems
that exist in other nonindustrial societies: the traditional attitudes
which see children as economic assets, the suspicion of those whom
the program must target, the corruption and incompetence of the
bureaucracy who run the program, and the still inherent inadequacies
of the current contraceptive devices in this kind of environment.

A government official charged with the propagation of birth control literature and devices claims that the traditional opposition of the
Catholic church is not a major factor in the problem. He said he welcomed the anticontraception statements of Pope John Paul II, arguing that they help the government program by drawing attention to
the problem, the ignorance of which, especially among the poor, is
the major concern of those trying to stem the population by artificial
means.

Unemployment is increasing as enormous numbers of new
workers come on the labor market. The labor force has risen since
1970 at an even faster rate on an average annual basis than has the
general population, 6.2 percent versus 3.8 percent. Official government estimates—which are patently ludicrous—have set unemployment at 7 percent. Based on income statistics in the census of 1970,
there appeared to be 4.9 to 5.8 million unemployed—37 percent to 45
percent of the labor force—or underemployed, that is, people whose
contribution to the gross domestic product is nil, or who work less
than 40 hours a week, or who earn less than the minimum wage. Both
the Echeverría and the López Portillo administrations attempted job

creation through enormous deficit financing schemes that brought about the runaway inflation and the enormous foreign borrowing.

One way of measuring the failure of the program to create new jobs is to place the 731,000 estimated new jobs inside Mexico in 1981 against the deportation of 866,800 Mexican illegals from the U.S., as reported by the Immigration and Nationalization Service that same year. U.S. immigration service's statistics do not attempt to cull out those illegals who have been deported more than once—though a very large number is assumed—nor estimate those who escaped the INS' surveillance. But the rough comparison does suggest how far the Mexican government program has failed—even during a boom year and by using highly inflationary methods—to meet the needs of its workers, and the extent to which illegal migration to the U.S. is a safety valve for the Mexican population problem.

Any discussion of the problem of Mexican emigration to the U.S. must start with this proposition, agreed to by Mexican and American observers: large Mexican emigration to the U.S. will continue. That proposition is based on five factors:

1. The enormity of the Mexican population "surplus" and the "porous" nature of the long land border, make inevitable the continuing entry of large numbers of Mexican nationals.

2. Mexican analysts, and many American students of Mexico's problems, contend that the exploding Mexican population must have the migratory escape valve if stability is to be maintained below the border.

3. The American tradition of welcoming new arrivals will continue with Mexicans and other Latin Americans despite prejudice and discrimination against them, particularly in the Southwest.

4. An important factor in support of migration is the beneficial effects of new emigrants on the U.S. economy—"stoop labor" for Southwestern agriculture and untrained but cheap labor for the service industries.

5. Although more ambiguous than many "professional Hispanic" spokesmen in Washington admit, the Mexican-American community has strong familial ties to Mexico and will to an unknown extent support a continuing emigration.

Emigration from what is now Mexico into what is now the Southwest of the United States is as old as the Spanish Conquest in the fifteenth century. But contrary to popular folklore, the claim of Mexican-American "nationalists" to a privileged role in the Southwest because they preceded other Americans is flimsy. Partisans of a more liberal policy toward Mexican emigration often use the spurious argument that "it belonged to them," to justify "an open border," or the right of Mexicans to emigrate and populate the American Southwest without restriction.

As Mario Cantu, a restaurateur with a Chicano radical background in San Antonio, who has been imprisoned for arms smuggling to Mexican terrorists, puts it: There were probably not more than 100,000 people in the whole area between Louisiana and San Francisco at the time of the American annexation, and most of them were Indians, who drew little distinction between the two colonizing forces coming at them from the north and the south; and, furthermore, large numbers of the population were Anglos (English-speaking Americans in Spanish-speaking areas of the U.S. Southwest). Therefore, Cantu says, the region "belongs" equally to all the immigrant ethnic groups that now inhabit it.

Whatever the Spanish-Mexican claims at the time of the U.S. annexation, Mexico had only been able to colonize parts of present-day New Mexico from the whole area. Northern Mexico, from the pre-Columbian times and the earliest Spanish colonial period, had a sparse population. Even today, the large Mexican border cities owe their size to the trade and migration between the two countries. In 1821, when the first Anglos from the U.S. began to colonize it, Texas had fewer than 4,000 Spanish-speaking inhabitants. And this despite extensive efforts by the Spanish colonial authorities in the eighteenth century to colonize the region to protect it from the encroaching British, and then American, French, and Russian (in California) hegemony. And by the time of the Texas Revolution in 1836, Anglos outnumbered the Spanish-speaking inhabitants five to one. There were only 61,000 inhabitants in present-day New Mexico and southern Colorado, the most successful of the Spanish-Mexican colonies in the Southwest, when the Treaty of Guadalupe Hidalgo was signed in 1848 ending the Mexican War, and there were already substantial numbers of Anglos among them. Arizona had only two thousand non-Indian inhabitants even after the Gadsen Purchase extended the border southward to include booming little Tucson with its one thousand people. And there were perhaps 7,500 Spanish-speaking settlers in California at the time of the American takeover.

There are few Mexican-Americans in the whole Southwest who can make claims to the area on the basis of their ancestry—like their fellow Americans, they are the sons and daughters, and grandchildren, and great-grandchildren of emigrants, albeit from neighboring Mexico rather than from across the seas.

The history of Mexican emigration into the Southwest is confused —and not only because some Mexicans were living there when the

U.S. acquired the areas after the Mexican War. Until the 1930s large stretches of the border were simply lines on paper in Washington, and no adequate records were kept. From 1886 to 1893 there were no statistics at all on border crossings, and even later in the century, most figures were estimates based on the small "head tax" charged emigrants who passed through official checkpoints. No visas were required from U.S. consulates. Nor was there great movement on the Mexican side of the border since northern Mexico was desperately poor and sparsely populated.

Cheap labor for U.S. expansion of agriculture in the Southwest and for building the railroads was recruited in China and Philippines. Nine-tenths of Mexico's population were rural, agricultural laborers still held in peonage under the large *latifundio*. The construction of railroads from the U.S. into Mexico during the 1900–1910 period made migration to the U.S. easier, and some 24,000 are reported to have legally migrated in that period. Because the railways were also employers, concentrations of Mexican-Americans appeared in faraway places such as Chicago, and continued to grow. ("The Second City" now has the largest Mexican-American population of any city in the U.S. with the exception of Los Angeles.) It also helps to explain why *barrios* have grown up in large cities near the railroad facilities or the stockyards, and the differences in caste which are so pronounced in the Mexican-American community. And, finally, it explains why *this overland migration made the Mexican-American emigration experience so radically different from that of the Europeans.*

"Drawn to these segregated enclaves, later arrivals either from Mexico or rural areas in the United States faced problems which were not identical with those of more experienced earlier residents, despite the identity in culture and traditional institutions. . . .Among other national groups the relative suddenness of their urbanization suggests that an overwhelming proportion started out occupying approximately equal status and were confronted by common problems of adjustment, with differentiation developing later."[4] But it was the violent period in Mexico, beginning in 1910, that spurred the movement which resulted in the large Mexican-American minority in the Southwest. Perhaps as much as 3 percent of Mexico's population moved north annually during some of the troubled years, reaching a peak in the 1920s, even though by this time the actual fighting in Mexico had stopped and because of mounting pressures, the U.S. put a brake on the inflow. Official U.S. statistics, probably only vague approximations, indicate that at the least a million Mexicans had entered by 1930 due to the upheavals of the Mexican civil war. An intensified effort to control the border after 1924 resulted in a growing number of illegal entries.

The movement toward illegal entry was aided and abetted by labor contractors who sought recruits for the burgeoning California and Texas agriculture. They made use of "coyotes"—local runners who helped emigrants across the border, and showed them how to escape visa fees, literacy tests, and head taxes. They were the precursors of today's army of border smugglers who usher people, drugs, and arms, as well as less valuable contraband, across the long and still largely unpoliced border. But after 1928, when the Depression began to be felt, the mass movement to California of poor whites from the drought-ridden farms of the South and West, caused Mexican emigration to drop off sharply.[5] Official figures for the 1930s record only 27,000 Mexicans entering the country on permanent visas. As the Depression deepened and the unemployed Mexicans in urban areas of the Southwest became a visible drain on local government budgets, a program for forced repatriation developed between the federal border patrol and local authorities—and even Mexican consular officials. Between 1931 and 1934, the city of Los Angeles sent fifteen trains with an average of one thousand Mexicans each back south. Cities as remote as Detroit and St. Paul, Minnesota, pressured Mexicans —and often American citizens tangled in the net of dual nationality —to return to Mexico in programs to repatriate indigents. Again, there are no accurate statistics, but guesses run to as many as 300,000 persons returned to Mexico in this manner—though some came back either as emigrants, or as proved American nationals.

World World II brought a new development, the "bracero" (*brazos* = arms, therefore, fieldhand) program by which the U.S. government arranged the importation of Mexican agricultural workers to replace the many Americans drafted for the military. An executive agreement between Mexico and the U.S., ratified by the Congress in August 1942 and extended in 1951, was to continue for twenty-two years. The peak of exchange was reached in 1959 when more than 135,000 men were admitted to work temporarily in the U.S. and then returned to Mexico. The volume declined markedly toward the end of the period but the braceros were replaced, at least in part, by "wetbacks" (*mojados*, a term of derision in Mexico), workers who crossed often for the same kind of work but without legal authorization. In 1953, an official U.S. government report estimated that for every legal agricultural laborer, four illegal aliens were being picked up by the border patrol.

Another twist occurred in 1964 when the Department of Labor imposed a new criterion for legal entry of temporary workers, which required certification that jobs for which they were being recruited could not be filled by domestic labor. The end of the bracero program and this new regulation altered the conditions of Mexican entry and led to a plateau for legal entrants of under 50,000 a year. But, of course, the illegal migration has continued apace; and although all numbers are suspect, it has presumably reached the millions, though many of them are only temporary residents who eventually return to Mexico. The number of forced repatriations crossed the million mark in 1984—with the probability that for every illegal returned, some four or five remained in the country.

Thus, Mexican emigration to the U.S. has a varied past: it has fluctuated violently, generally reacting to conditions south of the border. Because of the geographic proximity of their homeland, Mexican emigrants—far more than Europeans or Asians—have tended to think of themselves as temporary migrants, and the back and forth movement has been traditionally very large, and probably more so in recent times as transportation has become more available and less expensive. And Mexican emigrants—because of their language, the constant flow of new arrivals into relatively concentrated geographical areas, and the history of destructive and vicious descrimination against them in the Southwest—have tended to remain less assimilated into the general population and more a national subgroup in the U.S. than many other emigrant groups.

But even this complicated background of Mexican emigration hardly prepares one for the rat's nest of claims and counterclaims of the situation today. As a 1951 study of Mexican emigrants to southern California by a group of U.S. academics demonstrated, any attempt to categorize the Mexicans who come into the U.S. becomes extremely difficult.[6] These scholars break them down into five categories: (1) temporary illegal, long-distance migrants, mostly single males (mostly from Mexico's western central plateau, one of the traditional areas of migration to the U.S.) who come for long if temporary periods of work in the U.S. leaving their families behind in Mexico; (2) temporary, legal, long-distance migrants—"green carders"—entitled to work and live in the U.S. on a permanent basis, usually older males; (3) borderland migrants who commute regularly from hones in the Mexican border town where they can live more cheaply; (4) long-term, long-distance, illegal immigrants, who come either clandestinely or on tourist or student visas which they cannot extend, mostly married, who settle but with no legal basis; and (5) permanent legal immigrants, perhaps 70 percent of whom previously lived in the U.S. illegally, whose employers or relatives helped them obtain permanent status. But, the authors point out, these categories are not mutually exclusive and "they do not even begin to capture the full diversity of situations and motivations which one encounters among the Mexican immigrant population of southern California."

One government source estimates that 900,000 illegal Mexican nationals were counted in the 1980 census.[7] But, the authors reckon that this only sets a possible minimum figure for the number of Mexican illegals in the country. Mexican government estimates conclude that there are between 800,000 and 1.9 million "undocumented" Mexicans working in the U.S. over the course of a given year and contends that most of these sooner or later return to Mexico. Another estimate is that by 1975, the U.S. already had 3.5 million Mexicans, both legal and illegal, permanent and temporary, in the work force. A 1977 estimate by the Los Angeles police force put the total illegal population in that city alone at 650,000 people, of whom most would have been of Mexican origin—a claim vigorously disputed as grossly exaggerated by academics working in the field.

There is agreement, however, among most students of the Mexican migration problem that several new patterns have evolved in the past decade:

1. There has been a sharp increase in illegal immigration, reflected in the greater number of illegals being apprehended and returned to Mexico by the Immigration and Naturalization Service.

2. There has been a shift toward more permanent residence and longer periods of residence in the U.S. by the newer arrivals, apparently reflecting both the increasing economic pressures in Mexico and the new opportunities for integration in the U.S.

3. Emigrants are arriving in greater numbers from nontraditional centers of emigration from Mexico to the U.S. —the southwest and southeast instead of north and central areas of Mexico from which had come the great migrations of the 1920s and 1930s.

4. The Mexican influx to the U.S. is becoming more diffused around the country, no longer remaining in the traditional barrios in the Southwest.

5. Although relatively small in statistical terms, the U.S. is now receiving a heavy migration of upper middle-class and upper-class Mexicans, uncharacteristic of Mexican emigration (except for small numbers of Porfiristas who arrived in 1910).

Again, quantifying these observations is difficult and the expert observers vary widely in their estimates. But it is obvious that if the economic situation continues to deteriorate in Mexico, for all the reasons presented here, there are likely to be increasing attempts by Mexicans to emigrate to the U.S. Following the 1982 devaluations,

the border surveillance organizations on the U.S. side were reporting a 50 percent increase in the flow of illegal crossings. Figures
for the return of deported illegals seemed to reflect this, although it
could be argued that this was the result of greater vigilance by U.S.
officials. Many observers saw even the Simpson-Mazzoli immigration
bill, defeated in Congress in 1984, as a stimulus to Mexicans to try
to make it into the U.S. before more stringent U.S. legislation went
into force.

That large numbers of emigrants now entering from the states
of Oaxaca, Chiapas, and Tabasco in southern Mexico present a host
of new problems for the populations of these states are culturally different from the older sources of Mexican migration. They tend to be
poorer, less integrated into the modern Mexican economy, and more
"Indian"—both culturally and racially—than the northerners and the
people of the central plateau. Some Mexican experts also contend
that because they come from areas which in the past spoke Mayan
rather than Nahuatl (the language of the Aztecs and many of their
conquered peoples), they constitute a quite different ethnic group and
pose different problems of integrating with Americans. They also appear to be more desirous of returning to their native villages than
other Mexican emigrants—at a time, paradoxically, when the number of those staying on longer or permanently is increasing.

Although the statistical information is scarce and subject to
debate, proof that the Mexican emigrants are staying longer is
evidenced by their moving into occupations other than simple agriculture labor which was once virtually their only source of employment. The writers of the study on southern California point out that
there has been an expanding opportunity for Mexicans and Mexican-
Americans in nonseasonal, unskilled, and semi-skilled urban jobs in
Southern California since 1970. And a visitor sees anecdotal but striking evidence: A trade union official who has watched events in Los
Angeles for more than 35 year points to unions in the garment industry where Mexican labor has almost totally replaced blacks in
recent years. A bus driver for a rental car agency in San Diego explains that his English is poor because has has not been in the country
for long. An airport hotel bellboy in Albuquerque is obviously a recent
arrival.

Again, as to the dispersion of the Mexican emigration outside the
Southwest, statistical evidence is poor. But the constant news reports
of an increasing number of Mexicans in eastern cities where the community has been traditionally small indicate this trend, not to mention reports covering other sections of the country—for example, of
expulsions and difficulties of Mexican labor in the timber industry of
Oregon, Washington, and other parts of the Northwest.

Perhaps no trend is as hard to document as the arrival in the U.S. of a new group of members of the Mexican elite. Their numbers may be small, but there is constant gossip in Mexico City among professionals concerning those who have bought homes in the U.S. or who have sent their children to the U.S. A representative of one of the international Jewish welfare organizations reports that non-Jewish Mexican friends—mostly upper middle-class—constantly approach him to ask about the mood and the intentions of the small but relatively prosperous and influential Jewish community in Mexico. "The Jews have a nose for catastrophe, and I want to know what they are doing," was the way one typical inquirer put the questions to him.[8] During the pre-1981 boom, purchases of homes in the U.S. by individual wealthy Mexicans through American banking facilities in the Southwest reached into the billions of dollars. Houston, for example, has thousands of young and middle-aged Mexican professionals who have entered businesses there in what appears to be a permanent exile.

What is clear from this brief resumé of Mexican emigration to the U.S. is that today it stems both from the "push" of Mexican conditions and the "pull" of U.S. conditions, though in the past it was largely conditions inside Mexico that dictated the level of migration. The threat to U.S. stability lies not in a continuing Mexican emigration which would supply the U.S. with a reservoir of new workers, enrich our cultural diversity, and provide us with the kind of emigrants whose ethos has been one of the mainsprings of the American society's growth and progress since the founding of the Republic. But, looking back at the results of the eruptions of 1910–1924, what would happen if there were a new such period of instability in Mexico? Would Washington wake up one morning after the first shots in a new upheaval in Mexico to find literally millions of refugees scampering across the poorly defended U.S. southern border? That is the nightmare which Americans have to consider.

Since 1924, numerous intercultural factors have laid a new network between Mexico and the U.S. The new Mexican highway system, the profusion of radio and television, dominated by American programming, and the growth of the border cities all suggest that, in the event of a new upheaval, the flow of refugees from Mexico would be enormous. The extent to which this idea has become commonplace among Mexicans is demonstrated by two recent *romans-à-cléf: El Golpe, Operación Incruenta*, by Manuel Sánchez Ponton, and a sequel, appropriately entitled, *Estampida*.[9] The novels present a scenario in which a right-wing coup fails to rescue Mexico from its present crisis, a commonly held belief of future events by many middle-class Mexicans today. The huddled *pacíficos*, who in an earlier period tried to keep out of the way of the fighting and the banditry, this time are poised to flee to the U.S. And recall, not only is the Mexican population five times bigger than it was in 1910, but the restraints on movement which existed in that largely rural Mexico no longer obtain.

It is no exaggeration then, to speculate that literally millions of Mexicans might flee their country *if*, once again, there were a societal breakdown. Nor is it clear what the American response would be to a catastrophe for which no preparation has been made either in Austin, Sacramento or Washington.[10]

Chapter 8: **Law and Order on the Border**

Only the relative isolation of much of the Mexican border prevents it from becoming *the* major concern of U.S. authorities fighting crime and disorder.

For some three-quarters of its route from the Pacific to the Gulf of Mexico, the border runs through some of the loneliest desert in the world before it reaches the Rio Grande at El Paso. In much of this area, one can travel for miles—and days—without seeing anyone but the occasional U.S. law enforcement officer, perhaps only a Department of Agriculture employee chasing a stray cow to prevent the spread northward of the hoof- and-mouth disease that periodically infects Mexican cattle.

The Border Patrol has some four hundred officers, mostly engaged in chasing illegal immigrants. (One federal officer reckons that about 80 percent of the law enforcement activity on the border deals with immigration, the rest with drugs and smuggling.) They have helicopters, small aircraft, and ultramodern detection devices to help them halt the constant infiltration of the border. But it is not through these isolated areas, for the most part, that the illegal emigrants try to enter; when they do, there is an occasional tragic death due to thirst and exposure in the desert.[1] The main movement of Mexican illegals into the U.S. takes place near the large centers of population, at San Diego, El Centro, El Paso, Brownsville, and other major urban centers that abut on the border. And the Border Patrol must catch them at the point of entry if they are to be apprehended. For once across into the downtown areas of any of theses cities with their large Mexican-American populations, it is unlikely that they will ever be caught, except in expensive and ugly raids on factories or other enterprises where the illegals are working. Increasingly, many of the undocumented migrants move north of the border cities toward anonymity and jobs in the big cities in California, the Middle West, and even the South and the East.

The jig-saw puzzle of who is a Mexican, who a Cuban American, Salvadoran or Dominican, or a half dozen other Latin American nationalities (or who is Puerto Rican and therefore an American citizen) is harder and harder for even officialdom to resolve. Spanish accents are revealing, of course, but rarely are the emigration officers expert enough to detect the differences. And they can be disguised.[2]

The tragic elements in this situation and the growing disparity between the law and the reality of the border are creating a terrible problem for the authorities. "But if the immigration issue is a confusing one for the nation—Gallup polls indicate strong popular support for tighter immigration controls, but contemporary movies and Top 40 songs romanticize the plight of the aliens—the Border Patrol sees things in clearer and simpler terms," writes Todd Ackerman after a visit to the border in an account sympathetic to those who must enforce the law.[3] "The butt of ugly portrayals in the popular press, stereotyped as 'villains to a noble people looking for a better way of life,' they're defensive about their image and skeptical of the media. . . . For the most part, they are dedicated men: hard-shelled, patriotic and adroit at separating feelings from actions. Moral qualms are not their line of work. Instead they see themselves as upholders of the law, just as the military sees itself as defenders of the land. To a man, they're 'doing a service for their country'."

The lawlessness which surrounds immigration on the border is bound to produce a spiral of fraud and violence. Ruthless "coyotes" smuggle the aliens past the U.S. authorities at from $300 to $1,000 a head. A typical week in San Diego, Ackerman reports, will result in as many as 40,000 aliens being apprehended, and instead of serving prison sentences and being fined, they are simply turned back to Mexico. The estimate at this entry point is that as many as two aliens make it into the country for every one that is caught.

Into this atmosphere of fear and violence—there are often shootouts on the California border—have wandered an unlikely coalition of religious leaders determined to blunt the government's policy toward illegal aliens. More than 150 religious congregations across the country, according to the *National Catholic Register*, including Protestants, Roman Catholics, and Jews, in churches as far removed from the border as New York, were offering "sanctuary" to illegal aliens in 1984. (*The New York Times* reports the number had risen to 270 by midsummer 1985.) They are sheltering or transporting Central American refugees who cross the border in defiance of the authorities. According to the Rev. John Fife of the Southside Presbyterian Church in Tucson, "I think we have every legal right to do what we are doing. The current U.S. policy [in Central America] is a violation of the humanitarian ideals the country was built on. Every group that has studied the situation in Central America has informed the Reagan Administration that these are political refugees, not economic. We have to understand the nature of evil in our time. The guys in the Border Patrol aren't bad guys. The evil is in huge, impersonal bureaucracies, disconnected with reality, that make policy." The rather acerbic reaction of a U.S. Immigration and Naturalization Service official in Washington, D.C., was that while his service knew that they had the legal right to enter the churches, there were so many illegal aliens outside, they really had no time to correct this infraction of the law. But by Nov. 20, 1985 Immigration Commissioner Alan C. Nelson, in a letter to the House Judiciary Committee, cautioned that the whole concept of church sanctuary "was eliminated from law in England centuries ago and has absolutely no basis in American law."

And eleven members of the sanctuary movement were put on trial in Tucson, Arizona, in 1985 as a result of a nine-month government investigation the year before. They were charged with multiple conspiracy of conspiring to bring illegal aliens into the country and transporting and harboring them. The trial judge, Earl H. Carroll, condemned some of the government's practices of infiltrating the churches but said that it did not warrant the dismissal of the suit. And in January 1986, a suit was brought by two national church bodies, the Presbyterian Church (USA) and the American Lutheran Church, joined by four local churches in Arizona to halt the government from secretly taping their assemblies in search of illegal aliens. The government answered their legal brief by contending that infiltration was a normal and legal part of criminal investigation. The churches charged that the government's investigations—which included paying informers to infiltrate the operations of the church to smuggle illegal aliens across the border—were a violation of the constitutional guarantees of religious freedom. Rep. Peter W. Rodino, Jr. (D., N.J.), wrote Attorney-General Edwin Meese 3rd asking into the Justice Department's guidelines on the whole issue and whether it "distinguishes between entering a church for the purpose of making arrests as opposed to entering a church to gather evidence for a criminal case."

The convoluted controversy was an example of how what had been localized border problems were becoming regional, even national issues, as the Mexican crisis deepened. For while the sanctuary movement leaders had eschewed any connection with Mexico, other than using the facilities of fellow believers south of the border to transit it, the possibility that they will one day see Mexicans as well as Central Americans as victims of political persecution who must be given entry to the U.S. is not far fetched.

The growing numbers of migrants and their increasing impact on local environments,[4] even those far from the border, are ending the once geographic isolation of the southern border. Sitting in a beautiful old Mexican *posada* having a quiet dinner in Laredo, Texas, old residents, with an acknowledged sympathy for Mexico and the wretched Mexican "mojado," (wetbacks), complain that the enforcement of the immigration law is producing a growing atmosphere of violence and fear in their area. And it is clear that if human beings cannot be stopped from moving back and forth across the border at will, other commodities will move as easily—if not more easily.

That may well be. The growing defiance of the law is creating a belt of vigorous criminal activity along the Mexico border. In 1984, it accounted for at least one-third of all the heroin imported into the U.S. A third of all the heavy equipment stolen in the West and the Midwest—particularly automobiles—ends up in Mexico. And this despite the deployment of a vast array of law enforcement talent on the border—the Immigration and Naturalization Service, the Border Patrol, the Federal Bureau of Investigation, the Drug Enforcement Agency, the Secret Service of the Treasury, the Central Intelligence Agency resources, and the local city, county, and state law enforcement organizations. That may be one of the problems. For in law enforcement, as in other relationships along the border, the welter of organizations on the U.S. side makes cooperation difficult. The highly centralized Mexican administration—whatever its other myriad failings—means all negotiations on border problems must go through Mexico City.

The U.S. has tried fitfully, with some slight intermittent success, to integrate the various agencies and approaches to the border problem. In 1976, the Organization of U.S. Border Cities and Counties (OUSBCC) was created to work out a coordinated local approach to the border issues that could be presented to the federal government, but funding was exhausted by 1980. That same year, the Southwest Border Regional Commission was organized, one of eight regional commissions, to provide planning and coordination to help solve economic and social problems in the areas. But by 1981, the four border governors who had participated in the organization voted to disband the commission as "an unecessary layer of federal bureaucracy." There was general agreement that the commission had become a political football between its original Democratic sponsors and the Reagan administration. Yet another organization came into being in the early 1980s, composed of governors of the border states —four from the U.S. and ten from Mexico—who meet annually and establish committees to work on individual problems. But these meetings have turned into highly social gatherings—particularly when hosted by the Mexicans who make an enormous effort to make them successful social events. One Mexican-American Congressman who attended these meetings says that rarely is anything of substance discussed, and while they provide a social environment in which good will can be built up between Mexicans and Americans, little else is accomplished.

The Reagan administration has also introduced two new commissions, the U.S.-Mexico Trade Commission, and the U.S.-Mexico Binational Sectorial Commission headed by the two foreign ministers. But there is little to suggest that these new bodies will accomplish any more than their predecessors. "The issues that face us at the U.S.-Mexico border are in many ways the same that face the [developed] 'North' and the [non-developed] 'South' as the dialogue in the international arena," writes San Diego State University Professor Norris Clement, a student of the border problems.[5] And they appear just as intractable of solution.

Yet, curiously, drug traffic enforcement—that most difficult of all law enforcement problems—was one of the issues during the late 1970s where there was extensive and successful collaboration between Mexican and U.S. authorities. In 1975, when the American heroin epidemic peaked, American authorities estimated that 87 percent of the heroin consumed in the U.S. originated in Mexico, earning the Mexican traffickers as much as $500 million annually. Because the Mexican manufacturing process turns out a product which is brown, rather than the crystalline white that comes from South America, southern Europe, the Middle East, and the Far East, it is quite easily identifiable.

In the mid-1970s, the U.S. persuaded the Turkish government to move in on its producers, which had been the largest source of America's clandestine drug trade; and the French, concerned about their own rising narcotics addiction, closed off "the French connection" whereby raw opium from the Middle East was processed into heroin in the south of France and then shipped to the U.S. and northern Europe. Mexican producers rapidly filled the void and became the principal supplier for the U.S.

In 1969, the problem along the border became so serious that U.S. officials determined to bring it to the Mexican government's attention. The efforts of the Mexican army since 1962 to eradicate drug crops manually and with fixed-wing light planes had obviously failed. So the U.S. introduced a crash program, a new set of strict border controls that virtually paralyzed the border crossings and, of course, the tourist trade. Although they were relaxed after twenty days, they succeeded in getting the Mexican government's attention and convinced Mexico City that there would be no cooperation in other bilateral areas important to Mexico unless they cooperated with U.S. antidrug authorities.

In 1970, the two countries entered into a joint program—with U.S. financing. But the methods used were insufficient. In 1976, López Portillo, inaugurating his administration with the prospect of extensive collaboration with Jimmy Carter, allowed U.S. authorities to manage a massive effort to halt the raising of poppies in lowland Mexico from which the heroin was processed. The U.S. deployed personnel and some seventy planes into Mexico and with the collaboration of the Mexican authorities isolated poppy-growing to small mountain patches in faraway localities. The latest techniques were used and herbicides were dropped from the air over poppy and marijuana plantations which had flaunted their presence throughout the early 1970s in northern and western Mexico. In 1975, an estimated sixty-five tons of opium producing 6.5 tons of heroin were captured. By 1977, at the high point of the eradication campaign, some ten thousand acres of heroin—enough to produce ten tons of opium—were destroyed.

But with the general breakdown in relations between the López Portillo regime and the United States, Mexican authorities insisted in the late 1970s that they take over the conduct of the campaign. The U.S., sensitive to Mexico sovereignty, agreed and especially as these requests came during the height of the oil boom when López Portillo and other Mexican officials felt that they no longer needed U.S. cooperation. In fact Mexico with its enormous oil reserves held the upper hand in any negotiations.

The result has been disastrous. By 1982, forty-hectare fields of marijuana were discovered by U.S. intelligence in northern Mexico. Mexican enforcement soon became a joke. The surveillance aircraft, nominally in pursuit of these small mountain patches of narcotics simply overflew the large concentrations of flourishing drug plants.

By 1984, Mexico was supplying the U.S. heroin market throughout the West, much of the Midwest, and part of the South. A spectacular raid on marijuana caches in northern Mexico late in 1984 netted authorities more than ten thousand tons—eight times more than had been estimated was grown in all of Mexico in a year. Only the large imports from South America and the new center of manufacture in the Pakistan-Afghanistan border areas (and the preference for white over brown heroin) have kept Mexico from again becoming the principal supplier to the U.S. And that may have happened again in 1985.

Unless American authorities can find some new way to force the attention of the Mexican government on the problem—or the De la Madrid administration, for its international image and to effect the maximum economic cooperation with the U.S. does so on its own—it will again assume epidemic proportions.

The drug problem is particularly difficult for De la Madrid. Although Mexican-American youth in the barrios of southern California and Texas have always been a prime target for drug abuse, the Mexican traffickers have never sought to establish markets in Mexico itself, where it is a relatively limited social malaise, largely among the members of the elite. (There has been a rapid increase in the use of cocaine recently in Mexico City, apparently an extension of the American phenomenon, where it has become the drug of preference among young, upwardly mobile professionals.) That may be simply because the traffickers fear that should they do so, Mexican authorities would come down on them with the violence and lack of juridical scruples that characterize the PRI regime when it moves against enemies of the state. It may also be that the Mexican government understands the hazards that vast sums of money paid for drugs consumed in Mexico would create and has made its feelings clear to potential violators in Mexico.

Whatever the reasons, the drug problem is a bilateral issue between Mexico and the U.S.—one that cannot be ignored by either side, and for which no international "Third World" rationalizations to excuse Mexico are possible. The Reagan administration—with Vice President George Bush in direct command of an intraagency task force, has made the war on drug abuse and international trafficking one of its principal goals. The new attorney-general, Edwin Meese, made it a subject of discussion in his first meeting with his Mexican counterpart in August 1985, and issued the usual perfunctory statement on the effective cooperation between the two governments. It is true that due to the killing of an American antinarcotics officer and his pilot in Guadalajara in the spring of 1985, the Mexicans moved in on some highly placed narcotics "kings." And De la Madrid did undergo the embarrassment of stopping the head of secret service from running for Congress in the elections of July 1985 because of his reported association with well-known drug dealers. But the drug traffic is so much a part of the skein of corruption and inefficiency in the Mexican government and its police that one has to wonder how effective any program will be so long as there is such an enormous market across the border.

That became all too apparent in January 1986 when a scandal broke in one of Mexico City's prisons. Caro Quintero, one of Mexico's most notorious drug kingpins, had an altercation with his jailers. Quintero had been arrested for his involvement with the murder of the U.S. Drug Enforcement Agency officer in Guadalajara and his pilot and friend in the spring of 1984. Quintero's lawyer complained that Quintero had been beaten by his guards and that $6 million in U.S. currency and television receivers, hi-fi equipment and other luxuries, had been stolen from his jail cell. Mexico City newspapers further reported that the prisoner, under indictment for drug trafficking, had been permitted to leave prison and dine at some of Mexico City's most fashionable restaurants. That De la Madrid was unable to maintain discipline around as important a prisoner as Quintero was one more indication of the erosion of responsibility in the government because of its vast corruption.

Drugs are bound to preoccupy future U.S. administrations, not only because of the growing popular crusade against drug abuse, but because of the increasing geopolitical connections. There is growing evidence that the Communist government of Cuba is in league with some elements of the international drug smuggling operations, and, moreover, that the leaders of the Sandinista regime in Nicaragua have been using it to raise funds and extend their influence. The government of Colombia at Washington's insistence, the principal source of cocaine, has tried to use its influence to halt the traffic. But Mexico because of its geographic proximity, poses a special problem.

The drug traffic is bound to have a basic priority with Washington negotiators in the whole bundle of issues between the two countries and with Mexico increasingly dependent on U.S. aid. And certainly De la Madrid, in his pursuit of "moral rejuvenation," must be sensitive to the issue.

The question is, of course, how to do it. The almost universal corruption of Mexican law enforcement officials arising out of their low salaries and their long tradition of *la mordida* (the bite, the bribe),[6] and the enormous profit in the drug trade will demand, as it did in the 1970s, direct American intervention in northern Mexico, with the grating infringement of Mexican sovereignty, and this at a time when Mexico City is already smarting under constraints imposed by U.S. banks and the International Monetary Fund. In the general deteriorating economic situation with falling real wages and a devalued peso, the evil flower of bribery and corruption is likely to blossom all over the country. And, undoubtedly, crime and corruption on the Mexican border—and the pervasiveness with which it penetrates into the U.S.—will be one of the major problems for U.S. law enforcement in the decade ahead.

Chapter 9: In Search of a Policy

The greatest impediment to the formulation of a consistent and effective American policy toward Mexico is the lack of a domestic constituency in the U.S. for any Mexico policy.

Although Mexico is traditionally the third or fourth customer of American business—it was number two in the oil boom years—the U.S. business community's relations with Mexico are so diffused that policies and policy issues can rarely be focused through one or a group of industries. That is not true with Japan, for example, which is, overwhelmingly, the largest foreign customer for U.S. foodstuffs and agricultural raw materials, and thus the U.S. agricultural industry constantly monitors Japanese trade policies. Likewise, because of the enormous competition, the American automobile and electronics industries keep tabs on Japanese imports and pricing methods. These groups form a knowledgeable constituency which may not always be able to muster an effective strategy to pressure for policy formulation, but which at least can define the issues for the public debate.

The inability to focus American concerns on Mexico is the result of the variety of the trade, the diversity of the exports and imports to Mexico. Of Mexico's varied imports from the U.S., only automobile parts, wheat, and corn bulk large. A result of Mexico's new industrialization is that she is heavily dependent on intermediate manufactures from the U.S. for her own finished products. And in the past, with virtually a free exchange of currencies, Mexican consumers had only tariff barriers against highly protected local manufactures to limit their demands on these imports. That explains, perhaps, why there is no powerful Mexico lobby among the exporters.

Nor does the Mexican-American community, for all its size, exercise any appreciable influence on policy toward Mexico. There is no comparison, for example, between the impact of the Mexican-American community on policy toward Latin America and the clout that American Jews have in making policy toward Israel and the Mideast—or for that matter, of U.S. blacks on policies toward Africa. The truth is that Mexican-Americans are too poor, too badly organized, and—perhaps above all—too ambivalent in their feelings toward their ancestral home to be able to lay out a U.S. policy toward Mexico. The complications of Mexican-American politics in Texas explain why pressure for a consistent policy toward Mexico may not come from this ethnic group until some time in the next century, if ever.[1]

An equally important factor in the formulation and implementation of a U.S. policy toward Mexico—or the lack thereof—lies in the inability of the U.S. to focus its efforts through one part of the federal bureaucracy. The Latin American section of the State Department has a notorious reputation for provincialism—there is less transferring of career service officers there than anywhere else in the system. (Although there was an attempt to remedy that through Kissinger's famous GLOP, Global Learning Operations Program, an effort to avoid overspecialization in the Department which turned quickly into a rationalization for a lack of expertise.) It called for a greater exchange of technicians in the Department from one region to another. U.S. diplomacy in Latin America has also suffered in the past from the lack of interest and prestige connected with postings in this hemisphere.

The U.S. ambassador to Mexico often finds himself at the center of a maelstrom of bureaucratic relationships between Mexico and the U.S. of which he is not even always aware, much less exercising control. One ambassador tells how he learned accidentally at a Washington cocktail party while on home leave of negotiations for a multimillion-dollar Export-Import Bank loan to the Mexican government which were then near completion.

Washington has periodically attempted to centralize its policy toward Mexico. The Carter administration, which made something of a fetish of the president's interest in Mexico, set up a series of consultative groups with López Portillo "at the presidential level," but they produced no significant results. Nor did Carter's later attempt, when he appointed a coordinator with ambassadorial rank, which only further confused the situation with "two ambassadors to Mexico."

Professor Sidney Weintraub, a former State Department political and economic career officer in Latin America, argues that it probably would not help to restructure the U.S. government's Mexico operations. "It may be that the decentralized U.S. negotiating style is inevitable, given the variety of interests that must be heard on each issue," he writes. "A czar in charge of Mexican affairs might be a powerless figurehead. It may also be harder for the United States to negotiate with Mexico than with most countries because the domestic part of each negotiation is apt to be extremely important. That is what makes illegal immigration so intractable."[2] In a sense, Ambassador Eugene Douglas, in what is essentially an upbeat article on U.S.-Mexican relations, is even more pessimistic: "Must we conclude . . . that the styles of government in the two countries are so different that the best the United States and Mexico can expect in their relations is to agree to disagree? The answer is a qualified affirmative. . . . the prospects of working out policy norms in formal intergovernmental agreements are dim. Yet, this conclusion does not necessarily validate the worst-case scenarios in U.S.-Mexican relations projected by many analysts."[3]

As the Mexican crisis deepens, the impacts will be felt immediately by the Mexican-American ethnics—particularly the bulk who live in the four Southwest border states. No one can read the history of this minority in the U.S. without deep sympathy for their past suffering and chagrin for our past failings. Despite the enormous heterogeneity of the Mexican-Americans in caste, education, and wealth, in talking with them today about their family histories in the Southwest, one comes to realize that many families have been victims of discrimination which predates their arrival in this country and explains their whole attitude toward society. *Los de Abajo*, a novel of the Mexican Revolution, speaks of these traditional animosities as they existed in the 1920s and which carry over into modern Mexico and into the Mexican-American community in the U.S. today.[4]

A portion of the Spanish-speaking population in New Mexico, for example, sees itself as a group apart, attributing its uniqueness to its descent from the first Spanish settlers in the region dating to the explorations of Juan de Oñate, El Adelantado, into what is now New Mexico, in 1598. De Oñate founded the village of San Gabriel de Los Españoles on the Chama River. These Spanish-speaking New Mexicans claim descent from Spaniards and Apache Indians, but not from Mexicans. Whether in fact that remains a genetic truth given the migrations backward and forward to Mexico and the racial melting pot that has always obtained in Mexico, may not be important. Other New Mexicans of Spanish-speaking ancestry dismiss the whole differentiation as anachronistic, an old one brought over from Mexico, *"los ricos y los pobres."* The fact is, wealth and education have created a subculture among a small number of "old families" in the state who distinguish themselves as "Hispanos" rather than as "Mexican-Americans" or "Chicanos."

A Sacramento city official explains that his parents, despite their forty years in the U.S., have by choice not taken American citizenship. But they are equally ambivalent about their Mexico identity. When a parent tells, in this case, the middle-aged son, that "they" won't ever accept him in their society, the "they" encompasses more than just *gringos*. It goes back to a history of persecution or deprivation in Mexico which drove them to emigrate to the U.S. In this particular case, the mother is a Yaqui Indian with that northwest Mexico group's long history of conflict and suffering at the hands of the Spanish colonial and then the Mexican federal governments, including mass deportations to the Philippines and Yucatán. A young bank executive in San Francisco, the quintessential ambitious young white collar worker on his way up, tells how his emigrant parents keep telling him that he ought to get a trade where he could work with his hands, for sooner or later "they" will force him to that kind of job. A very successful data processing consultant in Los Angeles tells how his parents fled Mexico in the 1920s, and he asks rhetorically: "Do you think I can identify with that mess of corruption and repression down there?"

Yet it is equally evident that the Mexican-Americans—perhaps more than any other ethnic group in contemporary America—give much allegiance to their cultural heritage. And incidentally, it refutes the fear of the Mexico City intelligentsia that *norteamericanismo* is a deadly peril for Mexico's society and its culture. That a Mexican ethos, however difficult to define, persists—and one can confidently predict, will continue to persist for generations—among Americans of Mexican descent is proof that it can withstand the perils of "American cultural imperialism" in "the old country" itself.[5]

The ambivalence of the relationship between Mexican-Americans and Mexico will be a crucial factor in the decades ahead. The "professional Hispanic,"[6] those largely self-appointed spokesmen for the Mexican-American community and other Spanish-speaking groups in the U.S., insist that relations with Mexico are a primary concern of Mexican-Americans. That might apply to a few highly politicized Mexican-Americans but not to the community as a whole. And, talking with these politicians, one is aware that their interest in Mexico, at least in large measure, is related to the spin-off effect they hope any U.S. preoccupation with Mexico would have on the Mexican-American community. That is, there is evidence that these Mexican-American politicians in California and Texas see the growing importance of Mexican-U.S. relations as an aid in removing, at long last, the veil from their past plight, from their existence as "the invisible minority."

It remains to be seen, of course, whether the growing political consciousness and participation among Mexican-Americans in the region will result in a strong "Mexico" plank in their political agenda.

Mexican leadership, until recently, has not only ignored the Mexican-American population in the U.S., but has considered it an embarrassment. It was living testimony to the failure of the Mexican government to provide a living to the large numbers of Mexicans who had to flee to the U.S., where—viewed from Mexico City— they live lives in cultural separation and subject to discrimination. Although rarely admitted, Mexican leaders in government and business, who are generally drawn from the leadership caste, have condescended to Mexican-Americans who, for the most part, are descended from Mexicans who lived in the mother country at the lowest economic and cultural levels. It is no secret that Mexico City does not appreciate the appointment of U.S. ambassadors who have Mexican ethnic origins. Neither the "cool" child of the 1960s, the academic in blue jeans, Julian Nava, Carter's ambassador to Mexico, nor the suave, European-sophisticated, jet-setter and movie star, John Gavin, Reagan's choice, has escaped Mexico's condescension—and its effects on U.S.-Mexican relations.[7]

The Mexican government remained officially ignorant of the Mexican-American community until the Echeverría administration, when the contradiction of his appeal to "Third Worldism" and Mexico City's disregard of Mexican-Americans forced an acknowledgement of the group, particularly those Americans whose politics were perceived in Mexico City as left-of-center.[8] This change of attitude in Mexico City coincided, of course, with a new activism among young Mexican-Americans—the so-called Chicano Revolution of the 1960s when Mexican-American activists agitated for greater rights and economic advantages.[9]

The Mexican effort had mixed results. Echeverría and his successor, López Portillo, bitterly resented the calls of Mexican-American radicals for amnesty for left-wing political prisoners in Mexican jails —some of whom had participated in armed revolts in the 1960s and early 1970s. And the traditional condescension of Mexican officialdom to Mexican-American visitors continued and was a major irritant for the Americans.[10]

It remains to be seen whether Mexico City will either want to exploit or know how to use the undoubted dormant pro-Mexico feeling that exists in the Mexican-American community as the group's political power expands. There may be worthwhile comparisons here with the Irish-American and his concerns for the native land of his ancestors after the massive emigrations to the U.S. before the turn of the century. The difference, of course, is that Irish passions—even admitting the emotion generated by contemporary tragedy in Northern Ireland—have cooled over the past fifty years as the problems were resolved, whereas the crisis in Mexico is likely to heighten in the next years and therefore impinge on the relationship of Mexican-Americans to Mexico. A time factor is also involved; that is, will the Mexican-American community come of age politically before the relations between the U.S. and Mexico climax and have to be met and at least partially resolved?

Mexican-Americans have been traditionally one of the lowest participatory groups in the U.S. political process.[11] That appears to be part and parcel of their inability to progress as fast as other arrivals in the American polity. Whether there is something basically different in the Mexican emigration or in the conditions of the U.S. at the time of their arrival, it is a fact that Mexicans have not only been poorly educated, had lower occupation and income standards, and faced discrimination—as have other U.S. immigrants—but the bulk of Mexican-Americans in the second and third generation have not made substantial progress. This situation has led to the contention that they are in this respect entirely different from the European or Asian emigrants.[12]

The attempt to make voting more attractive to non-English-speaking U.S. citizens among the Spanish-speaking population is a questionable effort. Amendments to the Voting Rights Act require local election officials provide foreign language ballots and voter material where more than 5 percent of the voting citizens are of a single minority who do not speak English adequately to participate in elections, or where the illiteracy of the group is higher than the national average (completion of the fifth grade). The law affects 376 jurisdictions in nineteen states. Richard K. Kolb questions the whole procedure because of its divisive effect on the American polity.[13] But he also offers evidence that it may be of no real avail. He points out that Kings County, California, spent $3,600 per each Spanish-language ballot with only eight voters using them. Another California county spent $6,619 without a single voter availing himself of the ballot.

There are obviously many reasons for the lack of political activity of Mexican-Americans in the past. Compared to other emigrants, there has been a low rate of naturalization and, therefore, of qualified voters. Discrimination in all its varied forms before the passage of the civil rights legislation and the radical Chicano movement of the 1960s also played a large role. (There is an anomaly, however, in that there has traditionally been more Mexican-American participation in Texas than in California, where discrimination has always been considered to have been less severe, giving rise to the speculation that discrimination played a positive role in stimulating the Texas-

Mexicans to use the political weapon as a way of striking back against discrimination.) And, of course, the whole array of social isolation, including language, contributed.

The question of bilingualism is also misrepresented in much of the Eastern liberal media. Many Mexican-Americans, some of whom participated in the civil rights movement of the 1960s, are of the adamant belief that bilingualism in education is regressive. One political veteran in Washington, himself a major figure in the first antidiscrimination suits filed in Texas in the 1950s, says: "If you want to lock the young people up in the *barrios* where the *caciques* can exploit them forever, then keep them learning in Spanish." Former Sen. Tetsuo Hayakawa, a semanticist, has the provocative thought that while it may be possible to talk in theoretical terms about a child mastering new ideas in his own languages, the fact is, those ideas are inextricably associated with the language in which they have been expressed and their real significance cannot be transferred to another language.

"Supporters of bilingual education today imply that students like me miss a great deal by not being taught in their family's language," writes Richard Rodríguez. "What they seem not to recognize is that, as a social disadvantaged child, I considered Spanish to be a private language. What I needed to learn in school was what I had the right —and the obligation—to speak, the public language of *los gringos*. . . .Without question, it would have pleased me to hear my teachers address me in Spanish when I entered the classroom. I would have felt much less afraid. I would have trusted them and responded with ease. But I would have delayed—for how long postponed—having to learn the language of public society. I would have evaded—and for how long could I have afforded to delay?—learning the great lesson of school, that I had a public identity."[14]

All of these arguments are perhaps as important, and perhaps in the long run more persuasive, than the more generally held contention concerning national unity. This holds that English is the unifying factor in our heterogeneous and pluralistic society, and to encourage the use of other languages (at government expense and with government encouragement) is to experiment with a dangerously divisive device, however well intentioned. The new secretary of education, William J. Bennett, launched an attack on the federal legislation and subsidies for bilingual education in the late summer of 1985 arguing that it had accomplished little, despite expenditures of over $1.7 billion since 1968. There were immediate outcries from the professional Hispanic groups. But Bennett is likely to win support, particularly in a budget-tightening era.

Bilingual education is one of the issues that is likely to show up the cracks in the Spanish-speaking communities, particularly among the Mexican-Americans, which many believe is beset by the "crab syndrome." These observers, within and without the Mexican-American community, argue that there is a greater propensity among Mexican-Americans than among other groups for the community to pull down any one member who appears to have worked his way up to leadership.[15] Most Mexican-American political leaders deny this bitterly. But in an interview with a retired California civil servant and former radical who had worked among many ethnic groups and in trade union politics, he seemed to confirm the charge. He said that his most difficult problem in serving the governor had been his inability to identify and establish communications with leaders of the Mexican-American community, a problem unknown to other ethnic groups.

One of the aspects of the Mexican-American society that sets it apart from other ethnic groups is its heterogeneity. The various waves of immigration, the class and race differences carried over from Mexico, the scattered residences in the Southwest and elsewhere, and the vast economic and cultural differences have all contributed to a variegated group lumped under the term Mexican-American. That may explain why, while Mexican-American cultural and political organizations are not new, they have tended to be regional and local even while claiming national status.

The first national organizations consisted of Mexican-Americans in the armed forces in World War II and the Korean War (they have today the highest enlistment percentile of any ethnic group). These veteran organizations, which took up the cudgels against discrimination of their veterans, created a new atmosphere among Mexican-Americans in the 1950s.[16] The liberating wind of the civil rights revolution that swept blacks and American Indians in the U.S. also hit "the invisible minority," the Mexican-Americans, in the 1960s. But there has been and continues to be a reluctance among them to identify their problems with those of the blacks.[17] They still have difficulty with self-identification which is evident in that the terms they use to identify themselves vary from region to region; for instance, "Latin American" or "Latino" in Texas, "Spanish American" in New Mexico, and "Mexican-American" in California.

"Chicano," the term favored by the activists and the militants, has been transformed from a pejorative term to a badge of honor, much as did the word "black." But it is not acceptable to many older and middle-class Mexican-Americans. The Chicano Revolution, as Mexican-Americans nationalists like to call it, remains an amorphous series of episodes in the 1960s, for like all Mexican-American experience, it is heavily influenced by the regional differences in the U.S. Largely it is the story of flamboyant, sometimes violent, reactions among Mexican-Americans to individual episodes of discrimination, much of which had been traditional in the Southwest and traditionally accepted by the Mexican-Americans.

The movement had little by way of rational, ideological format. Many of the Chicano radicals were plagued with "vulgar" Marxism, but few had made a serious study of either Marxism or Marxist-Leninism as preached by European Communist ideologues. And in any case, their traditionalism and their nationalism—which generally included a fervent attachment to Catholicism—prohibited their acceptance of its dogmas. The Chicano radicals were courted with the usual American Communist doctrine concerning ethnic minorities, and some Chicanos got involved with armed radicals in Mexico. But it was far better characterized by such romantic notions as Aztlan—the legendary original home of the Aztecs, the barbarian nomads from the north who conquered the older and more stable civilizations of central Mexico. Some of the Chicano radicals gave this name to the territories in the Southwest which were claimed before the Mexican War by Spain and then by Mexico. It would, come the revolution, become a new homeland for Mexican-Americans, either as part of Mexico or, for those who had only contempt for the compromised bourgeoisie in Mexico, as a new country.

Few of these notions ever got beyond the slogan and demonstration stage. Nor have Mexican-American studies, by and large, fared any better than black studies in our major universities. They have become a refuge for those students who either could not or would not meet the demands of the tougher professional and liberal arts faculties. By the 1980s, many of the most militant and sophisticated Chicano radicals of the 1960s, along with their highly emotional and not very accurate presentations of the whole radical Chicano approach to the community's problems and the nature of the U.S. society, had drifted back to the *barrio*, merged with the growing government bureaucracies, or taken their place as professionals in the upward mobility that has characterized the community in the last two decades.[18] (In Houston, more than a third of the population of the barrio, the traditional areas where Mexican-Americans reside, has moved into the suburbs, and the Spanish surname is often the strongest tie to the older community.) And there is still no national organization among the Mexican-Americans which can claim to speak for them as the National Association for the Advancement of Colored People (NAACP) or even the Urban League has for blacks.

Some of the budding politicians, who speak of the unity of the Hispanic minority and seek to lump together Americans of Puerto

Rican, Cuban, Mexican, and other Spanish-speaking origins, are totally unrealistic. For instance: Although the politically active Puerto Ricans and Mexican-Americans have in the past identified with the Democratic party and liberal issues, the Cuban Americans in Florida have plunged into Republican party politics because of its tough stance toward Castro. Then there is Gov. Toney Amaya, a Mexican-American who ran into trouble with his own Democratic party in the New Mexico legislature when he tried to take command of the national lobbying effort for Spanish-speaking voters. The legislature was resentful that he spent so much time out of state, and this included the New Mexican Spanish-speaking legislators.

Voter registration, the chief weapon of the political activists, may not be as potent a weapon with this group as sometimes argued, since these new voters often follow older voting patterns. The threat of the growing "Hispanic" vote in the Southwest may well have been exaggerated. It is true, of course, that the Mexican-Americans in the Southwest are growing at a faster rate than other elements of the population.

Official U.S. census figures released in January 1986 show that one out of every 14 Americans is a Hispanic, that is, a person who identified himself as speaking Spanish or who carries a Spanish surname. That is 7.2 percent of the total population. From 1980 to 1985, this Hispanic population jumped almost 16 percent to 16.9 million people.

Mexican-Americans were the largest single group within this commuity. They were counted as 10.3 million or about five times the largest other Hispanic group, the Puerto Ricans. The median age in the Hispanic group was 25 years in 1985, some 23.2 percent older than a generation earlier, but still not aging as fast as the U.S. population as a whole. The Mexican-Americans had the largest families, averaging 4.15 persons as against a national average of 3.41.

In 1983, 42 percent of the entrants to Houston public schools carried Spanish surnames—by the year 2000 there may be 25 million Mexican-Americans living in the Southwest. But there is as yet no proof that their political consciousness is being roused nor that their votes will be tied to any one party.

The returns, so far, have been mixed. The first Republican governor of Texas since Reconstruction, William Clements, may have lost his race for reelection in 1982 to a Democrat because he lost the Mexican-American votes in the Rio Grande valley, and this despite his appointment of many Mexican-Americans to state office and his appeal to their conservative social values. Whether the Mexican-American swing to Clements' opponent was a function of their growing numbers—from 11 million in 1970 to 14 million in 1980—or simply the personalities of the two candidates will be a subject of debate for many years. Meanwhile, an intensive voter registration campaign in East Chicago, Indiana, a predominantly "Hispanic" city, in the summer of 1984, failed to get more than a poor third showing for a Mexican-American candidate for mayor. "The [incumbent] mayor pitted the Puerto Ricans and the Mexicans against one another here, and everybody lost," an East Chicago woman running for a judgeship said after an election in May. "Whereas the Mexican-Americans in the Southwest, the Cubans in Florida, and the Puerto Ricans in New York are homogenous, we in the Midwest are not yet."[19]

Ronald Reagan won some 20 percent of the Mexican-American vote in the 1980 election despite the traditional attachment of the Mexican-Americans to the Democratic party (largely as a result of their hero-worship of John F. Kennedy, the nation's first Roman Catholic president). In 1984 in Texas, Reagan more than doubled the Mexican-American vote of 1980—over 40 percent—despite a much better Democratic "Hispanic" organization, including a network among left-wing Catholics.[20] The Democrats' appeal to Mexican-Americans stems from Jack Kennedy's appeal as an almost mystical figure for most Mexican-Americans in the southwest and his portrait hangs in tens of thousands of homes like another Catholic icon. Public opinion polling in the Mexican-American community shows that its attitudes toward many of the political issues of the day are not those of the professional Hispanic Democratic leadership in Washington and New York. The overwhelming majority of the Mexican-American community remains essentially conservative, particularly on the social issues which touch family life, such as abortion, allegiance to the Church, and old-fashioned flag-waving patriotism.

This basic orientation of the Mexican-American community may finally be having its effect on the organizations founded by more liberal or radical activists. The League of United Latin American Citizens (LULAC), which comes closer than any other organization to representing the Mexican-Americans nationally, has been moving right away from its liberal-Democratic Party origins. Oscar Moran, LULAC's new president, announced in March 1986 an agreement in which the Adolph Coors Co. would contribute to Hispanic community causes. Previous LULAC leadership had not wanted to be associated with the notoriously conservative Coors family enterprise. Moran said the agreement "builds another bridge for the Hispanic Community with corporate America. . . . It's time for Hispanics to make the system work for us, instead of trying to go against the system."

Whatever other developments may occur within the Mexican-American community in the U.S., however, it seems certain that if conditions degenerate south of the border, the process of entering the mainstream of American life for the individual Mexican-American will assuredly become even more difficult. Aside from the economic and political effects, which all Americans will feel, it would be a blow to the Mexican-American self-esteem. If, just as Mexican-Americans are beginning to come out of their long history of cultural isolation from American life, the world is to have a dramatization of a corrupt, violent, unstable, and repressive Mexico, it will rebound on the lives of upwardly mobile young Mexican-Americans. It would present the world with the arch-stereotypes of Mexican life and culture from which members of the ethnic community are trying desperately to distance themselves. If you speak to Mexican-Americans about this, the almost universal reaction is one of dismay and resignation—or, by some of the more activist politicians, a simple denial of the possibilities.

The flood of immigration from Mexico is the most serious difficulty for Mexican-Americans in their relationship with Mexico—as it is for policymakers in Washington. The debate in the summer of 1984 on the Simpson-Mazzoli bill aimed primarily at stemming the unmanageable tide of illegal emigration from Mexico, was a microcosm of the contradictions that abound in the issue. It was only the precursor of many more debates to come. That it was debated at all reflects the visceral understanding throughout the country that the situation is out of hand, that we have, as proponents of the legislation argued, lost control of our southern border. The discussion of the bill also defied convention. For conventional wisdom dictates that important and controversial legislation cannot be aired in Congress during a presidential election campaign.

The measure was opposed by the Hispanic Caucus, a group of nine legislators of Spanish-speaking origin, who represented not only the Southwest but New York (largely Puerto Rican) and southern Florida (largely Cuban). Although the Hispanic Caucus and other "professional Hispanics" have steadfastly opposed all attempts to restrict emigration from Mexico and to deal with illegal immigration, repeated polls among the Spanish-speaking population have shown a contrary sentiment. A Gallup poll conducted in October 1983 among Spanish-speaking Americans showed that 75 percent favored legislation that would make it "against the law to employ a person who has come to the U.S. without proper papers." The same percentile thought that "everyone in the U.S. should be required to carry an identification card such as a Social Security card." And 62 percent said they favored a proposal "that illegal aliens who have been in the U.S. for seven years be allowed to remain in the U.S."

In other polls conducted by V. Lance Tarrance Associates and Peter D. Hart Associates, 51 percent of Spanish-speaking Americans favored reducing legal immigration to fewer than 450,000 a year, and 64 percent said that "tough restrictions on illegal immigration are the right approach because illegal immigrants take jobs away from American workers and give employers a way to avoid paying decent wages."[21] These results confirm am ambiguity about immigration, legal and illegal, among the Spanish-speaking community in the U.S., almost never reflected by the Hispanic lobby in Washington.

When the Simpson-Mazzoli bill came up, few—including Speaker of the House "Tip" O'Neill—expected that it would be discussed, much less passed. O'Neill, who opposed the bill, had prevented its introduction on the floor in 1983. But, to his embarrassment, in 1984 the Speaker had had to yield to pressures from the Senate to put it on the agenda when House opponents failed to prove their metal. Not only did the bill touch almost every facet of American social and political life, but the emotional issue brought out a host of factions: the ideologically motivated lobbies; the business community because of proposed sanctions against employers hiring illegals; the trade unions who want to see illegals curtailed but oppose importation of *braceros*; and the libertarians and religious with their concerns for human rights and families; and opposition to any kind to a national domestic identity system with which the legislation flirts.

In the end, Congress failed, after having struggled for three years with the issue in the waning hours of the congressional session before the 1984 presidential elections. Yet Congress went home with a consensus that something had to be done about immigration. Rep. Henry J. Hyde, a Republican conservative from Illinois, summed it up: "The legislative process worked. But there was an ambivalence that could not produce the necessary consensus for any version of the bill. Too many people, for different reasons, did not want a bill." Liberal House Democrats, led by Rep. Barney Frank of Massachusetts, wanted strong civil rights protection for illegal aliens written into the bill. Sen. Alan K. Simpson, the Republican conservative from Wyoming and chief sponsor of the legislation, accepted these strictures in an attempt to get a compromise piece of legislation—but with "the gravest reservations." The Reagan administration, while in theory in support of the Simpson-Mazzoli legislation, was worried about the cost of administering it. The heavy Californian influence in the administration sympathized with the complaints of the agribusiness community, which has for so long depended on the importation of seasonal workers from Mexico for crop harvesting. And libertarians in the administration feared the implications of the bill in new regulations for business, restrictions on the movement of people inside the country, and the right to work where and when one chooses.

The administration became even more cautious when presidential aspirant Walter F. Mondale attacked the bill as discriminatory during his campaign against Reagan, and the White House staff— led by the wary Chief of Staff James J. Baker—feared dramatizing the issue since Reagan had promised to sign the bill. Perhaps the final blow—which destroyed hopes for passage in a conference committee between the House and the Senate—was the argument that the measure, in its attempt to limit illegal emigration, would bring on discrimination against Mexican-Americans in their place of employment since employers would have to prove the U.S. identity of their own employees.

Although the sponsors of the bill maintained, and they were generally believed, that they did not intend discrimination, in a presidential election year with the media in hot pursuit of a phantom highly exaggerated Hispanic vote, the issue conclusively ended any hope of passage of the legislation in 1984. But the issue would assuredly return, again and again, to legislative halls. Whether new legislation introduced in 1985 (this time sponsored by Simpson and the prestigious Democratic chairman of the House Judicial Committee, Rep. Peter Rodino of New Jersey) would make its way through the new Congress could well be dictated by events in Mexico and the flow of illegal immigrants.

One of the often-heard remedies for the wholesale emigration from Mexico, is that the U.S. should undertake a huge foreign aid program which would create employment and economic opportunities in Mexico. But, considering the enormity of the problem, such a program could only be remedial at best. Prof. Sidney Weintraub of the University of Texas at Austin, in a closely reasoned article,[22] writes that there is no assurance that a modest rise in economic opportunity would lead to a decrease in emigration in the foreseeable future. He argues convincingly that most emigrants do not come from the absolute bottom of the social and economic scale, that there are psychological and social factors involved in emigration, and that modest increases in economic opportunity would not satisfy them.

"Because of its large population," Weintraub writes, "bilateral aid cannot be used with any emigration-inhibiting effect in Mexico. In addition Mexico has never wanted U.S. aid on a bilateral basis. Neither has Mexico wanted official U.S. government encouragement to private companies to invest in Mexico. For all practical purposes, therefore, the only U.S. foreign economic policy instrument that is relevant for seeking to curtail emigration pressure from Mexico is trade policy. A general lowering of trade barriers would help Mexico to some extent, but probably not significantly if this were done on an MFN (most-favored nation, or equality with other exporting countries) basis because of Mexico's general lack of competitiveness in world markets for manufactured goods. Discriminatory tourist allowances in favor of Mexico could encourage U.S. tourists to go there, but this would have an uncertain effect on Mexican emigration. The U.S. is not likely to grant Mexico trade preferences in the absence of reciprocity." Weintraub concludes by pointing out that some countries have been able to get around a surplus of labor in recent decades, but only by pursuing successful overall economic development programs.

To some extent the *maquiladora* program between Mexico and the U.S. is an attempt to help Mexico solve its social and political problems with economic aid. The *maquiladora* plants are U.S. (and Japanese and European) manufacturers who have set up shop, for the most part, just across the border, and who receive special customs and tax advantages from both governments. They may import parts and other raw materials from the U.S. and other countries without payment of customs as long as their products are reexported to the U.S. market or other foreign markets. The advantages for the manufacturers are that they can employ cheaper Mexican labor, sometimes cheaper raw materials (electrical power, natural gas, etc.), and sometimes escape expensive U.S. environmental manufacturing standards. The Japanese and Europeans save in transport to the U.S. markets as well.

The operations have on the whole been extremely profitable for the U.S. multinationals and some smaller U.S. companies. Two billion-dollar U.S. automobile operations, one by Ford which is already operating, and one proposed by General Motors, will test the concept. And the Mexican government profits, despite its big tax concessions to the operations, because the *maquiladoras* are dollar earners which today is crucial for the Mexican economy. There are, moreover, some 250,000 jobs being created directly or indirectly in the border areas by these operations.

Yet it is questionable whether the *maquiladoras* are, indeed, an exercise in statecraft as far as U.S.-Mexican relations are concerned. The growth of the *maquiladoras* in the border areas have added to the migration into the border cities leaning up against the U.S. frontier, and have attracted far more workers from the job-scarce

Mexican hinterland than they can provide. Some 75 percent of the workers are women, and social workers are perturbed by what that means for families drawn to the plants. The men tend either to become immediate candidates for illegal migration to the U.S., or, even worse, they drift into quasi-illegal border activities. That is almost inevitable given the enormous macho characteristics of Mexican life even today which require that the male be dominant in every aspect of family relationships.

There is talk of extending the concept to plants operating further inland both to spread the employment effects into Mexico's interior and as a wedge in a new program to emphasize exports, which most Mexican economists advocate. But aside from the fact that the plants would immediately lose some of their economic advantage (like running into infrastructure problems that the foreign manufacturer escapes in the border areas), other problems threaten. One Japanese manufacturer who has located his *maquiladora* in a non-border area reports that his problems with the state and federal bureaucracy in that area have become unmanageable. A source who speaks for the Japanese business community says there will be no more Japanese *maquiladoras* built in nonborder areas, even should the present lull in Japanese investment in Mexico, arising out of the financial crisis, dissipate.

Other ideas have been explored. Given the depth of the crisis in Mexico with its possible repercussions for the U.S., some Americans in the Southwest and a few Mexicans argue that, with the evolving U.S.-Mexican relationship, Mexico must get imaginative, special economic and political treatment from the U.S. *The New York Times*, ever ready to get on a trendy bandwagon, editorialized Feb. 4, 1986, "Make a Side Deal With Mexico." "Unlike other debtors, Mexico has almost unlimited quantities of oil and a rich neighbor that remains critically dependent on foreign energy supplies. Isn't there room here for a special deal?

" . . . Just a few months ago Mexico still had some prospects for a bootstrap recovery (sic). . . . The United States should not and probably cannot try to negotiate debt concessions for only one country, no matter how close. That is a task for the International Monetary Fund and the private banks that provided most of the outstanding loans to big Latin debtors.

"But Mexico is inextricably linked with the United States, geographically and historically; its political and economic stability are a unique concern for Americans. And oil provides a way to affirm this special relationship with a special deal."

The *Times* goes on to suggest that special purchases of oil be made from Mexico for the strategic reserve, purchases that would compensate Mexico for the loss of oil revenue because of the worldwide oil price fall. "With Washington struggling to reduce Federal budget deficits, spending an extra $3 billion on oil might seem profligate. But the White House and many in the Congress nevertheless want to spend extra billions on national defense. It is hard to imagine a more cost-effective investment in national security—and financial stability—than helping Mexico to help us fill the strategic reserve."

That special treatment could include massive aid shifts—probably from other parts of the world—as well as trade concessions for Mexican exports aimed at the U.S. market. Whether such a policy is acceptable to the xenophobic Mexican elite which runs the country is questionable. Nor is it at all clear that such altruism on the part of the U.S., even were it possible given the U.S. domestic political scene, would be productive in the long run. Subsidization of any economy in any country risks running against market forces and ending up as a boondoggle or worse. That would seem to be particularly dangerous in Mexico, given its long history of inefficiency and corruption. The tally for massive U.S. aid all over the world since the end of World War II—excluding the rebuilding of the European industrial play by the Marshal Plan, which *rebuilt* industrial plants—has been neither greatly innovative nor successful.

Whatever the merits of such a program, at the present, it has no domestic constituency in the U.S. and is not realistically attainable even were it to become a major goal of the Washington administration. Given the U.S. political system, such a program most probably would not be generated until the Mexican crisis was so far advanced that long maturation programs would no longer be effective.

Not the least obstacle to such a policy is America's one-dimensional perception of Mexico, the result of the domination of the issue by the New York banks.[23] Having foolishly lent Mexico billions on a program built upon false assumptions in the late 1970s, the banks must now try to put the best face they can on the issue. Thus the De la Madrid deflationary program which seeks to maintain the country's international credit standing at any cost—including a drastic decrease in economic activity and growth—is presented not only as successful (as it is) in creating surpluses in the balance of payments temporarily but as a long-term program. And this it cannot be. The austerity program has a short lifespan economically, given Mexico's desperate need to get on with high growth, or politically, since its huge population is already living at abysmally low levels of subsistence. Furthermore, as lender after lender among the regional and world banks withdraw from Mexico's capital market because of their losses, the access to new capital which the country must have is vanishing.

If the refinancing provided by the New York banks cannot fuel the dynamism of the Mexican economy—as seems likely—any new arrangement will only accentuate the conflict between the need for investment capital and service charges on the debt. No matter how painful it may be for the U.S. banking system, if Mexican stability is to be enhanced in the longterm and Mexico is not to end up an abandoned baby on the American Southwest's doorstep, the bulk of the $100 billion foreign debt is going to have to be written off completely or set aside for very extended payment, and new lending under rigid standards will have to be forthcoming.

But beyond the financial problem, as crucial as it is, is the false sense of security that the New York banks have given many American observers about the state of Mexico's economy and political system. The U.S. Federal Reserve System chairman, Paul Volcker, in particular, has been party to the propaganda and false analysis. One can justify it—as one high Washington official did in an off-the-record interview—as an effort to save the international banking system. And while history is replete with victories that were won by creating false perceptions rather than facing awful truths, it remains to be seen whether that is to be possible in the case of Mexico. In the end, no juggling of statistics, of loans, of interest payments will be successful if confidence is not restored among *Mexicans* in the future of their country and its economy. That, as has been said repeatedly, is not a function of econometrics nor of financial analyses; it is a political decision. Mexico will have to turn its back on the political posturing of the past three decades if her policies are to be reversed and confidence is to be restored.

Chapter 10: In a World Perspective

Driving along a highway that skirts the Rio Grande on a beautiful winter's afternoon, an Easterner is suddenly struck by the breadth and sweep of the American West. (The Spaniards and the Mexicans have, by the way, always called it the *Rio Bravo* [fierce] which may be significant of our views of reality, for the river is not large, nor at its lower extremities is it wild.) It is a long way on such a day from Laredo to Brownsville, two Texas border towns. But one reason it is longer than usual is that much of the road that parallels the river is a two-lane highway and it is crowded with traffic. As you drive along you see Mexican license plates as well as Texan and other U.S. tags. But reflecting on borders in other parts of the world—Hong Kong and Communist China, West Berlin and East Berlin, or even France and Italy—you realize how little concern either the U.S. or Mexico has shown for barriers.

Were there to be an emergency along this border that required a U.S. military response or a deployment of American security forces, even the infrastructure could not support it. Apparently no one considered, when the federal interstate highway system was being built, that a route which ran from Brownsville at the Gulf of Mexico to San Diego on the Pacific Ocean might be useful to our national defense. Most of the traffic on our southern frontier is, after all, north and south through the border. In other areas further west, the border is, of course, even less well defined or policed. Tom Miller in a travelogue along the border has described how porous it is even at the formal crossing points.[1]

Should the U.S. one day face any of a variety of possibilities—destabilization in Mexico, chaos on the border, a flood of refugees, armed infiltration—it would demand an immediate reordering of military priorities of a magnitude not seen since Pearl Harbor. The deteriorating Mexican situation as described here gives life to that possibility. Yet there is no real contingency plan for such redeployment. And it is this more comprehensive nature of the coming preoccupation with Mexico that is more important than the bilateral problems themselves; that is, the problems a crisis for overall American world strategy that a crisis inside Mexico is likely to pose. While a crisis in Mexico would present enormous immediate problems— refugees, arms smugglers, drug traffic, Soviet and Cuban intrigues— its greater danger lies in the effect on U.S. world strategy. American policy worldwide would be skewed by the sudden dramatization of a Mexican crisis. In the South as well as in the Southwest, trouble in Mexico would be trouble at a geographic proximity that America has not witnessed in the twentieth century—with the exception of the Cuban Missiles Crisis in 1962.

For more than fifty years, the United States has concentrated its energies in both the diplomatic and security fields in, first, fighting World War II, chiefly in Western Europe and the South Pacific, the Middle East, and Southeast Asia, and second, in trying to secure the frontiers of the free world after the outbreak of the Cold War in Central Europe and on Fukushima and Taiwan Straits in East Asia. The ebb and flow of that tide has preoccupied Washington since 1948. It has meant occasional victories and occasional losses for the U.S. and its Western allies and Japan. The inactivity on our Western Hemisphere borders—again with the important exception of the 1962 Cuban Missiles Crisis—left our planners, our policymakers, and our administrative officials, academia and think tanks free to ignore Latin America.

Increasingly, that will not be the case. Already the international financial system is rocked by the major debtors, largely in Latin America, who cannot pay their borrowings—Mexico, Brazil, and Argentina, and an accumulated debt of considerable proportions among other Latin American countries.[2]

Just as the OPEC price increases and the embargo of petroleum in 1975 brought foreign policy issues home to every American at the gasoline pump, the Latin debt problem may also eventually redound in higher interest rates and the failure and merger of some major American lending institutions. But, as the United States comes "home" to this Hemisphere and Latin America, it finds a different Latin America than when last we made a determined effort to secure our interests there on the eve of World War II. For the ideological battles in Latin America have been sharpened by the trends of the last forty years. The economies which have failed to produce adequate growth for the mushrooming populations will now be at the mercy of ideologues of both left and right. That polarization has already taken place in Mexico where one set of Marxists calls for a new autarchic road to development. Pseudo-intellectual gibberish that passes for analysis of the economic and social development in the region in the last decades has become the norm.[3] One finds the Latin American shelves of our college bookstores loaded with this sort of brazenly rhetorical nonsense disguised as social, economic, and political criticism, thrashing over half digested nineteenth-century Marxist terminology and concepts that no longer have validity precisely because, as the authors acknowledge, the world has changed. One has to lament that this is the raw material with which our young scholars are trying to construct a basis for dealing with what will be major U.S. problems tomorrow.

Another concept, which has become identified with the neoconservative trends in the U.S. and Western Europe, calls for a return to the liberal philosophies of the nineteenth century in economics. Ironically, although Latin American leaders in the last century were dominated by concepts of European liberalism, the Latin variety put an emphasis on anticlericalism and rationalism in cultural affairs— on openness to new scientific ideas—rather than on the economic liberal aspects which were so strong in British liberalism. Perhaps the heritage of Spanish intervention in the economy was just too strong to overcome. In any case, today's advocates of laissez-faire in Latin America come on the scene as an almost new political philosophy and may have more in common with the American neoconservativism than with their own old liberal traditions.[4] That juxtaposition of forces— and perhaps Mexico typifies them better than any other country in the region—promises enormous frictions and dynamism in the coming decades.

Geographic proximity, if nothing else—even though modern communications have minimized its differences to some degree will dictate U.S. concern and involvement. For just as American isolationism in the 1930s failed, ultimately, to isolate the U.S. from the conflict in Europe, no amount of retreat within the Vietnam Syndrome will save the U.S. from paying a price for living in the same hemisphere with the chaos that is descending on the Latin states. The danger is that Washington—notoriously a one-crisis city—will find it difficult to focus on an ailing Mexico and Latin America without abandoning its worldview. Imagine, for example, a situation of disruption in Mexico with hundreds of thousands of refugees plunging across our southern borders. How much support would there then be for continuing a U.S. troop commitment in Western Europe? How much for our substantial forces in South Korea, the "trip wire" that prevents another attempt by the communist North to take over the peninsula and from threatening Japanese security, so important to the West as the second national economy in the world?

That simply means that the growing Latin American fragility—
and the possibility of a major upset of the regime in Mexico—must
become an integral part of the international strategic concept for the
defense of the West. It is from this vantage point that many of us
have viewed the events in Central America from the beginning of the
1970s.[5]

The self-evident fact of the crisis in Latin America makes such
documents as the Linowitz report—a policy statement on Latin
America prepared during the Carter administration—incredibly
naive. Only an extremely parochial leadership in Moscow could fail
to see the possibilities for provoking trouble in this region so as
to occupy American talents and power—especially since the disrup-
tive forces have had considerable aid and comfort from European Social Democrat bureaucrats (including Willy Brandt, chairman of the
Socialist International). Even important high level advisers in the
French government of President Francois Mitterand, who despite
his commitment to socialism has been a steadfast U.S. ally in op-
posing the Soviets, including Regis Debray, once Boswell to the
Argentine-Cuban revolutionary, Che Guevarra's Johnson, have aided
and abetted the forces of destabilization in Central America.

Although a few people at middle-echelon posts in the U.S.
government take a pessimistic view of events in Mexico, there is
no high-powered and sustained U.S. effort to monitor the situation,
much less to prepare for a crisis.

The Justice Department does have a classified emergency plan
in the event of an extraordinary influx of Mexican refugees, or one
aspect of the overall problem. The plan was developed as a result of
the landing of the Mariel Cubans in April 1980. That grew out of a
bizarre episode in which a group of Cuban dissidents crashed into the
Peruvian embassy in Havana in search of political refuge. The Cuban
Communist regime took the occasion to teach a lesson to the Latin
American governments which have traditionally offered sanctuary in
their embassies—the so-called right of asylum. When the Peruvians
refused to return the six, the Cubans flooded the embassy with some
10,865 persons within thirty-six hours, from Good Friday to Easter
morning. Negotiations began. The Cuban Communist government,
in a show of bravado before world public opinion, announced that
"whoever wanted to go could." The Carter administration, which
had initially offered to take 3,500 of the refugees, switched and offered a new policy of "open arms and open heart." Cuban émigrés
in Florida were authorized to go to Cuba with whatever transport
they could arrange to pick up their relatives. Castro responded by
(1) stepping up the defamation campaign against those who sought to

leave, (2) setting up El Mosquito camp near the port of Mariel for those who wished to leave, (3) substituting people—prisoners from jails, inmates of mental institutions, etc.—for those who wished to leave in order to damage the reputation of the wave of emigrants who departed. Somewhere between 2,500 and 3,000 boats of all descriptions crossed the Florida Straits bringing some 125,000 Cubans. "The slowness with which the Carter Administration made the decision of participating in the migration of 125,000 Cubans brought to Key West from Mariel by exiles or their agents, wreaked havoc in the bureaucratic process of receiving and assimilating the vast numbers of refugees who arrived day after day. The lack of coordination among the different levels of government—city, county, state, and federal —overwhelmed by the tide of Cubans fleeing their country, rendered the Immigration machinery pitifully inadequate."[6]

The obvious parallel to what could happen in the Southwest should there be a sudden destabilization in Mexico is easily drawn— and has obviously been drawn by the Justice Department officials who have prepared the plan.

But the mechanism of the U.S. government is such that it rarely can respond to anything less than a three-alarm call. There is a vested interest in viewing the Mexican situation with rose-colored glasses. And there is a legitimate fear that other views may be self-fulfilling prophecies in a volatile society so intellectually subservient to the fads and lore of its North American neighbor. In that sense, this volume may be provocative. But the unfortunate likelihood is that its pessimism will soon be reflected in daily events.

Notes

Introduction

1. "Why I Quit the CIA," *The Washington Post*, Jan. 2, 1985.

Chapter 1

1. Senate Armed Forces Committee, hearings on Central America, Feb. 23, 1983, Washington, D.C.

2. Ramón Eduardo Ruíz, Preface, *The Great Rebellion, Mexico 1905–1924* (W.W. Norton & Company, Inc., 1980).

3. Patrick Romanell, *Making of the Mexican Mind: A Study in Recent Mexican Thought* (University of Notre Dame Press Paperback, Notre Dame, Indiana, 1967, University of Nebraska First Edition, Lincoln, Nebraska, 1952).

4. John Kenneth Turner, *Barbarous Mexico*, Introduction by Sinclair Snow (University of Texas Press, Austin & London, 1969). This is a reprint of a famous muckraking book—Sinclair draws parallels to *Uncle Tom's Cabin*—which had much to do at the time with influencing U.S. sentiments toward the *Porfiriato*. Like *Uncle Tom's Cabin*, it was a rather naive and uninformed presentation of Mexico's complex problems.

5. John Womack, Jr., Preface, *Zapata and the Mexican Revolution*, (Alfred A. Knopf, Inc., and Random House, Inc., New York, 1969).

6. Lorenzo Meyer, "Historical Roots of the Authoritarian State in Mexico," *Authoritarianism in Mexico*, José Luis Reyna &

Richard S. Weinert, eds. (Institute for the Study of Human Issues, Inc., Philadelphia, Pa., 1977).

7. Octavio Paz, "From Independence to the Revolution," *The Labyrinth of Solitude, Life and Thought in Mexico* (Grove Press, New York, 1961).

8. Jonathan Kandell, "Letter from Mexico—Young Writers Discover the Urban Novel," *New York Times Book Review*, Nov. 11, 1984.

9. Several versions were made with the film footage Eisenstein turned in Mexico, including one more faithful to his original intent produced by Sol Lesser in 1933, entitled *Thunder Over Mexico*. Ephraim Katz, *The Film Encyclopedia*, (Thomas Y. Crowell, New York, 1979).

10. *El Exílio Español en México, 1939–1982* (Fondo de Cultura Económica, Mexico, D.F., 1982), a propagandistic compilation at the instigation of the late Castroite *Excelsior* columnist, Manuel Buendía, in celebration of the resumption of relations between Mexico and post-Franco Spain, is nevertheless an impressive summary of personal biographies of the exiles and their Mexican activities, and a documentation of their enormous impact on every facet of Mexican life.

11. Patricia W. Fagen, *Exiles and Citizens, Spanish Republicans in Mexico* (University of Texas Press, Austin-London, 1973).

12. Ibid.

13. That is not to say, of course, that large numbers and influential members of the Spanish emigration were not only not Communist but even dedicated anti-Communist, some enormously effective in refuting much of the Stalinist propaganda, e.g., the essayist Victor Alba who for many years wrote on Mexican and Latin American events for the anti-Stalinist New York publication, *The New Leader*, and the famous London-based historian, Salvador de Madariaga.

14. Burnett Bolloten, *The Spanish Revolution* (The University of North Carolina Press, January 1979).

15. The Italian-born Vidali (who before Spain had undertaken Stalinist activities in Argentina) ended his career in Trieste in the post-World War II period after Marshal Josef Tito's break with Stalin; and gossip in left-wing circles held that he was there to plot Tito's death, as it turned out unsuccessfully, as he had plotted Trotsky's in Mexico. Still later he was an Italian Communist senator after Trieste rejoined Italy. Vidali has also

been reported as the murderer of Julio Antonio Mella, a charismatic leader of the Cuban Communist party who sought exile in Mexico from the Machado dictatorship in 1929. See Ralph de Toledano, *Lament for a Generation* (Farrar, Straus & Cudahy, New York, 1960).

16. Isaac Don Levine, *The Mind of an Assassin* (Farrar, Strauss and Cudahy, New York, 1959).

17. "Meanwhile, in Mexico, Castro proceeded to assemble recruits for an armed invasion of Cuba. Their training was under Alberto Bayo, a one-eyed Spaniard born in Cuba, who served in the Spanish air force, helped overthrow the monarchy and was promoted to colonel in the Loyalist forces. . . . After the Loyalist defeat he emigrated to Mexico, became a Mexican citizen and a powerful figure in the Caribbean Legion." Nathaniel Weyl, *Red Star Over Cuba* (The Devin-Adair Co. Publishers, New York, 1960).

18. See John Reed, *Insurgent Mexico* (International Publishers, New York, Reprint, 1969), for a more realistic presentation of what events of the period must have been like. John Reed was then a young radical reporter but had not joined the iconography of the world Communist movement with his account of the Great October Revolution. (One can ignore the highly propagandistic introduction which is largely specious).

19. "In 1807 Napoleon was contacted by D'Esmenard, resident in Spain, who assured the emperor that Spain was decaying and with little effort her colonial commerce could belong to France. But of more immediate importance to Napoleon was, of course, the state of affairs in Europe. His lack of success in calming the Spanish 'ulcer' and in humbling England was complicated by the attitudes and actions of the Spanish colonists. For not only were the colonies providing financial assistance to the Spanish resistance which followed the Napoleonic invasion of 1808, but now he found England at the side of the colonial authorities. These dilemmas forced Napoleon to decide for Spanish colonial independence in 1809 in hopes of cutting off aid to his enemies. . . . Father Hidalgo's *grito de Dolores* came suddenly, before the French had anticipated, and too early for the Napoleonic agents to capitalize upon it or even to play a leading role in it. The eminent Mexican historian Ernesto de la Torre Villar has demonstrated, however, that Hidalgo himself may have been influenced by Napoleon's agents." Harold D. Sims, "Napoleon and Latin American Independence," *Americas*, Vol. 25, No. 8-9, August-September, Washington, D.C., 1973.

20. Colin M. MacLachlan and Jaime E. Rodriguez O., Preface, *The Forging of the Cosmic Race, a Reinterpretation of Colonial Mexico* (University of California Press, Berkeley-Los Angeles-London, 1980).

21. See, for example, Roderic A. Camp, *Líderes Políticos de México, Su educación y reclutamiento*, trans. Roberto Ramon Reyes Mazzoni (Fondo de Cultura Económica, México, 1983).

22. Octavio Paz, *The Labyrinth of Solitude, Life and Thought in Mexico*, trans. from the Spanish by Lysander Kemp (Grove Press, Inc., New York, 1961).

23. When the writer visited the lavish National Archaeological Museum in Mexico City in the winter of 1983–84, although official descriptions made no mention whatsoever of ritual human sacrifice and cannibalism as integral parts of the Aztec pre-Columbian culture, Mexican guides in English, French, and Italian were titillating foreign visitors with excruciatingly detailed accounts of these practices as they worked their way through the displays.

24. Peter H. Smith, "Is there a power elite?" *Labyrinths of Power, Political Recruitment in Twentieth-Century Mexico* (Princeton University Press, Princeton, N.J., 1979).

25. See a forthcoming study, Stephen Haber, "The Political Economy of Late Industrialization: Mexico, 1880–1940," doctoral dissertation, Department of History, University of California, Los Angeles, Cal.

26. See "Decimo censo: el otro México," *Proceso*, July 30, 1984, Mexico D.F., Mexico.

27. Raymond Vernon, "Economic Policies and Performance," *The Dilemma of Mexico's Development* (Harvard University Press, Cambridge, Mass., 1963).

28. Mexico's soft-drink industry, which has bottling facilities and distribution all over the country, is a mixed blessing of the new age. Commercial carbonated beverages provide hygienic beverages to millions who would otherwise not have access to safe drinking water and the sugar content of the beverages is an important part of the caloric intake of poorer Mexicans. The average per capita consumption is 125 litres of soda pop per year. But researchers expressed concern about the large amounts of caffeine consumed and pointed out that more nutritious fruit juices are generally available at lower prices.

29. The Opus Dei movement among Catholic laymen around the world is a clandestine organization of progressive and "modern"

capitalists attempting to improve the social and political character of the society. Its most significant appearance was in Franco's Spain in the last years of the dictatorship when it paved the way for liberalization of the economy, rapid economic progress, and the peaceful transitions to the post-Franco regime to a popularly elected government through participation of its members in the latter-day Franco cabinets.

30. *The Washington Post,* July 13, 1985.

31. "It is clear that the first thing we must do is to broaden the nation, that is, to devolve initiative and liberty of action. The principal obstacle is centralization which afflicts us [and which] resides in the bureaucracy. . . . As for the PRI, hopefully it will recast itself, its inheritance as the party of the Mexican Revolution. Thereby it would learn to share power with the other parties and groups." Octavio Paz, "PRI: The Perfect Hour," *Vuelta 103,* June 1985.

32. See "Manifiesto para un México Justo y Libre," Un proyecto de Constitución Democrática, Comisión de Derechos Humanos, (DHIAC), Guadalajara, 1985.

33. David Gardner, *Financial Times,* July 5, 1985.

34. Rosas, the PAN candidate for governor in Sonora, only half humorously pointed out that his party had received no votes in one municipality where he had some 300 resident relatives.

35. "Las Elecciones de la Crisis, Hechos de la Semana, Análisis Político," Coparmex, Nos. 113, 116-117, 119, 120-121, 123, 124, 125, México, D.F., 13 July to 9 August, 1985.

36. Juan Miolina Horcasitas, "Entre Reforma y la Alquimia: La Costumbre electoral Mexicana," *NEXOS,* Mexico City, July 1985.

37. *Washington Times,* July 18, 1985.

38. "CSIS Latin America Election Studies Series," The Mexican Midterm Elections, Report No. 3, July 31, 1985, Center for Strategic & International Studies, Georgetown University, Washington, D.C.

39. Details of the vote fraud in Sonora, where a PAN candidate for governor was expected to make a strong race, were given to David Gardner, *Financial Times* correspondent, by an alleged PRI official who worked in a government-sponsored "Operation Niño" designed to produce a victory for the PRI. *Financial Times,* London, July 7, 1985.

40. "Latin Laggard," *Economist,* Nov. 17, 1985.

41. *The Washington Post*, July 11, 1985.

42. These accusations were followed in the immediate post election period by the publication of a book by the so-called *Partido Laboral Mexicano*, a group affiliated with the Lyndon LaRouche movement in the U.S. but with important PRI connections in the *Ministerio Gobernación*. In the style of LaRouche's journalism, a book, *El PAN: el partido de la traición*, "de un equipo," Editorial Benengeli, S.A., Mexico, D.F., 1985, painted a paranoidal fantasy of U.S. involvement, including a chapter largely devoted to this author.

43. *The Washington Post*, July 11, 1985.

44. *Economist*, July 27, 1985.

45. Letter to the Editor, Mexican Ambassador to the U.S., *The New York Times*, July 18, 1985.

46. Regulo Cortes Lazaro, "Elecciónes: Legitimidad Revolucionaria o Sanción Electoral?" *Divulgación*, Organo de Difusión Ideológica de P.R.I. en el D.F., Agosto 1985, México, D.F.

47. Steve Frazier, "Mexico's Rigged Elections Hurt Its Image and Its Credit Rating," *Wall Street Journal*, July 12, 1985.

Chapter 2

1. *The Making of Modern Mexico*, Frank Brandenburg (Prentice-Hall, Inc., Englewood Cliffs, N.J., 1964).

2. "Why did Wilson, who three months earlier had said it would be a 'crime against civilization' to lead the United States into war, decide at last that 'the right is more precious than peace'? . . . Only Wilson can answer that, and he never did. One answer has been offered by a man whom the President trusted and made the recipient of all his papers. When Wilson, in the last letter he ever wrote, a week before his death, asked Ray Stannard Baker to write his official biography, he said, 'I would rather have your interpretation than that of anyone else I know.' Baker's judgment of the Zimmerman telegram (an offer by Kaiser Wilhelm in the event of a victory of the Central Powers to restore the American southwest to Mexico) is that 'no single more devastating blow was delivered against Wilson's resistance to entering the war.' . . . It was the last drop that emptied his cup of neutrality." Barbara Tuchman, *The Zimmer-*

man Telegram, (Macmillian Publishing Co., New York, 1958, 1966).

3. "Shortly after the American decision for war in April 1917, Colonel House confided to British Foreign Secretary Arthur Balfour that Wilson would have found it difficult to go to Congress, except for the 'famous German telegram to Mexico' and the startling events in Russia that saw the Tsar overthrown and a movement begun toward democracy in that great country. . . . As House's confidence implied, Wilson was upset—but not for precisely the reasons contemporaries imagined. From his perspective, German meddling in Mexico had little chance of success; it was the dying gasp of the old diplomacy. It was laughable. But the success of the Mexican and Russian revolutions *was* in question. How the war ended might determine their future. Should Mexico and Russia continue to remain the scene of international rivalries, the revolution would have little chance— little chance of remaining open to liberal influences." Lloyd C. Gardner, *A Covenant with Power: American and World Order from Wilson to Reagan*, (Oxford University Press, New York, Toronto, 1984).

4. *Nomenklatura: The Soviet Ruling Class*, Michael Voslensky (Doubleday, New York, 1984).

5. How widespread was the concept of the Mexico Model as a solution to the problems of instability and economic development in the nonindustrial world is indicated by a conversation of the author with the then U.S. ambassador to India John Kenneth Galbraith who compared favorably what he saw as the similarity of the monopoly rule of India by the Congress Party and the PRI in Mexico. Both, he said, were forms of "democracy." Sol W. Sanders, *A Sense of Asia*, (Charles Scribner's Sons., New York, 1969). Octavio Paz answers this argument specifically with " . . . the party (PRI) is not an ideological party, it is one of groups and interests—a circumstance which, if it has favored venality, has also saved us from the terror of any sort of orthodoxy. The variety of tendencies that exist within it resembled the Congress party of India, except for this important difference: the Mexican party has no internal democracy and is dominated by a group of hierarchs who, for their part, give blind obedience to each president in turn." Octavio Paz, "Developement and Other Mirages," *The Other Mexico: Critique of the Pyramid*, (Grove Press, Inc., New York, 1972). Another answer came from Willy Brandt, former chancellor of West Ger-

many and chairman of the Socialist International. Brandt argues essentially that standards of freedom and morality apply to the non-European parties. Willy Brandt, *La Alternativa Social-democrata: Cartas y conversacciones*, (Editorial Blume, Barcelona, 1977).

6. For simplicity I have referred to the party which grew out of the 1920s as the PRI (*Partido Revolucionario Institucional*). The government party has actually gone through three name changes: *El Partido Nacional Revolucionario* (PNR) formed in 1929 was transformed into *El Partido Revolucionario Mexicano* (PRM) in 1938 and, finally, into the PRI in 1946.

7. *Excelsior*, May 30, 1984.

8. John Barron, *KGB, The Secret World of Soviet Secret Agents* (Readers Digest Press, New York, 1974).

9. Peter H. Smith, "Is there a power elite?" *Labyrinths of Power, Political Recruitment in Twentieth-Century Mexico*, (Princeton University Press, Princeton, N.J., 1979).

10. "Mexico's Elections Emphasize Nation's Political Stability," *New York Times*, (advertisement), July 9, 1976.

11. Also see Riding's news article on Mexico in the *New York Times*, Section E, Sept. 16, 1984.

12. *The Miami Report, Recommendations on United States Policy toward Latin America and the Caribbean—a community's call for response to economic and political crisis*, (University of Miami, Coral Gables, Fla., Jan. 3, 1984).

13. See the annual *informe* (state of the union message) of the president, López Portillo, Sept. 1, 1982.

Chapter 3

1. "The long history of Masonic influence in Mexican life dates back to the eighteenth century . . . The important York ritual entered Mexico with the assistance of Joel Poinsett, first American diplomatic minister accredited to Mexico, who in 1825 was instrumental in obtaining credentials from the Grand Lodge of New York. . . . To the young Mexican aspiring to a solid future in government, business, education or the military, Freemasonry is not indispensable; but few educated Mexicans, except for militant Catholics, choose the generally slower path

of building a career without Masonic affiliation. The lodges are not centers of political maneuvering, but they are sources of liberal instruction where the Mexican can prepare himself to comprehend what the Revolution is about and to lead his nation along acceptable Revolutionary lines." Frank Brandenburg, *The Making of Modern Mexico* (Prentice-Hall, Inc., Englewood Cliffs, N.J., 1964).

2. Roderic A Camp, *The Political Technocrats in Mexico and the Survival of the Political System*, Latin American Research Review, Vol. 20, No. 1, 1985.

3. *Wall Street Journal*, Sept. 10, 1984.

4. "Tip de 'El Norte'," "Lo Que Todo Mexicano Debe Tener Presente, *El Norte*, Dec. 6, 1983 (reprint).

5. May 16, 1984.

6. The incident recalls the whole saga of the Indian Planning Commission which in its inception was dominated by a physical scientist, P.C. Mahalanobhis, a Bengali statistician. He persuaded Prime Minister Jawaharlal Nehru that through a mechanistic approach, Indian raw materials and human resources could be integrated for a massive program of attack on Indian poverty. U.S. gifts of early computers to Mahalanobhis' Indian Statistical Institute in Calcutta were the "scientific" sheen to what was a ludicrous, simplistic, and in the end, tragic, approach to the nation's problems. But Mahalanobhis' "Plan Frame"—with the assistance of a number of Soviet bloc and Western econometricians dedicated to intervention in what had been a market economy with colonial distortions—set the pattern of Indian government intervention and state capitalism, from which the Indian economy has never recovered. Sol W. Sanders, "India Today," *New Leader*, New York, April 9, 1956.

7. *Wall Street Journal*, July 15, 1985.

8. Peter Montagnon, "Mexico's pace-setting way forward," Euromarkets Correspondent, *Financial Times*, September 12, 1984.

9. A rather optimistic presentation of the whole short-term scene appears in *Business Week*, Oct. 1, 1984.

10. Latin American Executive Officers Roundtable, February 1984, as quoted in *The Costs of Default*, Anatole Kaletsky, A Twentieth Century Fund Paper, Priority Press Publications, New York, 1985.

11. *El Financiero*, a Mexico City newspaper, June 4, said: "The total amount of the flight of capital during 1977–83 is beyond calculation."

12. Peter Montagnon, "Mexico likely to ask for earthquake relief loan," *Financial Times*, Sept. 28, 1985.

13. *World Financial Markets*, Morgan Guarantee Trust Co., April 1986.

14. *Excelsior*, June 1, 1984.

15. In 1985, the brokerage houses handled some 30% of all financial transactions—up from 8% only one year earlier according to one financial group in the private sector.

16. *Wall Street Journal*, Sept. 10, 1984.

17. *Financial Times*, Aug. 14, 1984.

18. Lawrence J. Brainard, "Current Illusions about the International Debt Crisis," *The World Economy*, (London, March 1985).

19. George W. Grayson, *The Politics of Mexican Oil*, (University of Pittsburgh Press, Pittsburgh, Pa., 1980).

20. A major accident at the El Cactus natural gas refinery in Monterrey is laid to aging equipment not replaced.

21. Interview with PEMEX President Ramón Beteta, *Business Week*, Aug. 13, 1984.

22. *Ensayo sobre "Nacionalism Revolucionari,"* Union Social de Empresarios Mexicanos de Monterrey, A.C., Monterrey, June 24, 1985.

23. Eudocio Ravines, *Capitalismo o Socialismo, disyuntiva del siglo*, Editorial Diana, Mexico, 1980.

24. A story that circulated in Mexico City political circles was that López Portillo appointed Durazo with his gangster connections because American organized crime from New Orleans was moving in on Mexico City rackets and the new president sought to fight fire with fire.

Chapter 4

1. Cuauhtemoc, unlike his predecessor, the equivocating Moctezuma, is one of the heroes of the cult of Indianism in modern Mexico. The bloody area seems to be haunted. Again, in September 1985, during the two massive earthquakes, the area was the scene of bloodletting. Thousands of Mexicans were trapped in their government-built apartment homes when the

earth tremor struck. There were accusations even before the earthquake that the apartments were jerrybuilt, examples of corruption and government malfeasance.

2. Roberto Newell G., and Luis Rubio F., *Mexico's Dilemma: The Political Origins of Economic Crisis* (Westview Press, Boulder & London, 1984).

3. One of the less-known facts about the rise of Fidel Castro is the aid extended to him and his brother, Raul, by democratic forces in the region, which were allied to the U.S., when they led a guerrilla movement from the Sierra Maestra mountains of southern Cuba against the Batista government. A lifeline of arms and supplies—as well as advisers—operated from Costa Rica. Castro had the support of Costa Rican democrats and other Latin Americans at a time when Batista's regime epitomized corruption and oppression, and while Batista was still supported by the Communist party of Cuba. Those involved were the same Costa Ricans who had been aided by the CIA in the 1946–1948 civil war in that country, the first attempt in the post-World War II period by Moscow to set up a Communist regime in this hemisphere. This background belies the oft-repeated charge in American liberal circles that it was the refusal of Washington to accept Castro that drove him to the Communist side in the international confrontation. See for a brief mention of this, along with documentation on aid from other U.S. sources to Castro before he took power, Nathaniel Weyl, *Red Star over Cuba: The Russian Assault on the Western Hemisphere* (The Devin-Adair Co., Publisher, New York, 1960).

4. Juan Vives, *Les Maîtres de Cuba*, (Editions Robert Laffont, Paris, 1981). Vives tells his personal story from 1958 when at 14 he joined Castro's forces as a protégé of Che Guevara, worked his way up in the Cuban secret services, came into conflict with the Cuban revolutionaries, and was finally released from a Castro prison through French intervention in 1980.

5. See Alfonso L. Tarabachio, *American Studies of Clandestine Tactics and Technology Series, Cuba: Technology of Subversion, Espionage, and Terrorism* (Technical Research Sciences Division, International Association of Chiefs of Police, Gaithersburg, Md., 1976).

6. Members of the Committee for the Americas apparatus have worked openly in the U.S. During the spring of 1980, preceding the national presidential campaign in the U.S., several of its most prominent members toured the U.S. meeting members

of the Democratic party. They sought to influence the internal workings of the Democratic primaries to take a more conciliatory policy toward Havana than even the Carter administration had done. When I spoke to one of the journalists attending one of the series of luncheons and dinners with the Cubans, he described the meeting as simply an effort for an exchange between Cuban and U.S. intellectuals. Apparently unaware that he was dealing with higher echelon members of Cuban intelligence, he stamped any such suggestion as "paranoidal conspiratorial."

7. The Mexican Left has a slogan: "Central America begins at Juchitán." This small town in Oaxaca state in the Isthmus of Tenhuantepe was taken over by a coalition of Communists, other leftists groups, and left-wing religionists. It has been the scene of violent clashes between the central government and local radical organizations as well as between Left and Right, and has figured prominently in the activities of the liberation theologians.

8. Or, as a representative of a major U.S. bank and one of the principal lenders to Mexico, a Mexican national, put it in an emotional outburst during an off-the-record interview in Mexico City, this kind of concession to Havana is seen by many Mexicans as the price of peace and "for not having our president assassinated like Kennedy."

9. Charlotte Hays, "Redeeming the poor of the world; Is Liberation Theology heresy, or a path to freedom?" *National Catholic Register*, Los Angeles, Calif., August 5, 1984. This article is a brief and objective presentation of the controversy—although it perhaps neglects the conspiratorial aspects of the liberationists, particularly a group of French and Spanish Dominican and Jesuit fathers working in Central America with strong Mexican and U.S. connections.

10. The East German Communists are generally tasked with providing communications and intelligence in their aid to Moscow's Third World client nations, and they are represented in relatively large numbers with the Sandinista junta in Managua.

11. U.S. intelligence reports indicated that during the forced removal of the refugees, the Mexican authorities came into conflict with local Mexican residents sympathetic to the Guatemalan refugees and that some of them, too, were forcibly moved to the new sites.

12. Mexico has retreated somewhat, too, from its position adopted in conjunction with France in a joint statement in 1981 calling

the Salvadoran Communist guerrillas "a representative political force." In late August 1985, after five years, it announced it would send an ambassador to El Salvador and establish full diplomatic relations with the Duarte government.

13. See "II. The Praxis of Intervention," *Revolution Beyond Our Borders: Sandinista Intervention in Central America*, U.S. Department of Defense, Washington, D.C., September 1985; and David Nolan, *FSLN: The Ideology of the Sandinistas and the Nicaraguan Revolution*, Institute of Interamerican Studies, Graduate School of International Studies, University of Miami, Coral Gables, Florida, 1984.

14. Bertrand Wolfe, *A Life in Two Centuries* (Stein and Day, Briarcliff Manor, N.Y., 1981).

15. A member of the Kissinger Commission staff confirms that the figure was arrived at with simplistic calculations.

16. Perhaps the motive was the widely circulated report in Mexico City that Octavio Paz threatened to move to Paris in self-imposed exile.

17. And apparently for Soviet espionage, as well. When an East German physicist was arrested in the Boston area in 1984 for espionage against the electronics companies based there, it was found that he had been a visiting professor at the Puebla university since 1979 with a well-endowed department in an institution otherwise desperate for funds.

18. Mario V. Guzman Clarza, *El Dia*, Mexico City, Oct. 13, 1982.

19. Virginia Polk, "Estados Unidos y el Esfuerzo de Paz de Contadora en Centroamerica," trans., *Backgrounder*, Heritage Foundation, Washington, D.C., August 1984.

20. For a discussion of the Sandinista's international strategies and intentions, see David Nolan, *The Ideology of the Sandinistas and the Nicaraguan Revolution* (Institute of Inter-American Studies, Center for Advanced International Studies, Miami University, Coral Gables, Fl., 1981).

21. Although there was no public confirmation, it was widely believed in conservative political circles in Washington that the Mexicans had conducted "parallel" negotiations in the same hotel where the Nicaraguans and the Americans were meeting with the Nicaraguans and the Cubans in Manzanillo. For many conservative critics of the Reagan administration's Central American policy, this seemed to be a replay of the Panamanian talks with the Sandinistas with U.S. representatives that had preceded the fall of the Somoza regime in Nicaragua.

22. The Mexican line on settling issues in Central America has not only irritated the U.S., but has often found little sympathy with non-Communist Costa Rica, with its long tradition of friendship with Mexico. In one of the most brutal big power exercises of intimidation in the area, the Mexicans in late 1983 waged a vicious press campaign against the Costa Rican foreign minister, Don Fernando Volio, the respected head of the faculty of law at the University of Costa Rica. The Mexican foreign office made it known to President Luis Monge that despite his long association with Mexico—he had lived many years as a trade unionist official in the country—he would not be welcomed on a state visit unless the foreign minister were removed. Costa Rica, itself in an economic crisis that matches the depth and implications of the Mexican problem, in order to secure Mexican oil loans and import concessions, and to regularize its position with its long-time ally, accepted the Mexican dictate and Volio was dismissed.

President Alberto Monge of Costa Rica, in an interview in January 1984, told me that he considered Sandinista Nicaragua a menace to peace in Central America. He said that he could not tell me what had gone on during his conversations a few weeks earlier with De la Madrid, when I asked whether the Mexicans really believed as their foreign ministry had often been quoted as saying, that there was no Marxist-Leninist threat in Central America. Monge then told me somewhat enigmatically that "Los Mexicanos ahora conocen que Costa Rica es su mejor amigo en Centroamérica." Unfortunately neither time nor Monge's reticence permitted further questions as to whether this Mexico-Costa Rican amity would prevent aggression from Nicaragua against Costa Rica and if not, what Mexico would do to help Costa Rica. In any case, a few months later, Monge issued a statement, on the eve of a first-ever meeting between the European Economic Community and the Central American states, wherein he took the exact opposite view of the Sandinista threat. Monge then tried to push through the Costa Rican parliament a constitutional amendment which would establish Costa Rica's permanent neutrality. The Volio affair and the effort to establish a formal neutrality aroused such opposition in the country—particularly within Monge's own Partido Liberación Nacional which had from its inception in 1946 taken a stand against dictatorship in Central America—that the whole issue is at this writing in abeyance awaiting the installation of a new president in May 1986.

(One of the best kept "secrets" of the area, of course, is that what is called, in an oft-repeated cliché, the traditional democracy of Costa Rica was only possible because of direct U.S. intervention in the 1948 civil war in that country. The CIA set up and aided to victory a group of Costa Rican democrats fighting to keep the strange coalition of neighboring Somoza in Nicaragua and local Communists from setting up the first pro-Moscow regime in the region. Much water has gone over the dam since, but it gives the lie to the repeated charge that Washington has only aided right-wing dictatorships in Latin America and that U.S. intervention is predestined to end in political disaster.)

Chapter 5

1. There is a striking precedent for such an eventuality in what one Argentine friend calls the Kafkaesque politics of Argentina. The Montonero insurgency of the 1970s in Argentina had its origins in both the radical Left and the radical Right. That is why, initially, it was able to recruit from pro-Soviet elements, particularly among the elite in the universities, and also at the same time involve officers in the military. It is this situation in which both poles of the political spectrum were compromised, it explains why although the Argentine military governments were able to suppress the violence with counter-terror, the cleanup campaign has been so untidy and left so many loose ends. See Gerardo Schamis, *War and Terrorism in International Affairs* (Transaction Books, New Brunswick, N.J., 1980).

2. Dennis M. Hanratty, "The Political Role of the Mexican Catholic Church: Contemporary Issues," *Thought*, June 1984.

3. See the brief summary of liberation theological concepts in Chapter IV.

4. Mary Ball Martínez has described in some detail how far the Chiapas bishopric and its appendages have strayed from conventional Catholic thought and practice in her article, "Clerical Materialism in Mexico's Southeast," *The American Spectator*, April 1984.

5. See Juli Loesch, "We're losing the Hispanics," *National Catholic Register*, Los Angeles, Aug. 18, 1985, for a discussion of the movement away from Roman Catholicism to Christian fundamentalism within the U.S. Spanish-speaking community.

Many of the factors described here are relevant to Central America as well.

6. Mons. Javier Lozano Barragan, *La Iglesia del Pueblo— Teologías en conflicto*, (Centro de Estudios y Promocion Social, A.C., Mexico, 1983). The title makes the subtle distinction between the People's Church (Iglesia Popular) of the pro-Communists in Nicaragua and the liberation theologians and the Church of the People (Iglesia del Pueblo) of the Mexican Catholic neoconservatives. For a short but pithy review of the history of these politico-theological maneuverings in Latin America, see *Marxism and Christianity in Revolutionary Central America*, hearings before the Subcommittee on Security and Terrorism of the Committee on the Judiciary, U.S. Senate, Sen. Jeremiah Denton, R., Ala., subcomittee chairman, 98th Congress, Oct. 18–19, 1983.

7. A Mexican neoconservative priest argues that one of the increasingly difficult problems for his partisans in the Mexican church is the influence of left-wing U.S. Spanish-speaking priests or Mexican migrants moving back and forth to the U.S., particularly those migrants who come from the volatile southern areas and who tend to be less sophisticated than other Mexicans entering the U.S. He believes that liberation theology has considerable influence among the staffs of the sixteen relatively new and inexperienced American Spanish-speaking bishops, particularly Archbishop Patricio Flores of San Antonio. That is true, too, of the staff of the National Council of Bishops in Washington, which is extremely favorable to the liberation theologians and repeatedly has thwarted Central American antiliberationist bishops and priests who have tried to present their views in Washington Catholic circles. There is also the question of funds intended for the Guatemalan refugees in Mexico which flow from foreign Catholic charities to the bishop of San Cristobal de las Casas and his liberationist organizations in Chiapas. U.S. Catholic Relief Services, historically on the left of the U.S. Catholic establishment, is now headed by former Ambassador Lawrence Pazullo, the first lay head of the organization in its history. Pazullo was ambassador to Nicaragua during the Sandinistas' early days in power and was widely considered by conservatives to have sabotaged efforts by them to identify the regime as a danger to U.S. security interests in the region.

8. Ramón Eduardo Ruíz, *The Great Rebellion, Mexico 1905–1924* (Norton, New York, N.Y., 1980).

9. Domingo P. de Toledo y J., "Solemn Conmemoracion del 5 Julio en Maracaibo", "Mexico en la Obra de Marx y Engels", Tipografico El Pais, Maracaibo, 1940. This is a serious if somewhat prejudiced attempt to summarize all the writings of Karl Marx and Frederick G. Engels on the economic-historical problem of Mexico. The writer has some difficulty, however, in presenting their views as always sympathetic to Mexican nationalism which he espouses. The Spanish translations of Engels are taken from "The Revolutionary Movements of 1847" as presented in a German text in La Gaceta Alemana de Brucelas, Jan. 23, 1848.

10. Benjamin Gitlow, *The Whole of Their Lives*, (Scribner's Sons, New York, 1945); Samaren Roy, "M.N. Roy in America," *The Radical Humanist*, (New Delhi, March 1983); and Manual Gomez, "From Mexico to Moscow," (*Survey*, London, Oct. 1964).

11. A pamphlet published by Workers Party of America, 1009 N. State St., Chicago, Ill., dated Moscow, Aug. 21, 1923.

12. Bertram D. Wolfe, *A Life in Two Centuries*, (Stein and Day, New York, N.Y., 1981).

13. Mark Falcoff, *Small Countries, Large Issues: Studies in U.S.-Latin American Asymmetries*, American Enterprise Institute Studies in Foreign Policy, Washington, D.C. 1984.

14. Ibid.

15. Luis E. Aguilar, ed. *Marxism in Latin America*, rev. ed., (Temple University Press, Philadelphia, 1978).

16. *Fourth International*, November 1940, New York, N.Y.

17. For the remarkable details of the plot, see Isaac Don Levine, *The Mind of an Assassin* (Farrar, Strauss, and Cudahy, New York, 1959).

18. Maurice Malkin, *Return to My Father's House* (Arlington House, New Rochelle, N.Y., 1972).

19. "A Communist push along Mexico's border," International Outlook, *Business Week*, Dec. 21, 1981.

20. Baron, John, *KGB*, Readers Digest Press, New York, 1974.

21. During the 1985 elections, the 1982 presidential candidate of the PSUM, Arnoldo Martínez Verdugo, was kidnapped by members of the radical left-wing Partido de los Pobres. While the kidnapping appeared to be largely to raise funds, it also expressed a split inside the Mexican Left with some elements calling for a

more radical policy. El Partido de los Pobres had been connected with the guerrilla warfare in western Mexico in the 1970s led by its founder, Lucio Cabanas. *Hechos de la Semana, Analisis Politico*, No. 122, COMPARMEX, 4–12 de Julio de 1985.

22. Sylvia Ann Hewlett and Richard S. Weinert, "The State and Organized Labor in Brazil and Mexico," *Brazil and Mexico: Patterns in Late Development*, Institute for the Study of Human Issues, Philadelphia, 1982.

23. " . . . the CTM [is] undoubtedly the most powerful mass organization within the Mexican corporativist system—much more powerful than any of the organizations that make up the popular sector, in spite of the fact that the labor sector is not the largest. This means, in the first place, that there is no similarity between the sectors and their corresponding organizations, and, in the second place, that the real repositories of power are in a few organizations. The CTM is also an exemplary case from the point of view of its control over the masses and its power in national politics. After its great struggles during the thirties under the leadership of Vicente Lombardo Toledano, the CTM gradually fell into the hands of its most politically backward and opportunistic sectors, the political expression of this process being the emergence of the 'five little foxes' (Fidel Velázquez, Jesús Yuren, Fernando Amilpa, Alfonso Sánchez Madariaga, and Luis Quintero) . . . It has been argued that the power of the official trades-union leadership would not last a day if the state did not so openly support it, and there is a good deal of truth to that. If the state did not repress trade-union attempts to organize resistance to the corporatist system of political domination, rebellion in the ranks of organized workers would spread like wildfire, and the trade-union bureaucracy would be incapable of resisting the onslaught." Arnaldo Cordova, "Mass Politics and the Future of the Left in Mexico," *Mexico hoy*, Era, Mexico City, 1979. This analysis is obviously biased by a "revolutionary," or a dissident Communist view, but it has a great deal to recommend it if one examines the realities of Mexican trade unionism.

24. *Mexico: Trends in Economic and Socio-Political Development*, an editorial collegium headed by V.V. Volsky, editor-in-chief, (Science), Moscow, 1983, in Russian with a Spanish translation of the title but no foreign language translations as of August 1984.

25. Manuel Buendía, *La CIA en Mexico*, (Ediciones Oceana, CA, Mexico, D.F., 1983).

Chapter 6

1. Octavio Paz, "Mexico and the United States, Positions and Counterpositions," *Tiempo nublado,* Seiz Barral Biblioteca Breve, Mexico, D.F., 1983.
2. Patrick Romanell, *Making of the Mexican Mind* (University of Notre Dame Press, Notre Dame, Ind. 1967)(paperback), First Edition-1952, (University of Nebraska Press, Lincoln, Neb.).
3. José Vasconcelos and Manuel Gamio, *Aspects of Mexican Civilization* (University of Chicago Press, Chicago, Ill., 1926).
4. Octavio Paz, "The Pachuco and Other Extremes," *The Labyrinth of Solitude,* (Grove Press, New York, 1961).
5. Philip Wayne Powell, *Tree of Hate,* (Basic Books, Inc., New York, N.Y. 1971). Powell makes a brilliant if somewhat emotional presentation of the incredible misinterpretation of much of the Ibero-American world in Western historiography, including Mexico and its relations with Spain.
6. Ross, Stanley Robert, Francisco I. Madero, 2 ed., Grijalbo, Mexico City, 1977. José Fuentes Mares; *Juarez: los Estados Unidos y Europa,* (Grijalbo, Mexico City, Barcelona, Buenos Aires, 1963).
7. Robert W. Johannsen, *To the Halls of the Montezumas,* (Oxford University Press, Oxford/New York, 1985).
8. Daniel J. Boorstin, "Editors Preface," Otis A. Singletary, *The Mexican War,* (The University of Chicago Press, London, 1960).
9. Ibid.
10. This provided a minor footnote to the war: A group of U.S. army deserters, mostly Irish emigrants, through their allegiance to their Church and sympathy for their coreligionists, the Mexican Catholics, fought one of the bitterest battles of the war against the Americans at Churibusco. Near the site of that battle in suburban Mexico City today is the government's Museum of the Interventions.
11. Johannsen, op. cit.
12. This was said to me in an informal interview an English-speaking Mexican national, a Mexico-born offspring of an enormously successful American immigrant businessman.
13. An editor of one of Mexico's largest magazines, a former Jesuit and now a fervent Marxist, in discussing this subject told me of his shock in a conversation with his brother a few days pre-

viously. The brother had said, "What we need is for the U.S. to land the Marines down here, kill all the Indians, and make a modern country of us." I said his brother must surely have been joking; yes, the editor replied, but he allowed as how there was a certain undercurrent of seriousness in his brother's statement.

14. On Sept. 23, 1984, *The New York Times*, carried on its front page an article with the headline, "For Mexicans, Concern Rises on Civil Rights." On Oct. 6, 1984, *The New York Times* Op-Ed page featured an article by Carlos Fuentes, the well-known Mexican novelist who resides in the United States. Fuentes presented a detailed account of the inconveniences for left-wing Latin writers imposed by restrictions in the McCarran-Walters Immigration Act which forbids visas to Communists wishing to enter the U.S. without a special waiver. It might well be asked why Fuentes does not protest with equal vigor against much more onerous restrictions on movement and freedom of expression in his own country. *The Economist* of London in its Nov. 17, 1984, issue carried an article "from our Mexico correspondent" entitled "Latin Laggard," commenting adversely on local elections in Mexico in November 1984 and warning that "Mexico, the leading economy in Latin America, will prove, once again, a laggard in democracy." And in March 1985, *The Economist*, in a leader picked up the refrain. The tenor of this comment in *The New York Times* and *The Economist* may well be the forerunner of a new kind of reportage out of Mexico as the situation there deteriorates.

15. There was an old Washington saw not so far from the truth that nothing more than a thousand miles from Vienna really excites Kissinger's full intellectual concern.

16. A few years later, in Tokyo, I was treated to a hilarious description of a mission of one of Kennedy's minions to the veteran old Peruvian revolutionary Raul Haya de la Torre. Haya, whose release had recently been secured after twelve years of "sanctuary" in the Colombian embassy in Lima through the representations of the Kennedy administration, told how he had been visited by the Kennedy emissary, Arthur Schlesinger, Jr. Haya said: "I couldn't deal with that young man. He kept repeating 'land reform,' 'land reform,' 'land reform,' like a priest telling his beads. I explained to him that his proposals would destroy our economy, that what we needed was colonization in the vast lands we had across the Andes in the Amazonian Basin. But he just kept repeating 'land reform,' 'land reform,' 'land reform'."

17. Mauricio Gonzalez de la Garza, *La Ultima Llamada,* Editores Associados Mexicanos, Mexico City, 1987.

18. Francisco Ortiz Pinchetti, "Margarita sucumbió al poder, a la corrupción, a la magia, a la soberbia." *Proceso,* July 30, 1984.

19. Cole Blasier, Intro: "Revolutionary Change," *The Hovering Giant, U.S. Responses to Revolutionary Change in Latin America,* (University of Pittsburgh Press, 1976).

20. Daniell Lerner, *Passing of Traditional Society,* (Free Press, Glencoe, Ill., 1958).

21. For a romantic and informative travelogue of the border areas; see Tom Miller, *On the Border, Portraits of America's Southwestern Frontier* (Harper & Row, New York, 1981).

22. The metropolitan Juarez region, opposite El Paso, Tex., is nearing 4 million people; Mexicali, near El Centro, has 2.7 million; Tijuana, opposite San Diego, has 2.8 million.

23. Frank J. Call, "Problems and Cooperation between U.S. and Mexican Border Cities," *United States Relations with Mexico,* Richard D. Erb and Stanley R. Ross, eds., (American Enterprise Institute, Washington, D.C., 1981).

24. Oscar Lewis, *Five Families, Mexican Case Studies in the Culture of Poverty,* (Basic Books, New York, 1959); and Oscar Lewis, *The Children of Sanchez* (Vintage Books, New York, 1963).

Chapter 7

1. Francisco Alba, *The Population of Mexico, Trends, Issues, and Policies* (Transaction, Inc., New Brunswick, N.J., 1982).

2. See Apadicio Laquian's work on migration, Social Science Office, International Research Development Centre, Ottawa, Ont., 1971–77. This research indicates that contrary to Western prejudices, migrants from isolated rural areas in the Third World, generally improve their environment even though they move into fetid urban slums.

3. *The News,* Mexico City, Nov. 28, 1983.

4. Leo Grebler and others, "Patterns of Work and Settlement," *The Mexican-American People, the nation's second largest*

minority (The Free Press, Macmillan Publishing Co., New York, 1970).

5.   Among the "Okie" migration to California were large numbers of Mexican-Americans from Texas, the parents and grandparents of many Mexican-Americans in Calfornia today. They form a distinct subcaste in the highly heterogeneous Mexican-American population of the Southwest.

6.   Wayne Cornelius, Leo R. Chavez, and Jorge G. Castro, *Mexican Immigrants and Southern California; A Summary of Current Knowledge, Report to the Human Resources Committee of the Los Angeles Chamber of Commerce*, Program in U.S.-Mexican Studies, (University of California, San Diego, December 1981).

7.   Jeffrey S. Passel and Robert Warren, "Estimates of Illegal Aliens from Mexico counted in the 1980 U.S. Census," annual meeting of the Population Association of America, Pittsburgh, Pa., April 14–16, 1983, Population Division, U.S. Bureau of the Census, Washington, D.C.

8.   Both the Jewish and Lebanese communities were threatened by the highest Mexican authorities during the mass flight of capital in 1981–1982, an effort to discourage their sending their assets overseas. An official of the Mexican government talking to U.S. Jewish organization officials, used the fact that Lebanese as well as Jews were pressured by the Mexican authorities as "proof" that there was no antisemitism involved.

9.   EDAMEX, Mexico City, 1983.

10.   A great deal of effort and paper has recently been wasted on pleas for a generous and liberal immigration program into the U.S. Nathan Glazer, *Clamor at the Gates: The New American Immigration*, (Institute for Contemporary Studies, San Francisco, Ca., 1985), and Michael S. Teitelbaum, *Latin Migration North: The Problem for U.S. Foreign Policy*, (Council on Foreign Relations, New York 1985), and Kevin McCarthy, R. Burciaga Valdez, *Current and Future Effects of Mexican Immigration in California*, (The California Roundtable, Rand Corporation, Santa Monica, Ca., 1985). All these studies are paeans of praise for the principle of continued immigration and envoking the past benefits of American immigration. But they fail to deal with the central problem here. It is not whether or not we shall continue to invite foreigners to this country but under what circumstances. Given the world as it is and will be in the 1990s, reasserting control of our southern border—including permitting a healthy and large Mexican emigration—is essential. That

has little if anything to do with the argument of the value to our country of continued immigration which most Americans would accept without question.

Chapter 8

1. "By the time the sheriff arrives there is usually nothing left under the scorching sun but bones, perhaps just a skull, and some tattered clothing. Sometimes the sheriff beats the coyotes to the scene and there are identifiable bodies lying bloated on the desert floor. The sheriff believes they are the remains of young Mexicans, driven by economic desperation at home to risk marching 50 miles across what is perhaps the harshest stretch of uninhabited territory left in the United States to find work picking fruit in southwest Arizona. The unlucky ones run out of water or get lost reaching the valley of the Gila River. . . . No one disputes that hundreds of Mexicans regularly risk death in the desert." Robert Reinhold, "Bones Found on Mexicans' Desert Path to U.S. Jobs," *The New York Times*, Sept. 26, 1985.

2. In the beautiful U.S.-Mexican film *El Norte*, which unfortunately paints a melodramatic and politically naive picture of Guatemalan refugees, one realistic portion tells how they are told to pretend they are Mexican by mimicking their conversation and accent. The parody is very close to the reality.

3. Todd Ackerman, "Looking south at a rising tide: On the border, personal compassion and some tough moral issues," *National Catholic Register*, Los Angeles, California, July 29, 1984.

4. A Mexican-American California assembly woman, visiting Central America in 1983, reported that there were already 20,000 illegal Salvadoran emigrants in her Los Angeles district and they were causing friction inside the Spanish-speaking community by their demands on public services.

5. Norris Clement, "The Border," *SDSU Report* (San Diego State University, Calif., September 1983).

6. An anecdotal but not untypical experience illustrating the extent of the petty corruption: Searching for an address on the Boulevard Reforma, Mexico City's beautiful and principal thoroughfare, in early 1984, my driver and an assistant with whom I was driving halted to ask two policemen in uniform for

directions to the address. They asked for 300 pesos *mordida* for the information. When my driver showed his credentials as a former member of the police force, the bribe was cut to 100 pesos. In his book on the transgressions of El Negro Durazo, his former henchman claims that Durazo required each policeman to have three uniforms—two supplied by the government and another which he had to purchase from Durazo. The level of corruption of the Mexico City police is ubiquitous and a generally accepted fact of life in the city; for example, most parking places on the street are "sold" by foot policemen in the area.

Chapter 9

1. Perry Skerry, "Vendetta in the Valley," *New Republic*, Sept. 17 & 24, 1984, an intensive if highly colored anti-Reagan survey of the complicated scene.

2. "Organizing the U.S.-Mexican relationship," *United States Relations with Mexico, Context and Content*, Richard D. Erb and Stanley R. Ross, eds. (American Enterprise Institute, Washington, D.C., 1981).

3. Eugene Douglas, "The United States and Mexico," *Strategic Review*, Boston, Spring 1985.

4. Stanley L. Robe, *Azuela and the Mexican Underdogs* (University of California Press, Berkeley, Los Angeles, London, 1979).

5. It also suggests that the problem of the Mexico City intellectual may well be his alienation from his own society, in part through his own Americanization, rather than the competition from North American cultural forms that have invaded Mexico with the worldwide communications revolution.

6. The very term "Hispanic," an invention of the 1960s would-be politicians, is a misnomer. Very little except language actually unites the Mexican-Americans of the Southwest, the Puerto Rican and Spanish-speaking Caribbean communities largely concentrated in metropolitan New York and the Northeast, and the growing Cuban American community largely centered in southern Florida. Their backgrounds in their countries of origin, the way they came to the U.S., and their present adaptation to the American society are vastly different. That is demonstrated in everything from voting to consumption patterns.

7. And that is in spite of Gavin's very effective campaign to represent U.S. interest even when it ran up against the traditional vacuity of diplomatic protocol.

8. On a winter afternoon in Corpus Cristi, Texas, in 1984 I interviewed two Mexican-American brothers who work together. They told me about being invited by the Mexican government, as part of a delegation of Mexican-Americans, to the inauguration of Echeverría. One described the whole episode as nonproductive, saying the Mexicans had treated the American group with disdain, had wined and dined them, lectured them briefly, and then sent them home. He said that he and others in the group had expected to be treated as equals and talked with seriously about mutual problems. His brother, however, insisted that he, personally, and the Mexican-Americans generally, now had access to the highest echelons in Mexico, which made them a part of the U.S.-Mexican negotiating process.

9. Like so much in Mexican-American history and life, the origin of the term "chicano" is disputed. There is no doubt that it was, until very recently, a pejorative term. One Mexican source says that it had its origins among political prisoners during the troubles of 1904–1922. But there are references to *chicana*—whether the same word or not—in poetry at a much earlier time. It may simply have been the elision produced by a shortened version of *Me-hi-can-o*.

10. A Mexican American trade union official in El Paso told me with great indignation of an attempt by a young (and female and that seemed to have considerable significance for the American middle-aged male) Mexican government official who crossed the border to lobby him against the American immigration legislation then under consideration (1984) in the U.S. Congress. "Imagine what would have happened if I had crossed the border to try to persuade Mexicans on an issue in their government machinery," he said.

11. A rule of thumb for ward-heelers has been that American blacks vote about half as often as whites, and Mexican-Americans half again as much as blacks.

12. Pastora San Juan Caffrey, Barry R. Chiswick, Andrew M. Greeley, Teresa A. Sullivan, "A Portrait of the New Immigrants," *The Dilemma of American Immigration, Beyond the Golden Door* (Transaction, Inc., New Brunswick, N.J., 1983).

13. "Bilingual Ballots: Balkanization of the U.S., *Human Events*, Washington, D.C., August 18, 1984.

14. Richard Rodríguez, *Hunger of Memory, The Education of Richard Rodríguez, An Autobiography* (David R. Godine, Boston, 1982).

15. "Do you know why a pail of Mexican crabs does not have to be covered?" "Because if one tries to crawl to the top and out, the others will pull him down." The joke is so often told by Mexican-Americans to outsiders that it has become enshrined as a cliché.

16. Matt S. Meier and Feliciano Rivera, "Heroes, Second Class," *The Chicanos, a History of Mexican Americans* (Hill and Wang, New York, 1972).

17. "Leadership and Politics," *La Raza: Forgotten Americans*, Julian Samora, ed. (University of Notre Dame Press, South Bend, Ind., 1966). Although somewhat overtaken by events, this book is useful in capturing the mood of the mid-1960s when the Chicano radical movement flowered.

18. Stan Steiner, *La Raza* (Harper & Row, New York, 1970).

19. "Election Loss Perplexes Hispanic Politicians," *New York Times*, Aug. 9, 1983.

20. How to deal with the Mexican-American vote has been a hard-fought issue inside the GOP in Texas: Reagan "Populists" wanted the president to visit the Valley (the agricultural area along the Rio Grande where 75 percent of the population is Spanish-speaking) but the partisans of Vice President George Bush, the country club set that has long run the party in Texas, did not want to risk his prestige there. A compromise—in which the Reagan Populists were not permitted to bring on the presidential platform their Democratic conservative friends— resulted in a little publicized victory for Reagan's charm. Paralleling this problem is another that is hampering the GOP's efforts to enlist Mexican-Americans throughout the Southwest. It is the dominance of Spanish-speaking circles by the Cuban Americans. Despite denials by both sides, it is clear that the bitter traditional Mexican-cuban rivalry, dating back to Spanish colonial times, has been transferred to their descendants in the U.S.

21. "Public Opinion on Immigration," Pamphlet of FAIR, Federation for American Immigration Reform, Washington, D.C., 1984.

22. Sidney Weintraub, "U.S. Foreign Economic Policy and Illegal Immigration," *Population Research and Policy Review*, (Elsevier Science Pub., B.V., Amsterdam, The Netherlands, 1983).

23. Joseph Kraft, "The Mexican Rescue," paper sponsored by The Group of Thirty, New York, 1984.

Chapter 10

1. Tom Miller, On the Border (Harper & Row, New York, 1981).

2. Little Costa Rica, the model parliamentary democracy founded on the political settlement dictated by the CIA's intervention in the 1946–1948 civil war, has the highest per capita international debt in the world—with the exception of Israel—totalling almost $4.5 billion for a population of less than 2 million. Repeated efforts by the commercial bank creditors, the international agencies and the U.S. government have not begun to solve its problems. It is a classic case of social welfarism run rampant and of the international liquidity that followed the OPEC oil price increases of 1978, and the resultant worldwide inflation. If no solution is found soon, the economic problem threatens to engulf the political stability of the little country, surrounded as it is by states in civil war, such as Nicaragua and El Salvador. See Sol W. Sanders, *The Costa Rican Laboratory* (Twentieth Century Fund, New York, 1986).

3. A not atypical example: "These questions are not posed today as they were during the populist period. The advance of mass industrial society, urbanization, the revolution in communications, even the situations of dependent-*development* themselves, pose the political question of popular participation in such a way as to *exclude manipulative links with dominant classes through the state* as an option. Such links were the basis of populism's policy. The internationalization of production and of the market have advanced, and the state productive sector has expressed itself in capitalist form. For the ruling groups, the nation is embodied in the state as the stimulus for an enterprise economy. But, at the same time, for dominated classes, the paternalism of the traditional Latin American state (in both oligarchic and populist versions) has been broken. Although politically frustrated, the guerrilla movements did serve the function of disrupting this paternalism and putting an end to manipulative types of alliance which once tied the people to the state in the name of the nation." Fernando Henrique Cardoso and Enzo Faletto, *Dependency and Development in Latin America*, trans. Marjory Mat-

tingly Urquidi (University of California Press, Berkeley and Los Angeles, Calif., 1979).

4. See Luis Coppola, Jr., *Opcion Delta, Alternativa de Desarrollo*, (Edamex, Mexico City, 1983); and the books of Luis Pazos, closely identified in Mexico with Milton Friedman and the Chicago School of market economists and monetarism.

5. It is the answer to an astounding statement made by Robert Pastor, a member of the National Security staff and the chief adviser on Latin America in the Carter White House, who asked in a political conversation if this author did not understand that instability had always been a characteristic of Central America, which is why we had intervened so often with the Marines in the nineteenth and early twentieth centuries. My reply was that indeed it was understood but that there was a significant difference today. And when he stared blankly, I reminded him of the ability of the Soviet Union since the early 1970s to project world power into many regions of the world, even into the Caribbean with the help of its Cuban surrogate.

6. *"El Caso de la Embajada del Peru y el Mariel: Exodo masivo de cubanos,"* Reporte Oral, (National Endowment for the Humanities, Reencuentro Cubano, Inc., Washington, D.C., 1981).

Index